AF553824

MYTHICAL ORIGIN OF INDIA

CULTURE AND CIVILIZATION SERIES

MYTHICAL ORIGIN OF INDIA

Edited by
Dr. R.K. Pruthi

DISCOVERY PUBLISHING HOUSE
NEW DELHI-110002

First Published – 2004

Reprinted – 2025

ISBN: 978-81-7141-864-0

Mythical Origin of India

Published by:

DISCOVERY PUBLISHING HOUSE
4383/4B, Ansari Road, Darya Ganj
New Delhi-110 002 (India)
Phone: +91-11-23279245; 23253475; 43596065
Mobile: +91 9811179893 / +91 9871656464
E-mail: discoverybooksindia@gmail.com
orderdphbooks@gmail.com
namitwasan9@gmail.com
web: www.discoverypublishinggroup.com

Printed at:
Infinity Imaging Systems
Delhi (INDIA)

PREFACE

Aim of this volume is to provide a historical background for understanding various perspectives of civilization and culture of India. First chapter gives an account of mythical origin of the Indian culture and its antiquity mostly from the Western accounts, which is followed by a brief history of India upto the end of the Muslim and the British rule in India and their influences on the Hindus. Chapters which subsequently follow clarify the theme of book further.

We would like to express our grateful thanks and indebtness to the scholars and institutions whose ideas and essays we have compiled in this volume.

My publisher and his staff members have worked hard to accomplish this difficult task. They deserve my readers love and patronage.

R.K. Pruthi

Contents

1. Introduction

Like all the great races of mankind whose traditions go back to prehistoric times, the Hindus believe that they are of divine origin. They claim descent from the person of Brahma, the creator; the Brahmins (the priestly caste) from his head, the Kshatriyas (the warrior caste) from his arms, the Vaisyas (the trading and agricultural caste) from his thighs, and the Sudras (the menial caste) from his feet. The other races of men are believed to have sprung out of the darkness which Brahma, in the process of creation, 'cast away'.

This is not, however, the only account of creation found in Hindu sacred books. The mythical sage Manu, instance, claims, in his code, that he created for mankind though not the universe. He acknowledges, however, the superiority and precedence of Brahma, whom he recognises as his father.

"This universe," says Manu, "was enveloped in darkness, unperceived, undistinguishable, undiscoverable, unknowable, as it were entirely sunk in sleep. Then the irresistible, the self-existent Lord, undiscerned, causing this universe with the five elements and all other things to become discernible, was manifested.

He who is beyond the cognizance of senses, subtle, undiscernible, and eternal, and is the essence of all beings, and inconceivable, shone forth. He desiring, seeking to produce various creatures from his own body, first created the waters, and deposited in term a seed. This (seed) became a golden egg, resplendent as the sun in which he himself was born as Brahma, the progenitor of all the world......That Lord having continued a year in the egg, divided it into two parts by his mere thought.

With these two shells, he formed the heaven and the earth, and in the middle he placed the sky, the eight regions, and the eternal abode of the waters."*

Other writers on the subject of creation had their own theories, and in practically every Hindu sacred book will be found an account of creation substantially different from any other. And all these conflicting accounts are held to be equally sacred and true by a line of argument peculiar to the Hindu with which the reader will soon become familiar.

The Hindu conception of the universe is essentially cyclic; that is, they do not believe in an absolute beginning or end of the universe, but maintain that creation, existence and destruction are endless processes ever repeating. This does not preclude a belief in the creation or end of a particular universe. The present world of ours, for example, had a beginning and will have an end; but it is a mere link in the endless chain of universes that preceded it and is yet to succeed it. Our world was created by Brahma, and after a definite period will be destroyed and replaced by another world which will suffer a similar fate.

The Hindus have evolved an ingenious mathematical table for measuring this cyclic process. Their unit of time, in this respect, is the Kalpa or a Day of Brahma. The Kalpa is equivalent to 4,320,000,000 of our years and is divided into 1,000 Mahayugas or great ages of equal length. The Mahayuga is subdivided into four Yugas or ages, namely, the Kritayuga, the Thretayuga, the Dwaparayuga, and the Kaliyuga.

The Kritayuga is the Golden Age of the Hindus, and they believe that in this age all men are equal and good, and evil is entirely absent from the world; the length of the Kritayuga is 1,728,000 years.

Thretayuga is the second age, and evil appears in this age; its length is 1,296,000 years.

Though men of this age are not so happy as those of Kritayuga they are much happier and more religious than men of Dwaparayuga or the third age in which good and evil, equally strong, struggle for supremacy. At the end of Dwaparayuga, which lasts 864,000 years,

* Sacred Books of the East Vol. xxv, edited by Max Muller.

evil overcomes good and the world enters Kaliyuga, the fourth age of strife, sweat and toil.

As the Kaliyuga progresses evil gathers momentum till good is completely destroyed and the redemption of the world can only be brought about by its destruction and reconstruction. And for this purpose Vishnu, the second of the Hindu triad, will the Hindus believe, incarnate himself as Kalki, the destroyer, and bring about the end of the world by a deluge or by fire. The Kaliyuga lasts 432,000 years.

It is interesting to note that according to the Hindus we are now living in the sixth millennium of Kaliyuga, and there are as yet more than 425,000 years for the end of the world.

The Kalpa is a Day of Brahma. This divinity is not immortal but is destined to die like all other beings, human and divine. The span of Brahma's life is one hundred years (computed at the rate of 4,320,000,000 of our years per Kalpa or Day of Brahma). On completion of his terms of life, Brahma dies and the universe is engulfed in what is called Mahapralaya, the Greater Chaos, which destroys all gods, demons and humans. After one hundered years of Chaos, another Brahma is born, and the cycle is thus continued without end.

Mention must also be made of Pralaya, Chaos, which succeeds every Kalpa or Day of Brahma. This Chaos and the attendant confusion are believed to be caused by the Night of Brahma when this god goes to sleep. The Night of Brahma, obviously, is of equal length as the Kalpa, but in the morning, when Brahma wakes up, order is again restored and life and light reappear.

The Hindus have found out the age of their creator; the reigning Brahma has just completed the 50th year of his life.

Like the Hebrews, the Hindus have a legend of the flood. To understand this, the reader must have some idea of another division of the Kalpa, known as Manwantara. The Kalpa is divided into 14 Manwantaras over each of which presides a Manu or world teacher. The Hindu legend of the flood narrates how the present Manu was saved by Vishnu in the form of a fish from the Deluge that brought about the destruction of the world which immediately preceded ours. This is the story:

"There lived in ancient times a holy man
Called Manu, who, by penances and prayers,
Had won the favour of the Lord of Heaven.
One day they brought him water for ablution;
Then, as they washed his hands, a little fish
Appeared, and spoken in human accents thus:
'Take care of me, and I will be they Saviour! '
'From what wilt thou preserve me? ' Manu asked.
The fish replied: 'A flood will sweep away'
All creatures; I will rescue thee from that.
'But how shall I preserve thee? ' Manu said.
The fish rejoined, 'so long as we are small,
We are in constant danger of destruction,
For fish eat fish; so keep me in a jar,
When I outgrow the jar, then dig a trench,
And place me there; when I outgrow the trench,
Then take me to the ocean—I shall then
Be out of reach of danger.' Having then
Instructed Manu, straightway rapidly
The fish grew larger; then he spoke again:
'In such and such a year the flood will come;
Therefore construct a ship, and pay me homage.
When the flood rises, enter thou the ship,
And I will rescue thee.' So Manu did
As he was ordered, and preserved the fish,
Then carried it in safety to the ocean;
And in the very year the fish enjoined
He built a ship, and paid the fish respect
And there took refuge when the flood arose.
Soon near him swam the fish and to his horn
Manu made fast the cable of his vessel.
Thus drawn along the waters, Manu passed
Beyond the northern mountain. Then the fish
Addressing Manu, said, 'I have preserved thee,
Quickly attach the ship to yonder tree;
But lest the waters sink from under thee,
As fast as they subside, so fast shalt thou
Descend the mountain gently after them.'
Thus he descended from the northern mountain.
The flood had swept all living creatures:
Manu alone was left."*

* Monier Williams, Indian Wisdom.

In another version of the myth it is said that Manu took with him the Seven Sages and a pair of every living creature, who repeopled the world after the deluge.

PREHISTORY

The peoples now known as Hindus are not ethnologically homogeneous. Most of the Hindus have nothing in common except the name. Even their name *'Hindu'*, is of foreign origin. There is no common word of indigenous origin which is applicable to all the Hindus. The word *'Aryan'* was applied to the three higher castes, but the fourth and the fifth castes, who form the majority of the Hindus, used to be known by their caste or sub-caste names.

The Hindus consist mainly of the aborigines of India and the various races that invaded and settled down in the country upto the time of the Muslim conquest. From time immemorial India has been considered fair prize for the invader, and the races that burst into the country from the North West were numerous. They invaded the country in different periods of its history, conquered the inhabitants and settled down slowly absorbing their religion and culture. The Hindus and Hinduism are the results of these racial migrations and fusions.

Of all the races that conquered India, the Aryans are the most noteworthy. They have managed to dominate the cultural life of India from the time of their irruption into country down to our times. The Aryans, after their settlement in the country, were, no doubt conquered by more virile tribes from Central Asia; but the traditions and the culture of the latter were readily assimilated by the Aryans and they themselves thought it a privilege to be recognised as a unit of the Aryan social system. All the literature and social theories of the Hindus are so permeated with overt and insidious statements of Aryan superiority that even non-Aryan kings who managed to subdue the Aryans had to recognise the superiority of the conquered. Hindu literature, dominated by Aryan prejudices had, for a long time, misled even impartial historians, and till very recently it was generally believed that, prior to the Aryan conquest, India was a wild country inhabited by savages and cannibals to whom the conquerors brought the blessings of civilisation. Ancient Indo-Aryan literature describes the peoples whom the Aryans conquered as demons, monsters and Sons of the Night.

Recent discoveries at Mohan-jo-daro and elsewhere disprove this ancient assertion and show that the races whom the Aryans conquered were a civilised people, culturally far more advanced than the warlike Aryan nomads who invaded their country. Excavations at Mohan-jo-daro unearthed a civilisation which flourished in the Indus Valley five thousand years ago.

The inhabitants of Mohan-jo-daro, from what we can make out of the ruins of their city, were a refined artistic people who knew how to plan and build cities, palaces, and houses for the common folk, and who loved a peaceful life.

"The town (of Mohan-jo-daro) is well laid out. Its streets are at right angles, running due north and south and east and west. The main street which is 33 ft. wide had been traced for half a mile and is unpaved. The side roads are about half this width. The buildings are of burnt brick set in mud mortar.

No stone is used and the absence of any kind of ornamentation is conspicuous. The windows and doors open upon the main street and it is probable that some were several storeys high, with flat roofs. An unusual feature of the houses is the presence of bathrooms, and also of an elaborate drainage system, greatly in advance of anything known in later India. For this purpose, pottery drain pipes and receptacles were laid down, communicating with the street drain or gutter.

No temple has been discovered, but a large public bath, 39 by 23 ft., has been unearthed. This bath which was rendered water-tight, is provided with steps leading down to the water, a promenade, and compartments for the bathers. Ingenious arrangements for filling and emptying it are provided. Just to the south of the bathroom is a large building, over two hundred feet long and one hundred feet wide, which may have been the royal palace."*

Ornaments, toys, sculptures and beautiful works of art in bronze and clay have been discovered together with seals with inscriptions on them. Mohan-jo-daro folk had a genius for works of clay, and earthen pots and jars with patterns of concentric circles in black, or ornamented with figures of trees, birds and animals, are found in large numbers.

Though temples have not been discovered, there is sufficient proof to show that the people of Mohan-jo-daro had a fairly well developed religion. The supreme spirit they worshipped was the Mother Goddess;

---

* India, Rawlinson.

"she is represented in numerous pottery figures and on seals and amulets." The worship of Shiva and the Lingam also appear to have been widespread. These religious ideas, no doubt, influenced later Hinduism although the Brahmins with their predilection for Aryan practices never acknowledge the sources.

All this may not sound very impressive when compared to modern achievements. But 5,000 years ago this was something really remarkable and it gives us a picture of India radically different from that painted by Indo-Aryans. Mohan-jo-daro culture was widely distributed at least from the Punjab right down to the Mekran coast, if not farther east. The culture is believed to have been Dravidian.

The rich cities of the Dravidians very naturally attracted the attention of the warlike Aryan hordes who successfully invaded the country, and either enslaved the native population or drove them towards the east and south-east. From the scanty records left by the Aryans themselves, it can be seen that the battles were bloody and fierce. But eventually the Dravidians were subdued and the Aryans occupied the country.

After a time, the conquered and the conquerors began to mix freely and to intermarry. This probably alarmed the leaders among the Aryans who had an exaggerated idea of their racial purity, and codes began to be laid down prohibiting intermarriage and free social intercourse. Thus were laid the foundations of the caste system, the most rigorous social code in the world.

The Aryans were racial and not religious fantics. They found no harm in borrowing the gods of the conquered races and giving them a place, subordinate though, in their patheon. Nor were the gods of the conquered the only ones the Indo-Aryans admitted into their pantheon.

In course of time the fate that befell the Dravidians befell the Aryans too, and they, in turn, were conquered by foreign races. The Indo-Aryans had to make room for these people in their social system, and for their gods in the pantheon. But social intercourse with the foreign races had to be prohibited in order to preserve the racial purity of the Aryans.

Hence each community that was admitted into the all-embracing Hindu fold was organised into an independent social unit a definite status and a code of its own, and all social intercourse between any two communities was prohibited. In religious matters, however, a more lenient attitude was adopted. People were allowed to worship any gods they pleased and hold any views they liked as long as these did not seriously challenge the fundamental principles of social organisation.

These tendencies gave rise to the main distinguishing feature of Hinduism, i.e.: social tyranny flourishing side by side with religious anarchy. Down to the present day, Hinduism permits its followers to worship any deities they like or no deity at all, but transgression of social codes in matters such as inter-dining or inter-marrying may easily lead to excommunication.

HISTORY

Ancient Hindus had distinguished themselves in many arts and sciences, and the works they have left us on philosophy, medicine, architecture, etc., compare favourably with those of any other ancient race. But no historical work of any merit is found in the voluminous literature of the Hindus.

The real history of India begins only after the Muslim conquest, and upto that period Indian history remains mostly a matter of conjucture. There are some accounts of India which have come down to us from foreigners who visited the country as travellers or invaded it, and these together with what can be gleaned from the literature and monuments of the Hindus give us some inkling into the condition of the country and its people at certain periods. But we look in vain into the literature of the Hindus for a continuous history of India.

The first authentic account of India and its people come from the Greeks. Alexander invaded the Punjab and the Indus Valley in the fourth century B.C. and his historians wrote and account of the people they saw in India. The original was lost, but copious extracts were preserved in the writings of later authors. After Alexander's conquests there was constant contact, for a long time, between the Greeks and Indians, and some of the Greek governors of Alexander's empire entered into matrimonial relationship with Indian kings and sent envoys to them.

One of these envoys, the celebrated Megasthenes, wrote an account of India, Megasthenes was the envoy of Seleucus Nicator, the Greek ruler of the North West Frontier which Alexander had conquered, sent to his ally Chandragupta Maurya, the Hindu emperor of Magadha. Megasthenes lived in Pataliputra, (modern Patna) the capital of

Magadha, for a number of years and had plenty of opportunities of studying the people of the country.

The picture he paints of India is a very pleasant one. The country was prosperous and the people were contented and happy. The land was well-irrigated, and famines were unknown. The country was traversed by numerous highways connecting all the great cities of the empire and trade flourished. There was an efficient postal system. Profiteering was not permitted and the prices were controlled.

Pataliputra had a municipal government of its own administered by six boards each consisting of five members. The first board dealt with trade; the second with foreigners coming into and going out of the city; and third was concerned with registration of births and death; and the remaining three were in charge of commerce.

"Megasthenes tells us that a noble simplicity was the predominant Indian characteristic..........'No Indian had ever been convicted of lying.... In the whole of Chandraguptas's camp of 400,000 men there who no conviction for theft exceeding 200 drahmae (£8/). They were not litigious'."

Whatever might have been the high sense of integrity or honesty of the people, their king, as we shall see presently, was far from being an example to his subjects.

Chandragupta Maurya was the first great emperor of India and we have accounts of him, left by Greek writers and by Indians, which show that he was a remarkable man. He was of low origin, but ambitious and unscrupulous. By intrigue and murder he managed to usurp the throne of Magadha and extend the frontiers of the kingdom.

In all his activities he was ably assisted by his Brahmin adviser Chanakya or Kautilya, the Indian Machiavelli. Kautilya's Arthastra (manual of polities), written 23 centuries ago, reads strikingly modern. Treating the traditional Hindu theories of statecraft and diplomacy with contempt, Chanakya struck a line of his own. He held that deceit, treachery and violence were indispensable to a king, and that a kingdom could be properly ruled only through spies, exaction, and a powerful standing army.

However much we may deplore the methods of Chanakya, Chandragupta appears to have flourished under his guidance. He managed first to foment rebellion in the Punjab, which was at that time under the Greeks, and take possession of it. He then successfully conspired against the king of Magadha whom he murdered. He usurped the throne of Magadha and built a powerful and beautiful city called Pataliputra on the banks of the Son, which he made the capital of his vast kingdom. He organised a powerful army and defeated Seleucus Nicator, the Greek ruler of Western Asia, who tried to reconquer the Punjab from the Indian king. After his defeat the two kings seems to have lived on friendly terms.

Chandragupta loved the pleasures of the world. His palace was the wonder of all those who beheld it. "In the Indian royal palace," writes Megasthenes, "there are wonders with which neither Memnonian Susa in all its glory, nor the magnificence of Ecbatana can hope to vie."

He had a well-stocked harem and an army of dancing girls, and the chief courtezan of the palace received almost the wages of minister. Having won his kingdom by intrigue and maintaining it by violence, Chandragupta "took elaborate precautions against assassination. He never slept twice in the same bed, and all food and drink were carefully tested in order to guard against poison. No one could enter the palace precincts without a permit, and an army of spies and agents provocateurs was employed to watch what was happening in the city, and no methods were considered too unscrupulous for getting rid of enemies of the state.

He was surrounded by a host of slave girls who cooked and served his food, tended to his wants, massaged his limbs and entertained him with dancing and music. A body-guard of foreign Amazons kept watch over the palace day and night. Chandragupta seldom went abroad except on festal occasions, when he rode in solemn procession through the streets in a litter on the back of an elephant."*

The country, under this oppressive tyrant, prospered! The people lived in peace with one another and the ever vigilant monarch allowed neither a neighboring monarch nor an ambitious subject to disturb the peace of the land. He permitted no one except himself to oppress his people. The officers of the state were carefully watched by spies and those who showed a tendency to amass wealth by accepting illegal gratification were dismissed and punished. Hence though the government was bureaucratic, the officials went in fear of the king and seldom dared to oppress the people.

---

* *India,* Rawlinson.

Chandragupta died in 298 B.C. It appears towards the end of his life he became a penitent and died a Jain monk in the famous monastery of Shravan Belgola in Mysore. According to another story he committed suicide.

Bindusara, his son, succeeded Chandragupta, but little is known of his long reign. Bindusara's son Asoka ascended the throne in 273 B.C., and this emperor is recognised by all the greatest of ancient Indian monarchs.

Brought up in the tradition of Chanakya and Chandragupta, Asoka's first concern, on coming to power was to extend the frontiers of his kingdom. He led an army against the kingdom of Kalinga, the modern Orissa, with no better excuse than the desire to annex it. The people of Kalinga resented this wanton invasion of their and fought fiercely. In the end the brave Kalingas were defeated and put to the the sword. The carnage was terrible and Asoka was profoundly moved by the bloodshed and misery caused to millions of people through his ambition and love for power.

He turned away from the field of battle in disgust, determined no more to conquer kingdoms. The teachings of the Buddha profoundly affected the king, and becoming a convert to this faith, he devoted his whole energy to the spread of Buddhism and to teaching men how to tread the noble path of virtue.

Throughout his vast empire he caused stone pillars to be erected on which engraved rules of conduct for his subjects. Some of these edicts are still extant and we know a good deal of the character of the monarch from these." "The Law, wherever pillars of stone or tables of stone exist, must be recorded so that it may long endure." "The Law as enjoined by Asoka was strictly practical and suited to the popular understandings.

No mention is made of metaphysical subtleties. It consists of compassion, liberality, truth, purity, gentleness and saintlines of life, 'harkening to elders, reverence to elders, and seemly treatment of Brahmins and ascetics, of the poor and wretched, yea, even of slaves and of servants'."

The emperor extended his kindness even to animals. He abolished the royal hunt and brought the slaughter of animals to a minimum. Hospitals were built in the kingdom not only for the sick among humans but even for animals and birds.

Chandragupta's elaborate spy system was converted by Asoka into a body of 'Overseers of the Law' who had to report to him periodically on the progress of religion in their jurisdiction. Though a Buddhist, he established complete religious toleration in his kingdom. The harsh and oppressive laws of Chandragupta were abolished and force was treated as necessary evil to be used only in case of extreme necessity. In his edicts he adjures his successors to bear in mind, "if ever they are tempted by the lust of empire, the worthlessness of conquest by force. 'The conquest of the Law,' he assures them, 'is alone a conquest full of delight'."

Asoka's attempts to lead men to the path of virtue were not confined to his own kingdom. He sent Buddhist missionaries to all the known parts of the world. Not only were great cultural centres like Alexandria, Asia Minor and Greece visited by these missions, but even the animistic and wild tribes of Central Asia were brought under the civilising influence of Buddism by the efforts of Asoka's missionaries.

The empire of Asoka extended from the Hindu Kush to the Bay of Bengal, from Kashmir to Mysore. The vast dominions were well governed and the example of the saintly emperor inspired the civil servants and the people. The great highways that traversed the length and breadth of the empire were safe for tradesmen and pilgrims, and the land was prosperous in the extreme.

"Asoka has been compared at various times to Marcus Aurelius, Saint Paul and Constantine. But no Christian ruler has even attempted to apply to the government of a great empire the principles of the Sermon on the Mount, or to announce, in a public edict addressed to his subjects, that 'although a man does him injury, His Majesty holds that it must be patiently borne, as far as it possibly can be borne.'

Two hundred and fifty years before Christ, Asoka had the courage to express his horror and remorse at the results of successful campaign, and deliberately to renounce war as a means of policy, in spite of the fact that his dominions included the unsubdued tribes of the North-west Frontier and was able in practice to put an end to cruelty to man and beast, and establish complete religious toleration throughout India. Asoka fulfilled Plato's ideal of the state in which 'kings are philosophers and philosophers kings.' "*

---

* *India,* Rawlinson.

Asoka died died in 232 B.C. after a reign of over forty years. Towards the end of his life he joined a Buddhist monastery and lived the life of a recluse.

We know little of Asoka's successors. They were not equal to the task to them by Asoka, and in the beginning of the 2nd century the Mauryans were overthrown by a Hindu chief who founded the.short-lived Sunga dynasty and established Brahminism as the state religion of the empire.

The Mauryan empire disintegrated soon after Asoka's death, and India against fell into chaotic conditions in which every chieftain fought for dominion and supremacy over his neighbour. The ever vigilant tribes of Central Asia, finding their opportunity in the weakness of Indian rules, made several inroads into the country.

Kanishka, the chieftain of one of these tribes known as Kushans, established himself in the north-west of India, and from Peshawar extended his kingdom eastwards and towards Kashmir. Like Asoka, Kanishka too came under the influence of Buddhism and was converted by the celebrated Buddhist scholar Asvaghsoha. Kanishka appears to have tried to emulate Asoka. He strenuously worked for the spread of the Buddhist faith.

To reconcile the differences of the various sects that had by now sprung up in Buddhism he convened a council of the leaders of the different sects. The council met at Kundalavana Monastery in Kashmir and was attended by about 500 monks from different parts of the country. After six months of discussion they seemed to have come to some sort of an agreement.

Though a great patron of art, literature and religion, Kanishka was, after all, a newly converted barbarian from the north and lacked the poise of Asoka, born and brought up in the land of the Buddha. The Buddhism that emerged out of Kanishka's efforts was the Mahayana or Northern Church, 'which differs as much from the primitive Buddhism of the Hinayana, or Little Vehicle of the South, as Medieval Catholicism does from the simple creed of the Christains of the century.'

Situated at the extreme north of India, Kanishka's capital Purushapura (Peshawar) was a meeting place of the civilisations of the east and west. Kanishka was great builder and his capital was embellished by many magnificent buildings. Of these the wooden tower of Purushapura, over six hundred feet in height, erected to enshrine certain relics of the Buddha deserves particular mention. "It consisted of fourteen storeys, and was crowned by an iron pinnacle, surmounted by a number of copper gilt umbrellas...Its side were adorned with numerous images of the Buddha, and it was many times restored. It was still standing in the 6th century A.D. and foreign visitors to India regarded it as one of the wonders of the world." But because of the impermanence of the material used, the tower did not survive the ravages of time and has not come down to our own times.

The Kushans cultivated friendly relations with the Roman emperors to the mutual advantage of both, and a brisk trade flourished between the Kushan empire and the Asiatic provinces of the Roman empire, both by land and by sea. The overland trade route ran through Balkh, and the sea route started from Barygaza (Broach) on the mouth of Narbada and ended in the Persian Gulf whence the merchandise went by land. This trade brought much prosperity to the Kushan Empire and the capital was wealthy to an unheard of degree.

The exact date of Kanishka's death is not known, but he is believed to have died in the third quarter of the second century A.D. A legend says he was assassinated by his people because of his tyranny. According to one account, Kanishka "is greedy, cruel and unreasonable; his campaigns and continued conquests have wearied the mass of his servants. He knows not to be content but wants to rule over the four quarters. The garrisons are stationed in distant frontiers, and our relatives are far from us. Such being the situation, we must agree among ourselves and get rid of him. After that we may be happy." Kanishka was a Buddhist, and this account of the great Kushan emperor was probably inspired by Brahmins.

After Kanishka's reign, India again relapsed into a period of disorder and strife. The beginning of the fourth century A.D. was, however, marked by the rise of the Guptas. The Guptas were orthodox Hindus. The Gupta empire reached the zenith of its glory in the reign of Chandragupta II, known in Indian legend as Vikramaditya. In the reign of this monarch, the Chiness traveller Fa Hian visited India on a pilgrimage to the holy places of Buddhism. Chandragupta had transferred his capital from Pataliputra to Ayoddhya, the city of Ram, but it appears he lived the better part of the year in Ujjan which was the centre of his activities as told in legends connected with his life.

Fa Hian tells us of the great car processions of Pataliputra, of hospitals founded by charriable persons throughout the country, and of physicians competent to deal with every kind of sickness. The caste system was in full swing and the low castes had to live outside the city walls. The people were intensely religious, whether Buddhists or Hindus, and temples and monasteries could be seen everywhere in India. There were great centres of learning, conducted mainly by priests, to which students and scholars from the different parts of the country flocked.

After the death of Chandragupta II, the Central Asian hordes again invaded India. The While Huns made many inroads into India and Mihiragula, who established himself in Kashmir in the beginning of the 6th century A.D., is described by Bhuddhist writers as a ferocious iconoclast who destroyed monasteries and shrines and massacred the priests. One of his favourite pastimes was to was to watch the death agony of elephants hurled at his command from the precipices of Himalayan hills.

The Huns penetrated deep into India. They overran the Punjab, but were prevented from expanding eastwards by a confederacy of Hindu princes who checked their advance. This, however, did not stop them from penetrating southwards as far as Gujarat and the sea coast. All these wild tribes settled down in India and were, in due time, absorbed in Hinduism; they too enriched its legends and mythology.

The strife between the different warring elements in the country continued till the seventh century when the rise of Harsha of Kanauj again restored order and peace for some time. Harsha was a lad of sixteen when he ascended the throne. "He went from east to west, subduing all who were not obedient. During this time the elephants were not unharnessed nor the soldiers unhelmeted. After six years of incessant campaigning he was able to rule in peace for thirty years without striking a blow."

Harsha's empire stretched from the Vindhyas to the Himalayas, from the Bay of Bengal to the Indus. South of the Vindhyas the Chalukyas ruled, and Harsha's attempts to reduce them were not successful.

We know more about Harsha and his kingdom than any of his predecessors because of the visit, in his reign, of the Chinese scholar and pilgrim Hiuen Tsang. This celebrity was an enthusiastic admirer of Harsha and he has left us panegyrics of the emperor and his kingdom.

Hiuen Tsang's descriptions of the customs and manners of the people show how little the Hindus have changed during the last fourteen hundred years. He writes: "The Kshatriyas and Brahmins are cleanly and wholesome in their dress, and they live in a homely and frugal way. There are rich merchants who deal in gold trinkets and so on. They mostly go barefooted; few wear sandals. They stain their teeth red or black. They bind up their hair and pierce their ears. They are very particular in their personal cleanliness. All wash before eating; they never use food left over from a former meal. Wooden and stone vessels must be destroyed after use; metal ones must be well-polished and rubbed. After eating they cleanse their mouth with a willow stick, and wash their hands and mouths".

The land was prosperous and the people were contented happy. Literature and art flourished in Harsha's reign. Harsha himself was a man of no mean literary talent and was the author of some works. The period was one of intense intellectual activity, and Harsha's religious toleration emboldened every thinker to propound his religious and philosophic theories fearlessly. Assemblies were often convened in which famous scholars discussed and argued abstruse subjects for days. These discussions were not always conducted in the spirit one expects of learned men. "On one occasion a professor of the Lokatya sect, who were extreme materialists, wrote out forty theses and hung them at the gate of Nalanda college, with the notice: 'If any one can refute these principles, I will give him my head as a proof of his victory.' Hiuen Tsang accepted the challenge and defeated his rival in a public disputation. He spared his head and made him his disciple."

Hiuen Tsang appears to have loved these discussions, and Harsha, as a mark of honour to the distinguished 'Master of the Law from China,' had a huge debating hall constructed, and invited all celebrated scholars of his kingdom to attend the discussion. During the debates feelings ran high and it was even feared that Hiuen Tsang's life was in danger, and Harsha had to declare that "if anyone should hurt or touch the pilgrim he should at once be beheaded, and whoever spoke against him should have his tongue cut out." This gave the pilgrim complete freedom to air his views, and we are told that Hiuen Tsang fought 'the followers of error' for eighteen days at the end of which 'there was none to enter the discussion.'

The favour Harsha showed the Buddhists brought upon him the ire of Brahmins who conspired to kill him. After many unsuccessful attempts the Brahnins fomented a rebellion, and Harsha was assassinated by his own troops.

Harsha was killed in 647 A.D. He was the last of the great Hindu emperors, and on his death India was again broken up into several petty kingdoms each warring against the other, and all living in fear of foreign invaders. We know little of this period of strife and turmoil, but when the curtain rings down again, we see the stage set for the Muslim invasion and the end of Hindu suzerainty in India. Before proceeding further with the history of North India, we may however, briefly survey the history of South India.

Though not possessing so eventful a history as that North India, the Deccan and the extreme south were prominent in the ancient world. From the very dawn of history, Malabar then known as Chera, had trade relations with great Mediterranean centres of civilisation. The Chera kingdom was ruled by a king whose titular name was Perumal. "The chief port was Muziris of Mushiri, the modern Cranganoor where there appears to have been a Roman colony and temple of Augustus." It was at this port that Apostle Thomas landed, preached the Gospel and founded the Church the members of which are even known as St. Thomas Christians.*

The most important South Indian kingdom in the ancient world was the Pandyan. Megasthenes mentions this kingdom and says that the Pandyan king possessed a powerful army and great wealth derived from trade. The principal articles of commerce were pepper, ginger, cinnamon, rice, coral, pearls, ivory, apes and peacocks.

Madura was the capital of the Pandyans and this city was famed throughout the ancient world for its wealth and splendour. The Pandyans were on friendly terms with the Romans and the trade between the two countries cemented their friendship. The Pandyan king is recorded to have sent an embassy to congratulate Augustus Caesar on his accession to the throne. A large number of Roman coins were found in South India, showing that Roman currency was legal tender in the principal

---

* Readers interested in the origin and growth of Christianity in India are referred to the author's auto work Christians and Christianity in India and Pakistan (Allen & Unwin, London.)

cities of the South. The Pandyan kings used to employ as bodyguards Roman mercenaries who are mentioned in Tamil literature as "dumb Mlecchas with their long coats and armours and their murderous souls, who might be seen acting as sentries at the palace gate."

To the north of the Pandyan and to the South of the Anddhras who ruled in the Deccan was the ancient Chola kingdom. The Cholas were of later origin but overran the Pandyan kingdom, waged successful wars with the Pallavas and the Chalukyas who had risen in the East and the North, and by the end of the 10th century A.D. had gained complete mastery ovetr South India. The Cholas were great builders and seamen. Their irrigation projects were on a stupendous scale and the whole country was well watered and cultivated. The Cholas had a powerful fleet and were the undisputed masters of the Bay of Bengal. Rajendra Chola Deva I (A.D. 1018-1035) even made a landing in Bengal and defeated the armies of Mahipala, the king of Bengal.

The Cholas waged incessant war with the Chalukyas who had risen in the Deccan. These wars had not reached a definite conclusion when the Muslims from the North invaded South India and put an end to all Hindu ambition.

MUSLIM CONQUEST AND AFTER

At the time of the Muslim conquest, we find India divided into a number of kingdoms ruled by clans called Rajputs. The origin of the Rajputs is obscure. Though at present the Rajputs claim to be blueblooded Hindus, the probability is they invaded India on the disruption of the empire of Harsha, took possession of North India and were absorbed into Hinduism.

The Rajput was brave to a fault and his loyalty has never been questioned. But few Rajput leaders could see beyond their clans, and no appeared to have been inspired by the greater interests of the race or the country. The Rajput was never so happy as when fighting, and no excuse was too trivial to pick up a quarrel. 'Too proud and indolent to undertake menial work, he spent his time quarrelling with his neighbour and raiding his territory. Haughty and punctilious, he seized upon the most trivial slight as an offence to be wiped out in blood; on one occasion, a sanguinary campaign was fought because a Raja when out hawking had picked up a partridge which had fallen over his neighbour's boundary.' The Rajput considered war as an end in itself.

Although a few Muslim generals had crossed into India before, and subdued the Hindu Kingdoms in the Indus Valley and the North West Frontier, the real invasion of India was started by Mahmud of Ghazni, known to the Hindu to the Hindus as the Idol Breaker. Year after year this audacious invader descended on the rich plains of Hindustan and carried away to Ghazni enormous wealth in gold, silver, precious stones and slaves. Jaipal the Rajput king of the Punjab could not stop him. His son Anandpal made a fervent appeal to the other Rajput kings of India to realise the danger and come to his aid; and for once the Rajputs apprreciated the need for unity and formed a confederacy to resist the invader. But the unwiedly and quarrelsome Rajput hosts were badly led and were no match for the disciplined armies of Ghazni.

Mahmud started on his expeditions in the month of October every and went back to his northern home, at the start of summer, laden with booty. He invaded India seventeen times and in his depredatory expeditions visited practically every city of northern India. Mahmud's most famous exploit was his raid on the temple of Somnath in Kathiawar. He destroyed the temple and carried away immense booty.

Mahmud had no territorial ambition and never cared to govern or annex the places he conquered. He was content with the booty he collected and left the Hindus to rule their improverished kingdoms as best as they could. The fact that Mahmud with an army, much inferior in numbers to the hosts of the Rajputs, plundered India seventeen times without meeting any serious resistance throws a sad reflection on the lack of organisation and discipline of the Rajputs.

In A.D. 1030 Mahmud died and the Rajputs enjoyed half a century's respite during which time they recovered sufficiently from the shock to indulge in internecine wars. Prithwiraj Chauhan, the Rajah of Delhi, the most powerful of the Rajput kings, abducted the daughter of Jaichand of Kanauj from the wedding hall and this led to a war between the two Rajahs.

When the Rajputs were thus engaged in their interminable quarrels, Mohammed Ghori who had overthrown the kingdom of Ghazni, invaded India. In his first attempt he was unsuccessful. But the next year he came again and defeated Prithwiraj who died on the battlefield. The Hindus died with their king or fled in panic and the carnage was terrible. When news of the defeat reached Delhi, the Rajput women, headed by the queen, committed mass suicide in the terrible rite called jauhar (mass suicide by fire).

The Muslims entered Delhi and established themselves in the city. Unlike Ghazni, Ghori believed in the Muslims occupying and ruling India, and he left his general Kutub-ud-din Aibek in Delhi to continue the conquests and bring the whole of India under subjection. Mohammed Ghori fell by the assassin's dagger in 1206 A.D., but his Indian conquests were ably ruled by Kutub-ud-din who now assumed independent sovereignty with his capital at Delhi. Kutub-ud-din was the first Sultan of Delhi, and to commemorate his conquests, he built the Kutub Minar, still extant, 'rightly considered by Fergusson to be unsurpassed by any building of its type in the world .'

Kutub-ud-din brought the whole of North India under subjection, and the other Muslim dynasties, that succeeded his, extended their conquests southwards. In fact, from the ascension of Kutub-ud-din to the throne of Delhi in the early part of the thirteenth century till the death of the Mogul emperor Aurangazeb in 1707, the Muslims were the undisputed masters of India. What Hindu princes remained in North India were vassals of the central Muslim power; but in the south some Hindu princes enjoyed a certain amount of independence, especially under weak Muslim rulers. It is, however worthy of note that an independent Hindu Kingdom (Vijaynagar) flourished in the Deccan for about two centuries. This kingdom was overrun by Muslims in the 16th century A.D.

The death of Aurangazeb and the disorder that followed marked the rise of the Maharathas and the Sikhs. The religious policy of Aurangazeb caused much discontent among the Hindus, and Shivaji, the great Maharatha leader, carried on an incessant war with the Moguls till his death, and this was not a little responsible for the weakening and the break up of the Mogul empire. The Maharatha power grew with surprising rapidity and it appeared as though the Hindus had reconquered India and brought the Muslims under subjection. The Muslims however, united themselves to check the power of the Maharathas. The confederacy was led by Ahmad Shah Durrani, the ruler of Afghanistan, who was alarmed by the rising power of the Maharathas whose activities had reached the Punjab as far as Lahore. The Muslims and the Hindus met on the historic battle field of Panipat near Delhi, and the Maharathas were defeated (1761) and put to flight. Durrani did not stay in India, but returned to Kabul leaving India in the hands of weaklings, and thus and paved the way for the British conquest of India.

The British who came to India as traders took advantage of the political confusion that followed the disruption of the Mogul Empire and by a steady policy of expansion gained complete supremacy over India and ruled the country from the nineteenth century till august 15th, 1947 when they relinquished control to Indians. Unlike the other conquerors who settled down in the country, the British were birds to passage who have left no lasting ethnic impression on the population of India, though the political institutions they have bequeathed are of an enduring nature.

THE MUSLIM AND BRITISH INFLUENCE ON THE HINDUS

We have seen that prior to the arrival of the Muslims all the peoples that invaded India and settled down in the country were absorbed into Hinduism. They received a definite status in Hindu society and their religious beliefs and traditions were incorporated in Hinduism. The main reasons for this were that the newcomers' religion was little better than primitive, and that they had no dogmas, philosophical or theological systems, and no powerful sacerdotal classes to guard them. The more intelligent members of the community were probably conscious of the superiority of the Indo-Aryan religion and were anxious that their community should be accepted into the Hindu fold.

The Muslim conquerors, on the other hand, had a traditional culture of their own and they believed that the salvation of mankind could be achieved only through their religion. They hated idolatry, and considered it their duty to efface it from the world. They had definite dogmas on religion and the slightest deviation from them, even in thought, was believed to lead to eternal damnation. While they held such strong views on religion, they had the most lenient social code in the world. They were free from many social prejudices and believed that all men were equal in the sight of god and social inequalities were man-made. Thus Islam is, in every respect, the antithesis of Hinduism with its idolatrous practices, social rigidity and leanings towards spiritual anarchy. It is obvious that these two religious could not absorb one another.

In their first onrush the Muslims were extremely violent towards the religion of the Hindus. They destroyed Hindu temples and idols, plundered and forcibly concerted the Hindu and put to the sword those who would not accept Islam. This worked very well at the time of Mahmud of Ghazni, who did not trouble himself with the government of Indian territories he conquered. But with the occupation of India by Muslims, they became responsible for the good government of the country and had to adopt a more conciliatory attitude towards Hinduism, the professed religion of the majority of their subjects.

The two religions influenced each other appreciably. The lower castes were attracted by the social status they stood to gain by conversion, and the proselytizing zeal of the Muslims made them embrace Islam in large numbers. The social democracy of the Muslims profoundly affected Hindu society and wherever Muslim influence has been predominant and prolonged, Hindu society dies not show its most undesirable caste features. Idolatry among the Hindus is less prevalent in provinces which had Muslims for masters for a long time.

The uncompromising monotheism and the simplicity of worship of Islam attracted many Hindu religious thinkers and these founded sects among the Hindus which were akin to Islam. One of the undesirable results of Muslim contact was, however, the adverse effect it had on the position of Hindu women in society. The status of Hindu women at the time of the Muslim conquest was anything but enviable; with the advent of the Muslims, the Hindus began to imitate the ways of the rulers and introduced the Purdah system in their society.

The contact with the British had its own effect on Hinduism. Although the British did nothing actively to force their social or religious codes on the Hindus, the tendency of all subject races to imitate their rulers resulted in the introduction of many social changes among the Hindus. The position of women was definitely raised both among the Muslims and Hindus because of the freedom enjoyed by women among Westerners.

The taboo prohibiting sea voyages, which contributed not a little to make the Hindus narrow-minded and conceited, was definitely broken under British rule, and many Hindus travelled abroad and were impressed by the achievements of the Western nations. They tried to teach their people that there is much good outside India which could be profitably adopted by the Hindus.

The spread of English education was instrumental in bringing home to the Hindus a political and social consciousness which eventually brought political independence to the country.

2. Loka

Swarga

Go forth, go forth on those ancient paths on which our ancient fathers passed beyond. There you shall see the two kings, Yama and Varuna, rejoicing in the sacrificial drink.

Unite with the fathers, with Yama, with the reward of your sacrifices and good deeds, in the highest heaven. Leaving behind all imperfections, go home again, merge with a glorious body.

—*Rig Veda:* hymn to the dead man (Wendy DonigerO' Flaherty)

Saptaloka

Seven steps to heaven

1. Bhoo-Loka. (Earth)
2. Bhuva-Loka. (Space between Earth and Sun, regions of Munis, Siddhas)
3. Swa-Loka. (Heaven of Indra, between Sun and the polar star)
4. Maha-Loka. (Abode of Bhrigu (Vedic sage) and other saints supposed to be co-existent with Brahma)
5. Jana-Loka. (Abode of Brahma's sons, Sanaka, Sananda, Saint Kumara)
6. *Tapa-Loka*. (Abode of deities—Vairagis are semi divine beings or Manes unconsumable by fire, and capable of translation to Satya-Loka). Manes are described in Kasi-Khanda as ascetics, mendicants, anchorites and penitents, who have completed a course of rigorous austerities.

7. *Sathya-Loka*. (Brahma-Loka) abode of Brahma. Translation to this world exempts beings from the process of rebirth.

Loka. A world, a division of the universe. Triloka (three worlds) are heaven, earth and hell.

There are also other interpretations, e.g., at the end of each *Kalpa*, or day of Brahma, the first three words are destroyed.

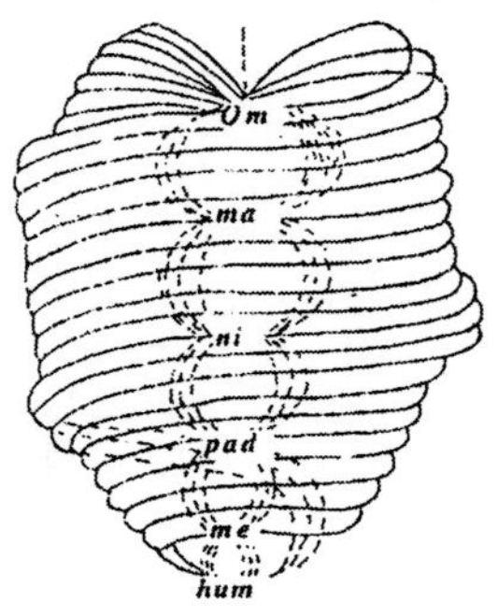

"Om Mani Padme Hum"

Brahma-Loke : (Abode of superior deities)

Pitru-Loka : (where Pitrus (fathers) the first pitrus were sons of gods; *Vaayu-Purana)*

Soma-Loka : (Moon and planets)

Indra-Loka : (Inferior deities reside here)

Gandharva-Loka : (Heavenly spirits)

Raakshasa-Loka : (Abode of *Raakshasaas* [evil spirit])

Yaksha-Loka : (Supernatural beings; attendents on Kubera, god of wealth)

Pishacha-Loka : (Friends, evil spirits).

Hierarchy of Lokas as enumerated by Sankhya and Vedaanta schools

"Planes of Existence".

'Om Mani Padme Hum' is a great Buddhist *mantra,* that reveals six planes of existence or consciousness. In this mantra there are six

syllables that correspond to the six planes of existence. viz. ***deva-loka*** *asura-loka, nara-loka, trison-loka, pretaloka, bikku-loka.*

A person using this manta *'Om Mani Padme Hum'*, relates himself to all these *lokas* and sends thoughts of compassion to them. Through this mantra he also relates himself to the whole universe and sends love and goodwill to other fellow beings in this universe.

The purpose of life or creation is to grow consciously towards the Divine, our Source—as the flower unfolding its beauty to the sun.—*Prabhushri.*

The correspondence is as follows:

'Om' : *Deva loka,* the sphere of angels or gods and goddesses.
'ma' : *Asura loka,* realm of demons.
'ni' : *Nara loka,* sphere of human beings.
'pad' : *Trison loka,* the sphere of animal natures.
'me' : *Preta loka,* the ghost land.
'hum' : *Bikku loka,* realm of utter darkness."

—Haridas Chaudhuri
—*"The Essence of Spiritual Philosophy"*

The Hindu thinkers had evolved not a linear, but a cyclic theory of time made up of *yugas, manvantaras* and *kalpas.* The universe is without beginning and without end going on recurrent phases of manifestation and dissolution.. The *yugas* or ages of the world are four in number.

In the first *yuga* called *krita,* whose duration is computed to be 4,800 years of gods (each year of gods being equal to 360 years of men), there is perfect and eternal righteousness and the *Dharma* is standing on all its four feet.

In the next three *yugas* viz. *treta, dvapara* and *kali,* consisting respectively of 3600, 2400 and 1200 years of gods, *Dharma* gradually decreases by one-fourth, remaining to the extent of only one-fourth in the present *kali yuga.* At the end of each *kali yuga* there is tremendous destruction after which the golden age appears again. This cycle of creation, destruction and recreation of the world goes on eternally.

First is *Krita* or *Sathya* meaning perfect. *Krita* or *Sathva Yuga,* the first of the ages is perfect or a four-quartered *yuga, Dharma,* the moral order of the world, during this age is firmly based.

Krita Yuga "Sathya"

This second *yuga* is the *Treta Yuga Treta* means three-quarters. During the *Yuga,* this world as well as the body of human society, is sustained by only three-fourths of its total virtue.

Treta Yuga

During *Dvapara Yuga* only two of the four quarters of *Dharma* are effective, reflecting a dangerous balance between imperfection and perfection, darkness and light.

Dvapara Yuga

And, finally, in the *Kali Yuga,* the present dark age, which began according to tradition in 3102 B.C. believed to be the age of the Mahabharata war, the world subsists on only twenty-five per cent of the full strength of *Dharma.* During this age, man and his world are at their wost with complete moral and social degradation.

***Kaalachakra* (Wheel of Time)**

The duration of each *Yuga* is computed by years of gods. A year of the gods is equal to 360 years of man. So

1. *Krita Yuga* 4,800
   4800 x 360 = 1,728,000
2. *Treta Yuga* 3,600
   3600 x 360 = 1,296,000
3. *Dvaapara Yuga* 2,400
   2400 x 360 = 864,000
4. *Kali Yuga* 1,200
   1200 x 360 = 432,000

Total 12,000 4,320,000

A day of Brahma = 1000 x 4,320,000 = 4.32 x 10^9 years

Each *yuga* or age represents a progressive decline in virtue, morality, happiness and longevity. In the *Krita yuga* the duration of human life was 4000 years. In the *Treta* 3000: In the *Dvapara* 2000. In the *Kali yuga* there is no fixed measure. We are at present in the *Kali yuga* which according to tradition began in 3102 B.C. the year of the *Mahabharata* war. The *Krita* is the golden; the *Treta* the silver; the *Dvapara* the copper and *Kali* the iron age.

The four *yugas* constitute the *Mahayuga* of 4,320,000 earthly years. One thousand *Mahayugas* or 4,320,000,000 earthly years make a *kalpa,* 'a day of Brahma'. "At the close of this day of Brahma, a collapse of the universe takes place, which lasts through a night of Brahma, equal in duration to his day, during which period the words are converted into one great ocean, when the lotus-born god (Brahma) expanded by the deglutition of the universe...sleeps on the serpent Shesha. At the end of the night he awakes and creates anew."

(*Vishnu Purana*)

> *,...at the end of the Kali-yuga there is pralaya, or destruction, and the cycle begins all over again. We are at present living in a Kali-yuga, although opinions differ as to how near we are to the final destruction, Given the incredible amassing of nuclear material over the last few decades, enough now to destroy not only mankind but all life on this planet many times over, it seems that we are nearer the end than is generally believed. But, then, we must also be nearer the new beginning, the dawning of the next Satya-yuga!*
>
> Dr. Karan Singh

A day and night of *Brahma* make up 8640 million years. 360 such days and nights constitute a 'year of *Brahma'* or 3,110,400 million earthly years. His life lasts for 100 such years, that is, 311,040,000 million years. This is the largest cycle in Hindu cosmology after which the whole universe returns to the world spirit until another creator god is evolved. Within each *kalpa* there are 14 *manvantaras* or secondary cycles, each lasting 306,720,000 years with long intervals between them. Each *manvantara* contains 71 *Mahaayugas,* a thousand of which form the *kalpa* of 4,320 million years.

At the end of each *manvantara,* the world is recreated and a new Manu appears as the progenitor of the human race. We are now in the seventh *manvantara* of the *kalpa* of which the Manu is known as *Manu Vaivasvata.*

The process of destruction after the end of each *kalpa* is described in the *Vishnu Purana.* "At the end of a thousand periods of four ages the earth is for the most part exhausted. A total death then ensues, which lasts for a hundred years, and in consequence of the failure of food all beings become languid and exanimate, and at last entirely parish. The eternal Vishnu then assumes the character of Rudra, the destroyer, and descends to reunite his creatures with himself. He enters into the rays of the Sun, drinks up all the waters of the globe and causes all moisture whatever, in living bodies or on the soil, to evaporate, thus drying up the whole earth...."

Time never stops

"Time never stops—it ever flows: the future rushes towards us to become the present, and moment by moment it merges with the entire past. In this river of time you and I stand, work and achieve.

With eyes fixed on the Goal, to strive on in the present becoming the architect of the future, is 'creative living'. In this we employ Time. We are masters of Time.

To live weeping for the past, wasting the present moments, shuddering with imaginary fears for the future is self destructive, 'suicidal living'. In this time employs us. We then become slaves of Time.

Surrender to Him all your regrets and fears, and work with blind audacity for Truth, in Truth, with Truth.

—Swami Chinmayananda

Jyotirvignyaana (Astronomy)

Astronomy in India, like in other civilisations, has very ancient origins. The earliest records of astronomical thinking in India can be found among the *Vedas* dating back to earlier than the Ist millennium B.C. Substantial progress was made in the Ist millennium A.D. with the primary interest in the study of the motions of the sun and moon in order to develop a working calendar to determine the times for performing the various religious ceremonies and agricultural operations. For the ancient Indian, the sun was the most important heavenly object and its heavenly path was considered sacred. The moon's path was observed in relation to the 27 "*nakshathras*" (lunar mansions) or asterims. It was found that the moon spends a day in each "*nakshathra*" and momentarily comes into a state of conjunction with the most conspicuous star in that group. Then the names of the lunar months, numbering 12, were given on the basis of the *nakshathra* on which the full moon occurred. These 12 lunar months total to about 354 days and sixty-two lunar months are approximately equal to sixty solar months. Thus every thirty months an extra month had to be added making that particular one a thirteen month year.

A very important feature of Indian astronomy is the cycle concept of time. This was developed from the concept of *'yuga'* or cycle. The *Mahaayuga'* or the great cycle, is conceived as a period at the beginning of which all the planetary bodies are in conjunction. This period is given as 4,320,000 solar years which is then divided into four mundane ages or *yugas'* in the descending order of 4:3:2:1. The last one is named as "*Kali Yuga*" or the Iron Age through which the world is currently passing and is believed to have started in 3102 B.C.

Aryabhata, the great Indian astronomer and mathematician of the 5th century A.D. differed from the other astronomers of the time in saying that the earth was not stationary but rotated about its own axis. The ancient Indians were aware of the seven moving celestial objects—Sun, Moon, Mercury, Venus, Mars, Jupiter and Saturn—which were generally termed as planets since the belief was that the earth was the centre of the universe around which the planets move. To these seven objects, two more were added—the demonic figures Rahu and Ketu, which are in fact the ascending and descending nodes of the moon, to facilitate the theories of the eclipses. The priestly astronomers of the era saw eclipses as caused by Rahu (the demon's head) devouring the sun or the moon. However, Aryabhata with his mathematical knowledge could provide an explanation in terms of the sun being obscured by the moon and the shadow of the earth obscuring the moon. Great importance was placed in the accurate forecasting of the eclipses as religious rituals were observed during the eclipses. Even now, these rituals are practised in many parts of India.

There were many other great scholars—Varahamihira, Bhaskara, Brahmagupta to name a few—who improved upon the knowledge of astronomy in India. Gradually, the interaction between the Indian astronomers and those from as far as Greece and Baghdad made very significant impact on the advancement of knowledge of that period.

The 2nd millennium A.D. saw the introduction of some simple instruments like the water clock for the measurement of time, among others. A versatile instrument, the astrolabe, which was known to the Greeks, travelled to India along with Arab astronomy. In the 18th century A.D., a major achievement in the usage of astronomical instruments of medieval origins was made by Maharaja Swami Jai Singh II of Jaipur, who erected huge observatories with large masonry structures for observing the celestial objects. Two of his observatories can be seen even today in Delhi and Jaipur under the exotic name of "Jantar Mantar" or the mysterious instruments. However, there are records to show that in 1689, a telescope was used for the first time on Indian soil to make stellar observations from Pondicherry, a coastal town in southern India. And the subject to astronomy in its new and modern form made inroads into India with the arrival of the Europeans about three centuries ago. Yet, even today many sections of Indian society continue to practice the astronomically timed age is old religious rituals of ancient origin sometimes meaningful and sometimes otherwise.

(G.S.D.B.)

Hindu Time Measure

Among the Hindus, 60 lunar years constitute one cycle. The first year of the cycle denotes the evolution of a new creative force which apparently is supposed to end in the last or 60th year after getting fully matured, when the new year gives rise to a new force.

The 60 lunar years are: *1. Prabhava, 2. Vibhava, 3. Sukla, 4. Pramoduta, 5. Prajotpatti, 6. Angirasa, 7. Srimukha, 8. Bhava, 9. Yuva, 10. Dhatu, 11. Eswara, 12. Bahudhanya, 13. Pramadi, 14. Vikrama, 15. Vishu, 16. Chitrabhanu, 17. Swabhanu, 18. Tarana, 19. Parthiva, 20 Vyaya, 21. Sarwajjtu, 22. Sarwadhari, 23. Virodhi, 24. Vikriti, 25. Khara, 2. Nandana, 27. Vijaya, 28. Jaya, 29. Manmatha, 30. Durmukhi, 31. Hevilambi, 32. Vilambi, 33. Vikari, 34. Sarwari, 35. Plava, 36. Shubhakritu, 37. Shobhakritu, 38. Kodhi, 39. Viswavasu, 40. Parabhava, 41. Plavanga, 42. Kilaka, 43. Soumya, 44. Sadharana, 45. Virodhikritu, 46. Paridhavi, 47. Pramadicha, 48. Ananda, 49. Rakshasa, 50. Nala, 51. Pingala, 52. Kalayukti, 53. Siddharthi, 54. Roudri, 55. Durmathi, 56. Dunhubbi, 57. Rudhirodgari, 58. Rakthakshni, 59. Krodhana, 60. Akshya.*

The Zodiac System and the Solar System

The zodiac is a broad band or belt in the heavens extending 9 degrees on each side of the ecliptic.

The ecliptic or the path of the Sun passes exactly through the centre of the zodiac longitudinally. It is an imaginary circle of 360 degrees and the ancients divided this zodiac into 12 equal parts of 30 degrees each, each being named after the constellation.

The zodiac, known as the Bhachakra in Sanskrit, revolves on its axis once in a day from east to west.

The planetary orbits which were recognised as having the most powerful influences on our earth are seven, besides the shadow planets, *Rahu* and *Ketu.*

According to *Suryasiddhaanta,* Saturn is the most distant planet from the earth. Jupiter, Mars, the Sun, Venus, Mercury and the Moon come next in the order of their distance from the terrestrial globe. The nearest planet to our own orbit is the Moon.

Body	*Time taken per degree of zodiac*
Sun	one day
Moon	1 hr 48 min
Mars	1½ days
Mercury	2/3 days
Jupiter	1/30 year
Venus	1 day
Saturn	1 month

PERSONALITY INDICATIONS

Aries (*Mesha*) the Ram

Qualities: Independent thinkers, are not strict followers of convention, lovers of scientific thought and philosophy, have their own idea of right and wrong, strongly bent upon educational pursuits, stubborn but frank, impulsive and courageous, tendency to gossip, easily influenced by flattery, martial in spirit.

The Sun in Aries: Active, intelligent, famous, traveller, wealthy, warrior, variable fortune, ambitious, phelgmatic, powerful, marked personality, impulsive, irritable, pioneering, initiative.

The Moon in Aries: Round eyes, impulsive, fond of travel, irritable, fond of women, vegetable diet, quick to decide and act, naughty, inflexible, sores in the head, dexterous, fickle-minded, war-like, enterprising, good position, self respect, valiant, ambitious, liable to hydrophobia if the moon is afflicted, large thighs, popular, restless, idiosyncratic versatile.

Taurus (*Vrishabha*) the Bull

Qualities: Have their own principles and ways, piercing intellect, not sentimental but appreciate truth, extremely good memory, high physical and mental endurance, business knack and good intuition, tendency to dominate others, liable to extremes, zealous and easily accessible to adulation slow to anger but when provoked furious like the bull, passionate, shine well as authors, book dealers and journalists.

The Sun in Taurus: Clever, reflective, attracted by perfumes and dealers in them, hated by women, slowly to action, musician, self-confident, tactful, original, sociable, intelligent, prominent nose.

The Moon in Tauras: Liberal, powerful, happy, ability to command, intelligent, handsome, influential, fond of fair sex, happy in middle life and old age, great strides in life, beautiful gait, large thighs and hips, phlegmatic afflictions, rich patience, respected, intrigues, inconsistent, wavering mind, sound judgement, voracious eater and reader, lucky, popular, influenced by women, passionate indolent.

Gemini (*Mithuna*) the Twins

Qualities: Wavering mind, active, jack of all trades but master of none, vivacious but tendency to be inconstant, subject to sudden nervous breakdowns, often conscious of their faults, liable to fraud and deception.

The Sun in Gemini: Learned, astronomer, scholarly, grammarian, polite, wealthy, critical, assimilative, good conversationalist, shy, reserved, lacking in originality.

The Moon in Gemini: Well read, creative, fond of women, learned in scriptures, able, persuasive, curly hair, powerful speaker, clever, witty, dexterous, fond of music, elevated nose, thought reader subtle, long life.

Cancer (*Kataka*) the Crab

Qualities: Intelligent, bright, frugal, industrious, sympathetic, morally not brave, attached to children and family, extremely sensitive, talkative, self-reliant, honest and unbending, love of justice and fairplay.

The Sun in Cancer: Somewhat harsh, indolent, wealthy, unhappy, constipation sickly, travelling, independent, expert astrologer.

The Moon in Cancer: Wise, powerful, charming, influenced by women, wealthy, kind, good, a bit stout, sensitive, impetuous unprofitable voyages, meditative, much immovable property, scientist, middle stature, prudent, frugal, piercing, conventional.

LEO *(Simha)* the Lion

Qualities: Have the ability to adopt themselves to any condition of life, ambitious and sometimes avaricious, independent thinkers, stick to orthodox principles of religion, tolerant of others' precepts and practices, lovers of fine arts and literature and have a certain amount of philosophical knowledge, voracious readers, capable of non-attachment and contentment.

The Sun in Leo: Stubborn, fixed views, strong, cruel, independent organising capacity and talents for propaganda, humanitarian, frequenting solitary places, generous, famous.

The Moon in Leo: Bold, irritable, large cheeks, blonde, broad face, brown eyes, repugnant to women, likes meat, frequenting forests and hills, colic troubles, inclined to be unhappy, naughty, mental anxiety, liberal, generous, deformed body, steady, autocratic, settled views, proud, ambitious.

Virgo (*Kanya*) the Virgin

Qualities: Exhibit their intelligence and memory when quite young, discriminating, emotional, carried away by impulses, love music and fine arts and acquire much power and influence over other people, liable to nervous breakdowns and paralysis, they can become great philosophers or writers.

The Sun in Virgo: Linguist, poet, mathematician, taste for literature, well read, scholarly, artistic good memory, reasoning faculty, efferminate body, frank, lucid comprehension, learned in religious lore, reserved, wanting adultation.

The Moon in Virgo: Lovely complexion almond eyes, most, charming, attractive, principled, affluent, comfortable, soft body, sweet speech, honest, truthful, modest, virtuous, intelligent, phlegmatic, fond of women, acute insight, conceited in self-estimation, reserved, conversationalist, many daughters, loqacious, astrologer, skilled in music and dance.

Libra (*Thula*) the Balance

Qualities: Keen foresight and reason out things from the standpoint of their own views, firm in conviction and unmoved by mean motives, susceptible to feelings of others minds, idealists, insensitive to what others say of them, as political leaders and religious reformers they exert tremendous influence over the masses, love excitement and have the power of intuition, not amenable to reason, great lovers of music, love, truth and honesty and do not hesitate to sacrifice even their lives at the altars of freedom and fairplay.

The Sun in Libra: Manufacture of liquors, popular, tactless base, drunkard, loose morals, arrogant, wicked, frank, submissive, pompous.

The Moon in Libra: Reverence and respect for learned and holy people , saints and gods, tall, raised nose, thin, deformed limbs, sickly constitution, rejected by kinsmen, intelligent, principled, wealthy, business-like, obliging, love for arts, far seeing, idealistic, clever, mutable, amicable, losses through women, loves women, just not ambitious, aspiring.

Scorpio (*Vrischika*) the Scorpion

Qualities: Youthful appearance, generous disposition and fierce eyes, fickle minded, love excitement, inclined towards sensuality, cultivate friendship with many people, philosophic disposition, proficient in fine arts and dancing, silent, dignified and think before they speak, good conversationalists and writers.

The Sun in Scorpio: Adventurous, bold, fearing thieves and robbers, reckless, and stubborn, unprincipled, impulsive, idiotic, indolent, surgical skill, dexterous, military ability.

The Moon in Scorpio: Broad eyes, wide chest, round shanks and thighs, isolation from parents and preceptors, brown complexion, straight-forward, frank, open-minded, cruel, simulator, malicious, sterility, agitated, unhappy, wealthy, impetuous, obstinate.

Sagittarius (*Dhanus*) the Centaur

Qualities: Generally inclined towards corpulence, conventional and businesslike, prompt and uphold conservative view, attracted towards the study of occult philosophy and sciences, unostentatious, god-fearing, honest, humble and free from hypocrisy, brilliant, affable.

The Sun in Sagittarius: Short-tempered, reliable, rich, obstinate, respected by all, happy, popular, religious, wealthy, musician.

The Moon in Sagittarius: Face broad, teeth large, skilled in fine arts, indistinct shoulders, disfigured nails and arms, deep and inventive intellect, yielding to praise, good speech, upright, help from wife and women, happy marriage, many children, good inheritance, benefactor, patron of arts and literature, ceremonial minded, showy, unexpected gifts, author, reflective mentality, inflexible to threats.

Capricorn (*Makara*) the Crocodile

Qualities: Knack of adopting themselves to circumstances and environments, modest, liberal and gentlemanly in business transactions, noted for their preservance and strong mindedness, very stoical to miseries of life, generous and philanthropic, great interest in literature, science and education, god-fearing and humble.

The Sun in Capricon: Mean minded, stubborn, ignorant, miserly, pushful, unhappy, boring, active, meddlesome, obliging, humorous, witty, affable, prudent, firm.

The Moon in Capricorn: Ever attached to wife and children, virtuous, good eyes, slender waist, quick in perception, clever, active, crafty, somewhat unselfish, sagacious, merciless, unscrupulous, inconsistent, low morals, niggardly and mean.

Aquarius (*Kumbha*) the Water-bearer

Qualities: Some of the greatest philosophers and seers were born under this sign, of winning manners and elegant disposition, highly intelligent, make friends very easily, pure in heart and always inclined to help others, shine as writers, good spokesmen, interesting conversationalists, extraordinary literary skills, intuitive and good judges of character devoted to their friends and spouse.

The Sun in Aquarius: Poor, unhappy, stubborn, unlucky, unsuccessful, medium height, rare faculties, self-esteem.

The Moon in Aquarius: Fair-looking, tall, large teeth, belly low, youngish, sensual, sudden elevations and depressions, pure-minded, artistic, institutional, diplomatic, lonely, peevish, artistic taste, energetic, emotional, esoteric, mystical, grateful, healing power.

Pisces (*Meena*) the Fishes

Qualities: Reserved in their manners, god-fearing, rigid in observance of orthodox principles of religion, stubborn, tendency to exert authority over others, proud of their educational and other attainments, restless and fond of history, antiquarian talks and mythological masterpieces, frugal in spending money, generally dependent upon others throughout their life, just in their dealings, lack self-confidence.

The Sun in Pisces: Pearl merchant, peaceful, wealthy, uneventful, religious, prodigal, loved by women.

The Moon in Pisces: Fixed, dealer in pearls and fond of wife and children, perfect build, long nose, bright body, subservient to opposite sex, handsome, learned, steady, simple, good reputation, adventurous, many children spiritually inclined later in life.

(*B.V.R. & G.V.*)

KAALAPURUSHA: PERSONIFICATION OF TIME

Janmakundali

The birth chart positions, the *navagraha,* the nine planets, plus *Rahu* and *Ketu* at the time of birth. The chart has 12 positions for the 12 months of the year. The diamond within the square, which represents the earth, is formed by two triangles. The one pointing upwards represents man and the other pointing downwards stands for women. The lines marking the three outer squares symbolise the three *gunas,* the three tendencies, *Sattwa* (ascending), *Rajas* (circular movement) and *Tamas* (descending).

First 24 years

पुरूषो वाव यज्ञस्तस्य यानि चतुर्विंशातिवर्षाणि
तत्प्रातः सवनं चतुर्विंशत्पक्षरा गायत्री गायत्रं प्रातः सवनं
तदस्य वसवोऽन्वायत्ताः प्राणा वाव वसव एते हीदं सर्वं।
वासयन्ति।।१।।

Man, truly, is the sacrifice. The twenty-four years which he passes (first) are the morning libation, for the metre Gaayathri is made up of twenty-four syllables, and the morning libation is related to the Gaayathri metre. With this the Vasus are connected. The Praanas indeed are the Vasus. for they make all this stable.

(3.16.1)

Chant: "O Praanas, Vasus, unite this morning libation of mine with the midday libation. May I who am a sacrifice not be lost in the midst of the Vasus who are the Praanas."

(3.16.2)

Next 44 years

अथ यानि चतुश्चात्वारिंशद्वर्षाणि तन्माध्यन्दिनंसवनं चतुश्चात्वारिंशद्रक्षरा त्रिष्टुप्त्रैष्टुभं माध्यन्दिनंसवनं तदस्य रूद्रा अन्वायत्तः प्राण वाव रूद्रा एते हीदं एर्वं रोदयन्ति।।३।।

Now, (his next) forty-four years are the midday libation, (for) the metre Tristubh is made up of forty-four syllables, and the midday libation is related to the Tristubh metre. With this, the Rudras are connected. The Praanas indeed are the Rudras, for they cause all this (universe) to weep.

(3.16.3)

Chant: O Praanas, Rudras, unite this midday libation of **mine with** the third libation. May I, who am a sacrifice not be lost in the midst of the Rudras who are the Praanas. He surely recovers from that and become healthy.

(3.16.4)

Further 48 years

अथ यान्यष्टाचत्वारिंशद्वर्षाणि तत्तृतीयसवनमष्टाचत्वारिंशदक्षरा जगती जागतं तृतीयसवनं तदस्पादित्या अन्वायत्ताः प्राणा वावादित्पा एते हीदं सर्वमाददुते।।५।।

Then (his next) forty-eight years are the third libation. The metre Jagati is made up of forty-eight syllables and the third libration is related to the Jagati metre. With this, the Adityas are connected. The Paranas indeed are the Aditya, for they accept all this.

(3.16.5)

Chant: "O Praanas, Aadityas, extend this third libation of mine to a full length of life. May I, who am a sacrifice, not be lost in the midst of the Aadityas who are the Praanas,"

(3.16.6)

Chants help overcome illness, pain etc.

"Chandogya Upanisad"

MANTRAS (CHANTS OF LIFE)

Mantra is a Sanskrit syllable or a group of syllables, used to concentrate cosmic and psychicenergies.

It is said of Shiva, the Supreme Spirit (Paramaatman), that his body is mantra (vidya). It is made visible in the shape of a sign (linga). The linga is composed of mantras and is regarded as the body of Siva, the place where he is present. Four of these mantras occupy the four regions of the manifested world and the fifth, Isana, lies beyond them, in the central direction. From there, it is at the same time everywhere, a subtle luminous presence. It condenses into a celestial light (divya-linga) equivalent to the vibrations released by the recitation of the respective mantras. The divya-linga, which is Tatpurusha, forms the central 'root pillar' (moola stambha) of celestial light; Vaamadeva however is the linga, installed and consecrated on its base. In the 'root pillar' everything has its origin and finally ends in it. Thus it is said it was called the linga. By the evocative power of the mantras, Siva is realised through the universe; the universe is His body (sarira); this body is of pure energy (saktika sarira), containing all the elements, itself the primordial substance (pradhana)' of the moving universe.

—Stella Kramrish

Mantras create positive vibrations and healing energy field in the surrounding. Hence, they have powerful effect on the psychic health of the person chanting them.

"Trikenu"
Recitation of Lord's name -A must
Hare Rama Hare Rama
Rama Rama Hare Hare
Hare Krishna Hare Krishna
Krishna Krishna Hare Hare

Hindu scriptures extensively glorify the process of chanting the body names of Hari. In the Sree Bhagawatam it is mentioned:

"My dearking, although Kaliyuga is full of faults, inebrieties, quarrel and hypocrisy, there is one good quality about this age—it is that simply by chanting the Hare Krishna mantra, one can become free from material bondage and be promoted to the transcendental kingdom."

—Shree Bhagawatan 12.3.51

Mantras are rhythmical formulae; they evoke a supernatural presence, each mantra conjures up a corresponding vision of that supernatural presence.

—Stella Kramrisch

Gaayathri Mantra

ॐ

Aum

भूः भुवः स्वः

Bhuh Bhuvah Svah

तत् सवितुर वरेण्यं

Tat Sabitur Varenyum

भर्गो देवस्य धामहि

Bhargo Devasya Dheemahe

धियो यो नः प्रचोदयात्

Dhiyo Yo Nath Prachodayat

The *Gaayathri* is a universal prayer which does not ask for mercy or pardon but asks for a clear Intellect, so that Truth may be reflected therein without distortion. *It can be used by men and women of all castes and creeds,* for it calls upon the Glorious Power that pervades the Sun and the Three Worlds, to arouse, awaken and strengthen the Intelligence, so that it may lead one through intense *saadhana* to success.

The *Gaayathri* is divided into three sections. The first section consists of the *Pranava*.

Aum, Bhuh Bhuvah Svah.

Here, the chanter contemplates the Glory of Light that illumines the three worlds or the regions of experience.

Tat Savitur Varenyum

The second section picturies the Glory, the Splendour and the Grace which flows from the Light:

Bhargo Devasya Dheemahe.

The third section is a prayer for final liberation, through the awakening of the innate intelligence that pervades the Universe as Light.

Dhiyo Yo Nah Prachodayat.

With the chanting of this mantra the chanter is purified and is transformed into a Vipraha (wise person. sage) as the mind gets purged of all the impurities.

"The Gaayatri Mantra should be carved on the doors of every laboratory in the world".

—*J.B.S. Haldane*

Mantra Shakthi

Mantra Shakthi is something which cannot be seen. It can only be inferred. For instance, when mantras are uttered and oblations are offered in the fire, we can see the offered materials being reduced to ashes and this is called Pratyaksha, or perception through direct observation. However, the material which is reduced to ashes gets concvered by Mantra to the person for whom it was intended. This cannot be seen, it can only be inferred and this perception by inference is called Paroksha.

MANU'S CONCEPT OF GURU-SHISHYA

The Guru

He is the real guru who can reveal the form of the formless before your eyes; Who teaches the simple path, without rites or ceremonies; without rites or ceremonies; Who does not make you close your doors, and hold your breath, and renounce the world; Who makes you perceive the Supreme Spirit wherever the mind attaches itself; Who teaches you to be still in the midst of all your activities.

Fearless, always immersed in bliss, he keeps the spirit of yoga in the midst of enjoyments

—*Kabir*

Guru and the God

Guru and God are standing in front of me,
Whom should pay my respect first
I bow down to my
Guru Because Guru has shown me the path to God.

—*Kabir*

Yassaaraswatha Vaibhhavan Gurukritam peeyusha paakodbhavam
Thallabhyam gurunaiva naiva hatathah paathah pratishtaa jushaa

The splendour of knowledge which is churned out of the cream of nectar (*ambrosia*) by the preceptor can be obtained only through the benevolance of guru; and it can never be acquired forcibly by any body with a conceited bent of mind.

Even to this day, Manu is considered the first law-giver by the Indians. By the time *Manusmrithi*—treatise on the do's and dont's for all categories of people in Ancient India—took its present shape several concepts that were floating in the traditional circles got crystallised.

Education was given prime importance during the Vedic period where rituals were an integral part of the life of nomadic Aryans. The imparting of the knowledge of Vedic rituals through word of mouth from generation to generation gradually paved the way for a systematic study of these *Vedas* and the *Vedangas,* the latter being supplementary to the study of the former. In this process, the concepts of the teacher. and the taught also tend to get clear.

In ancient Sanskrit literature we come across three words that stand for a teacher viz., *Aachaarya, Upaadhyaaya* and *Guru.*

However it must be born in mind that these concepts do overlap and that their exact position in the chronological sequence cannot be determined with any certainty.

Yasakacharya's *Nируktha* explains the term *aachaarya* etymologically in the following excerpt:

Why is *aachaarya* (preceptor) called so? Aachaarya (preceptor) makes the students understand right conduct.

Or he accumulates the meaning (of texts). Or he accumulates knowledge.

But sage *Aapasthambha* who, like Manu, wrote a normative treatise on the duties of different classes of people slighty differs from this view of *Yasak.* According to *Aapasthambha* he is *aachaarya* from whom one can accumulate knowledge per training to *Dharma.*

Vachaspatri while commenting on Yogassotra summaries the qualities to be found in *aachaarya* in these words:

"Aachaarya is one who accumulates the knowledge of the scriptures; establishes one on the path of right conduct and also, he too practises the right course of action."

Even *Amarakosha* speak of *aachaarya* as one who explains the mantras and also is guide of *Manthravyakhyakrudachaarya Aadeshta.*

Chanakya, the famous author of *Arthashaasthra* viz., *Kautilya* describes *aachaarya* as one who has an abundance of both general and specific knowledge of assorted subjects, who speaks pleasantly, who has a perfect control over his organs of sense and action, one who has the capacity to impart knowledge properly.

It is interesting to note that the contexts in which the term *aachaarya* appears in the *Upanishads* suggest its exclusive usage with reference to the Vedic knowledge.

Having explained the *Vedas*, the *aachaarya* instructs the disciple: speak the truth; practise the Dharma.

Although the term *aachaarya* connotes one who imparts Vedic knowledge, in some contexts it is used to denote a teacher who imparts knowledge in general.

'The knowledge acquired through a preceptor alone will lead one to the desired goal.' 'Now as to knowledge. The teacher is the prior form; the pupil is the latter form; knowledge is their junction; instruction is their junction; instruction is their connection. Thus with regard to knowledge.'

Thus the root *Ved* and the substantive *vidya* often appear in conjunction with *acharya*. These investigations into the connotations of the world *aacharya* lead to the following:

1. In the *Brahmana* texts *aachaarya* exclusively deals with Vedic knowledge. The episode of *Jhandilya* and *Saptharathavahini* and *Shathapathbrahmana* illustrates this view.

2. In majority of the usages in the *Upanishads* the term *aachaarya* connotes a preceptor of philosophical and metaphysical knowledge.

3. In some contexts in *Upanishads aachaarya* refers to teacher of knowledge in general.

Manu defines *aachaarya* in the'following words:

> *The divja who, after performing the sacred thread-ceremony, imparts Vedic knowledge to the student along with the knowledge of kalpa and 'rahasya' is called 'aachaarya.*

Some of the key-words used in this definition of *aachaarya* need further clarification. Though *divja* normally means all the three *varnas viz, Brahmana, Kshatriya, Vaishya.*, in this context it is restricted in its meaning only to *Brahmana.*

> *The participle 'upaneeya' refers to the ceremony – 'samskaara' – of initiating a student into the study of Vedic lore. Upanayana marks the beginning of studentship.*

An examination of the definition of *aachaarya* given by Manu makes it clear that by his time, the floative traditions with regard to the concept of *aachaarya* had crystallised.

The above discussion could be summarised as follows:

1. The world *aachaarya* can be derived etymologically from
   - *(a)* *aachaarya* = right conduct
   - *(b)* aacharith = to approach, to go to for instruction or
   - *(c)* *achinothi* to accumulate knowledge wealth or merit.
2. *Aachaarya* provides shelter to the *Anthevaasins* as the meaning of the latter would suggest.
3. *Aachaarya* gives his students a second birth by performing their *upanayana samskaara* through which they are initiated into the study of the and sacred lore.
4. *Aachaarya* emancipates the student's hold through the dissemination of esoteric knowledge.
5. *Aachaarya* is an institutional instructor of intellectual and objective knowledge.

Upaadhaya another term that usually denotes a teacher, though it is met with less frequently except in the vocative case in classical Sanskrit literature. In some contexts it may also be used pejoratively as in *Mudraraakshasam,* where Chanakya tries to mollify the sentiments of his student whom he had treated rather harshly:

'My child, it is only the heady feeling of being pre-occupied with onerous tasks that perturbs us and not the irascibility towards the students that is so commonly co-existent with the upaadhyaayas.'

Even Manu recognises *Upaadhyaaya* as a person who has chosen teaching as his profession for the sake of his livelihood and has only a limited of the subjects to be taught.

Guru is a 'word almost impossible to render by one English word. It is applied to anyone to whose authority defence is due —parents, elderly relative, teachers, persons of piety and learning' as Prof. S.K. Belvarkar so rightly observes. (of H.O.S. Vol. 21. p. 16 note 6).

Yajnavalkya defines *guru* broadly as one who performs the *samskaaras* and educates the student in the Vedic lore.

In the modern context the term *'guru'* has acquired a more universal meaning of being a 'super expert' in a field of knowledge. We often hear the term *guru* being used for someone who is at the forefront of his discipline. Hence the terms such as computer guru, political, management guru have become part of the language. *In Saura Purana, guru* is described as the destroyer of ignorance. A personal of the usage of the term *guru* in different contexts in *Manusmriti* reveals that it is used as a synonyms for *aachaarya* more particularly when the rules of conduct are prescribed for the *Brahmacharin* during the latter's stay at the teacher's residence. A closer examination of such contexts suggests that an emotional and personal value is attached to *guru*. Words like *bhakti, pujan* etc. are more often associated with *guru* than with *aachaarya.*

From secret these examples we may fairly summarise that in the their connotations the term *aachaarya* is objective and institutional whereas *guru* is subjective and personal. According to Manu, students can be classified into ten categories or contrarily ten types of people are fit to be educated by a teacher.

The son of one's own teacher, One who renders personal service. One who exchanges knowledge of one subject for the sake of another, One who is righteous, One who is austere, One's relative. One who is capable of acquiring and retaining knowledge, A wealthy person, a well-wisher, a dear-person—these ten are fit to be educated by a preceptor in accordance with the tradition.

A student should be interested in the fruits of *Dharma* or *Artha* or at least proficient in rendering personal service.

Classical Sanskrit literature is replete with stanzas that deal with the various qualities to be found in an ideal student. It may not be out of place to summarise these qualities:

Capacity to acquire and retain knowledge edge; Perseverance in efforts; Total freedom from lethargy; Absence of shyness in acquiring knowledge; Absence of complacency over one's own learning; aversion to comforts; an alert mind; Detached outlook towards home, parents etc.; Presence of mind even in adverse situations; Determination to succeed -Ever active mind; Maturity and Absence of anticipation of results.

The norms he prescribes for the student regarding his behaviour during his stay at his preceptor's house throw a flood of light on the life and social mores and the times.

(R.N.N)

Tripurashri (fifth sheath of Sri Chakra) is that of *guru* which is *Sarvarthasadhaka* (grants all prosperity) one should render *seva (guru). Guru grants* wisdom in the following maaner paving for immortality (1) *Sarva siddhi;* Attainment direct knowledge of the *aatma.* (2) *Sarva Sampat: (Nishkama)* wealth without desires. (3) *Sarva priyamkari;* perpetual pleasure. (4) *Sarva mangalakarini:* the feeling of Shiva auspiciousness. (5) *Sarva kamaprada:* supreme bliss. (6) *Sarva dukha vimochini:* freedom from all miseries. (7) *Sarva mrityu prashamani: immortality. (8) Surva vigna nivarini: removal of all differences. (9) arvanga sundari;* Beauty by removal of all superstitions and *maaya* (illusion). (10) Sava saubhagya dayini: Oneness with Shiva.

Guru-dakshina

An offering to the *guru,* in reverence to *guru's* teachings.
Brahma Vidya—Spiritual Education

Science of Spirituality

Brahma Vidya or "Science of Spirituality" is commonly understood to mean be coming and *Saadhu* a retiring to the wilderness abandoning all worldly responsibility. But it is not so. Self-realisation is the culmination of a life lived intelligently and made progressively more and more free from the chains of slavery imposed by nature on man due to his imperfections and the consequent discontentment and unhappiness. The entire scheme of *Brahma Vidya* is to make a person happier and contented in his daily life so that the spiritual unfoldment will take place within the individual automatically. Self-realisation is not the sudden acquisition of special knowledge, it is the culmination of the evolutionary process in man.

"The purpose of Spiritual Education or Brahma Vidya is to enable man to have a Vision of the Divine in Society. When man combines this Vision with Topas, he merges with God. The Vision of Divinity and merging with Divinity, are like the two poles; one positive and the negative. The positive and negative will join together and take you to a position where you will become Divine."

—Baba

All the activities that an individual undertakes in this world are done with the hope to obtain a greater amount of happiness and to achieve freedom from unhappiness (called '*Dukkha Nivritthi and Sukha Praapthi*). This is known in common parlance as 'A higher standard of living' and 'A higher standard of life' or popularly known as 'Success in Life' and 'Happiness in life'. In spite of the best planning by politicians, governments, scientists, economists etc., man's life remains full of imperfections and unhappiness. This has led to wars and revolutions. The reason for this is man's excessive preoccupation with the body and the senses. All the human effort and ingenuity is spent is creating more and more avenues for sense enjoyments and then wasting all the energies by indulging in those sense pleasures. Consequently even materially prosperous people are found to lead a life of unhappiness, sorrow, anxiety and tension. The joy, happiness and contentment in one's life and the ability to spread the same to others through love, kindness and other noble qualities form the basis for a higher standard of life. Hence it can be seen that a higher standard of living does not lead to a higher standard of life. It is the noble qualities of the head and the heart that go to make a happy life for any individual. Happiness is the capacity to generate within oneself the noble qualities of love, kindness, cheerfulness, optimism and integration and also the large-heartedness to share one's material prosperity with others around oneself. Thus we find that success and happiness in life will ultimately depend upon the condition and quality of the mind and intellectual equipment of the individual.

The remedy suggested by the spiritual masters to free a person from the slavery of the sense is through the process of *"Brahma Vidya"*.

—K.V.K. Thampuran

Nine circles of Bhakti Nava Ratna (Navavidha Bhakti)

There are nine steps in the pilgrimage of man towards God along the path of dedication and surrender.

1. *Shravanam*: Developing a desire to listen to the glory and grandeur of the handiwork of god and His awe-inspiring manifestation. This is the starting point. It is by hearing about the Lord again and again that we can transform ourselves into Divinity.

2. *Keertanam:* Singing about the Lord, His manifold exploits and magnificence.

3. *Smaranam:* Dwelling on the Lord in the mind and revelling in the contemplation of His beauty, majesty and compassion.

4. *Paadasevanam:* Entering upon the worship of the Lord, by concentrating on honouring the feet or footprints.

5. *Archanam:* This develops into a total propitiation of the Lord and systematic ritualistic worship, in which the aspirant gets inner satisfaction and inspiration.

6. *Vandanam:* The aspirant begins to see his favourite form of God wherever he turns, in all beings and all objects. So, he develops an attitude of *Vandana* or reverence towards all life and nature.

7. *Dasyam:* Established in his bent of mind, he becomes the devoted servant of all without feeling inferior or seeking superiority. This is a vital step, the stage of service which every person calling himself a social worker or volunteer has to reach. It is more fruitful than reciting the name and counting beads, or sitting for hours in meditation. The Lord is pleased only when you do thing the Lord desires. How else can you win His grace? How else than by nursing, nourishing and saving His children? How else, than helping them to realise Him as their Lord and guardian and cultivating faith in Him, through your own straight and sincere living?

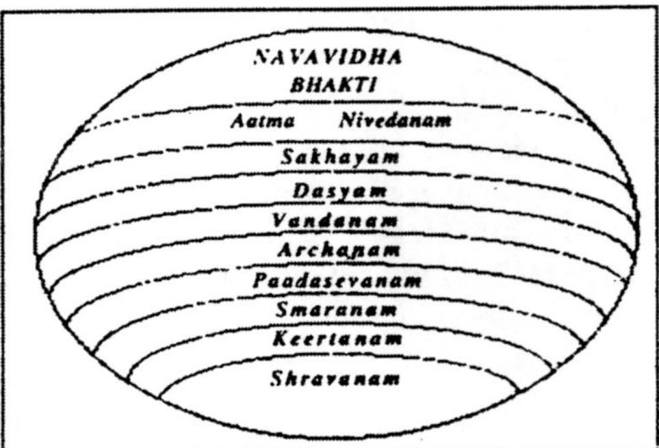

8. *Sakhayam:* This takes the seeker so near the Lord that he feels himself companion and the sharer of God's power and pity, and His triumphs and achievements. His *sakha* in fact, as Arjuna had become.

9. *Aatma Nivedanam:* This's is the prelude to the final step of total surrender or *Aatma Nivedanam.* The seeker through

his purified intuition knows and yields, fully to the will of the Lord."

—*Baba*

Nine aspects of piety

The following are the nine aspects of piety enjoined upon all persons to become virtuous.

1. *'Ṣatsanga'* or association with the virtuous
2. *'Harikatha'* or recitation of sacred hymns and songs.
3. *'Inswar Bhakti'* or love of God.
4. *'Theertha Yaatra'* or a pilgrimage to shrines and holy places.
5. *'Guru Pooja'* or worship of the preceptors.
6. *'Dhyaana'* or meditation.
7. *'Bhakta Seva'* or service of devotees of God.
8. *'Loka Kalyaana'* or welfare of all the creative being of the world.
9. *'Japa'* or constant recitation of the Lord's name.

The holy *vedas* are immortal and eternal. They are the most ancient spiritual text of Hinduism and claim to have no beginning or end. The devotional hymns and mantras to be chanted during a *yagna* are contained in the *Vedas.*

The *Yagna* begins with a ceremonial lighting of the sacred fire admidst the chanting of the *Vedas.* Everything is prepared in accordance with the instructions contained in the *Vedas.* The *kusha* grass seats for the participants, the ingredients for the *Yagna* eg. ghee, twigs....

By pouring three tins of sancified ghee into the *Yagna* fire, mankind gets in return the equivalent of three hundred tins of ghee. Its purifying effect is spread by the wind to the four corner of the world.

It is specifically mentioned in the *Vedas* that when the Vedic chants fill the air, rays of Divine Grace shower upon all mankind. Thus the *Yagna* promotes the welfare and prosperity of the world.

The *Devi Bhagavatha* also contains many potent mantras and mystic formulas. The 18,000 verses of this sacred text are recited during the *Yagna.*

Yagnas are performed for diverse reasons. The chanting of select mantras have been specially formulated by the *rishis* to awaken our latent spirituality.

However there is no need to have holy priests or costly material for the *yagna* or elaborate ceremonies.

There are other simple *yagnas* which any one of us can perform and derive happiness and mental peace.

Deva Yagna: Deva means Divine. Thinking of God...contemplating upon His multifarious activities....offering all actions to Him is called *Deva Yagna.*

Pitru Yagna: This is a sacrifice offered to one's ancestors beginning with one's mother and father. It is an expression of gratitude since they have brought us into this world. Performing various sacrifices ceremonies for one's deceased ancestors is also a form of *Pitru Yagna.*

Brahma Yagna: This *yagna* portrays an acquisition of the ageless wisdom which is enshrined in our sacred scriptures.

Atithi Yagna: The yagna is performed by providing hospitality to guests, to serve the sick and poor... provide food to the hungry and in being charitable.

Yagna (Sacrifice)

"The heart of man is itself the sacrificial fire altar. The pangs of desires are the tongues of flame; the evil that is in man is the offering that goes into the fire and the treasure of unruffled ananda is the ultimate gain. This is the real Yogna you have to perform everyday in your life. All these ceremonies are but a symbolic remainder and an inner prompting for you to act according to the dictates 21 *of Dharma, in everyday life. The Vedapurusha receiving these outer offerings is in you. Dedicate all your thoughts, world and deeds to Him. That is the real Yagna. Offer all bitterness in the sacred Fire and emerge grand, great and godly".*

—Baba

Bhootha Yagna: Bhootha Yagna consists of rendering service to all living beings. This includes kindness to animals...feeding them...protecting them in their natural habitat.

In today's world, most of us do not have the time, the knowledge of hymns and *mantras* and the necessary inclination to perform these *yagnas*.

However the efficacy of the purifying effect and spiritual potency of the *yagnas* is NOT LOST due to our non-observance of it. These ceremonies and religious rites can be viewed in another perspective...that of being entirely symbolic in nature.

The offerings to be made in the fire of Brahman is the EGO...(desire for) wealth, materialistic fame and power...Once anything is dropped into the fire it cannot be taken back because it is reduced to ashes. Our egoism..our desires..our hatred..our attachments..must be burnt out..turned to ashes..then only can it be called a *Yagna* or - sacrifice.

If we perform the ritualistic sacrificial rites without having the corresponding knowledge and spiritual wisdom, we can compare this form of *yogna* to one in which damp wood is placed and only smoke issues forth.

The perennial wisdom of the *Bhagavad Gita* details the importance of *Yagnas*. The mellifluous poetry of Lord Krishan's Divine song stands testimony to its ageless wisdom in today's world of imperfection.

The five *yagnas* have been explained by Lord Krishna in Chapter Four *(Shloka 25* and 26). Lord Krishna elaborates on the world *Yagna* considering all actions that are performed within attachment and do not stem from ego-centric desires.

Through Arjuna Lord Krishna teachers us to perform all actions in a spirit of dedicated activity. Such actions/*Yagnas* do not taint his consciousness. These actions could be performed for any personal/community/national cause which the individual is willing to perform. In this context the world *Yagna* has a more universal application.

The four essential constituents of a *Yagna* are explained by Lord Krishna in an oft-quoted *shloka* of the *Bhagavad Gita* (Chapter 4 *Shloka 24):*

"Brahman *is oblation;* Brahman is the clarified butter, etc., constituting the offerings; by *Brahman* is the oblation poured into the fire of *Brahman;* Brahman verily shall be reached by him who always sees Brahman *in all actions."*

The man who has realised *Brahman* perceives the instruments by which the oblation is poured in the fire as Brahman. All *Yagnas* arise from *Brahman* i.e. the sacrificial fire is also perceived as *Brahman*. The *Yagna* is being conducted by *Brahman* i.e. the performer of the *Yagna*. All *Yagnas* lead to the one and same goal: *Brahman*.

Many sacrificial rites or *Yagnas* are often specifically performed by people who are longing for a certain preconceived result. Such *Yagnas*/actions bind a person since they stem from egoism.

However if a *Yagna*/action is performed by one who has realised *Brahman*, then he is free from the binding effects of such an action.

Therefore it is obvious that right application of knowledge makes ever action a glorious *yagna*. The result of this form of *Yagna* is a greater amount of self-control (over the senses) and a consequent inner integration which leads to the inner flowering of the individual personality.

Dhyaana (Meditation—Union with Godhead)

धियोयोन: प्रचोदयात्-ॐ

"Dhiyo yonah prachodayat"

We mediate upon the supreme effulgence of the Divine creative sun, that the may give impulse to our intelligence.

Rig Veda, III. 62.10
Translation by David Frawley
(Vemadeva Shastri)

Grow in love, meditating on the Embodiment of Love, called Krishna. When the heart has not melted and softened to the cry of distress, when the fountain of love therein is blocked with the tinsels of pride, Krishna will not play the flute in your ear. You may claim to have spent decades in the service of Krishna, but without the key of love you cannot gain entrance to the *GoLoka* where he resides.

After long searches here and there, in temples and in churches, in earths and in heavens, at last you course back. Completing the circle

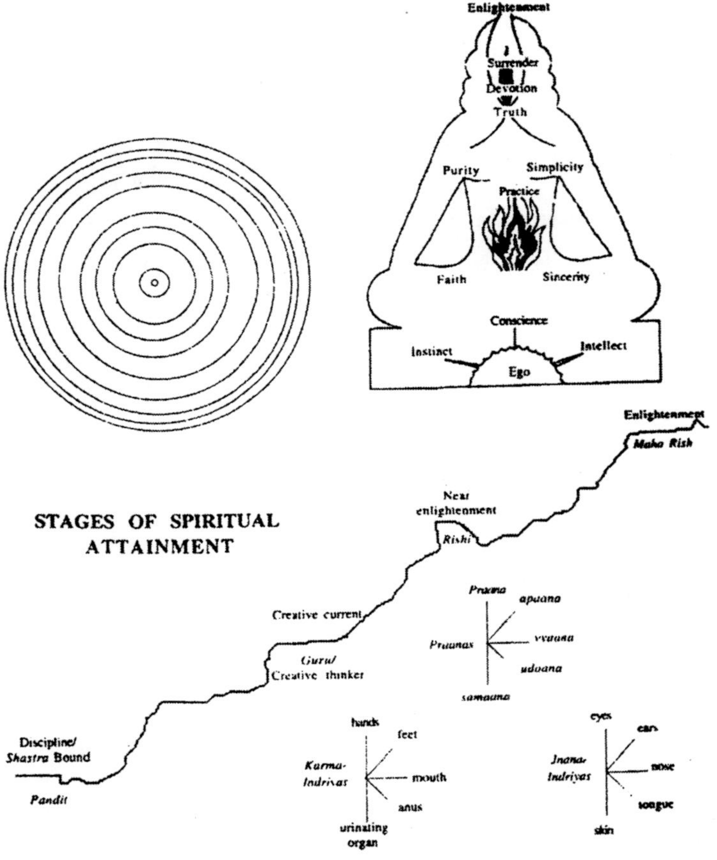

STAGES OF SPIRITUAL ATTAINMENT

from where you started, to your own soul and find that He for whom you have been seeking all over the world, for whom you have been weeping and praying in churches and temples, on whom you were looking as the mystery of all mysteries shrouded in the clouds in nearest of the near, is your ownself, the reality of your life, body and soul. That is your own nature. Assert it, manifest it. It is truth and truth alone, that is one's real friend, relative. Abide by truth tread the path of religious inquiry.

Meditation is nothing else but rising above desires; renunciation is the power of battling against evil forces and holding the mind in check.

—*Baba*

NIRVAANA

IV	*Turiva*	Enlightenment
III	Deep sleep	Near enlightenment
II	Dreaming	CreativeCurrent
I	Waking	Paradigm bound

The three states of Man (Waking, Sleep and Dream states)

The mind gets fixed during the time of sleep. Whether a person concentrates his mind or not, whether a person does *Ishvarabhakti* or not. automatically the mind gets happiness during the time of sleep. When the man gets up in the morning for a few minutes immediately after getting up, his mind is peaceful and calm and quiet. Inside the body of every living being, there is some *shakthi* or power. This is the *jeevaatman,* during the sleep, the *jeevaantman* gets merged in the *Paramaatman.*

"Only when one is able to combine the waking, dreaming and deep sleep states, or combine the gross, the subtle and the causal aspects of the body into one, that one will get a chance of having a glimpse of the divine soul."

—*Baba*

Mind *(Manas)*

Sparsha Indriyas	(recognise the objects of perception by touch): tongue, skin.
Praana: Praana-Vaayu	(located in the heart), *Apaanavaayu* (responsible for excretion),
Saman-Vaayu	(responsible for digestion), *UdaanaVaayu* (belching sound after eating), *Vyaana-Vayu* (when we are tired)
Gross body	*(Sthoola-Shareera)*
Subtle body	*(Shookshma-Shareera)*
Causal body	*(Kaarana-Shareera)*

TRAIDS OF THE FORMS

'AUM is the threefold form *aatman.* There are various triads of the forms of *aatman.* These are worshipped by the use of threefold OM.

"Whole universe is contained, is every point of space, You get darshan of divinity, on every human face.

"Trikenu"

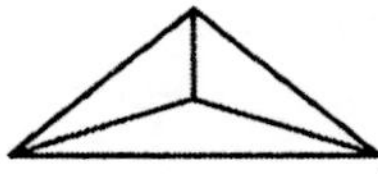

Om is the primordial, cosmic sound, the source of all words and thoughts. All other triads are variations of the triad 'AUM'.

		Triad	*Triad Forms*	
△	1.	A.U.M. (Om)	Sound form	△
△	2.	Brahma, Vishnu, Mahesh	Trinity form	△
△	3.	Generation. Operation, Destruction	GOD form	△
△	4.	*Bhuh, Bhuvah, Svah*	E,Y,Z, axis/space form	△
△	5.	Past, Present, Future	Time form	△
△	6.	Mind, Intellect & Egoism	Intelligence form	△
△	7.	Feminine, Masculine & Neuter	Gender form	△
△	8.	Fire, Wind, Sun	Light form	△
△	9.	*Sattawa, Rajas Tamas*	Guna form	△
△	10.	Lakshmi (Wealth), Saraswathi (Wisdom), Durga (Power)	*Shakthi* form	△
△	11.	Birth, Life Death	***Samsaara***	△
△	12.	Space, Time Causation	**Transcendent form**	△
△	13.	*Sathyam, Shivam, Sundaram*	***Transcendent form***	△
△	14.	*Sat* (Truth), *Chit* (Knowledge), *Aananda* (Bliss)	Transcendent form	△

Meditation in its highest form, say the *Upanishads,* is concentration upon the truth *Aham Brahmaasmi* (I am *Brahman).* As aids to meditation, various symbols of *Brahman* are accepted, of which the most important is the mystic syllable Om.

'Affix to the *Upanishad,* the bow incomparable, the sharp arrow of devotional worship; then, with mind absorbed and heart melt in love, draw the arrow and hit the mark, the imperishable *Brahman.* Om is the bow, the arrow is the individual being, and *Brahman* is the target. With a tranquil heart, take aim. Lose thyself in him, even as the arrow is lost in the target. In him are woven heaven, earth and sky, together with the mind and all the senses. Know him, the Self alone. Give up vain talk. He is the bridge of immortality. Within the lotus of the heart he dwells, where, like the spokes of a wheel, the nerves meet. Meditate on him as-Om. Easily mayest thou cross the sea of darkness.

The *guru* has perhaps no more important duty than to study carefully the personality and temperament of the pupils committed to his charge, and to prescribe to each, according to his nature, an appropriate method of meditation.

Meditation is the last step on the path of realisation.

"None beholds him with the eyes, for he is without visible form. Yet in the heart is he revealed, through self-control and meditation. Those who know him become immortal. When all the senses are stilled, when the mind is at rest, when the intellect wavers not—then is known, say the wise, the highest state. The calm of the senses and the mind has been defined as *Yoga*. He who attains it is freed from delusion.

Gather us in; Thou Love that fillest all; Gather our rival faiths within Thy fold. Rend each man's temple veil and bid it fall, That we may know that Thou hast been of old;

Gather us in.

Gather us in; worship only Thee; In varied names we stretch a common hand; In diverse form a common soul we see; In many ships we seek one spirit-land; Gather us in.

Some seek a Father in the heaven's above, Some seek a human image to adore; Some crave a Spirit vast as life and love; Within Thy mansions we have all, and more; Gather us in

—*George Matheson*

9 THE MYSTIC NUMBER NINE 9

All multiples of 9 added together ultimately become number 9. This can be verified (16x9=144;1+4+4=9).

The mystic number 9 is arrived at in this wise:

The universe is constituted of the three factors—time, space and causation.

The universe is constituted to the three *Gunas* (ingredients)—*sattwa, rajas* and *tamas.*

The Universe is constituted of the three functions—creation, preservation and destructions.

Thus this three times three making nine has become a mystic number. It exhausts the definition of the phenomenal universe.

Twice nine or eighteen makes the *Mahabharata* scheme complete.

The eighteen portions (*Parvas)* in the epic define in detail the career of man on earth.

The eighteen chapters in the *Gita* make *Yoga* philosophy complete.

The eighteen days' warfare makes the warriors' exploits complete.

Eighteen are the divisions of the armies of the contending parties—Pandavas and Kauravas. The one having seven divisions and the other eleven. Thus all the available human forces mobilised were eighteen in number.

—*Swami Chidbhavananda*

3. Glimpses of India Civilisation

India's cultural and civilisation is not only one of the most most ancient, but it is also one of the most extensive and varied. To it have contributed, throughout the ages, many races and peoples, who have either temporarily come into contact with India or have permanently settled within her borders, joining the ranks of her children and helping to evolve a distinctive Indian culture, the keynote of which is synthesis on the basis of eternal values.

The present volume digs deep into the past and reveals to our view the prehistoric glimmerings of this culture in the admirable Indus Valley Civilization which flourished over 4,000 years ago. It gives us glimpses of the Vedic civilisation when the grand spiritual foundations of Indian culture were laid, and of the Jaina and Buddhist movements which tried to spread the accumulated spiritual wealth among the masses and classes of the country and, the latter, also abroad.

Thus the foundations of the two great ideals of India—Synthesis of Cultures and Spiritual Regeneration of Man—have been truly laid in these early phases on which the future structure of India's culture has been raised.

INDIAN CIVILIZATION AND CULTURE

In one of his great poems, Bhārata-tīrtha (India as the Great Holy Spot), Rabindranath Tagore expressed, in beautiful language, how different peoples came into India from prehistoric times right down to recent centuries (which brought to the shores of India the modern European peoples) and have co-operated in building up a great culture which does not seek to exclude anything, but is all-inclusive, and does not take up an attitude which would deny to any people its right of self-expression.

As a matter of fact, the great culture of India is basically a Synthesis—a synthesis of not only blood and race, but also of speech and of ways of thinking (of which the different speeches are the outward expression) as well as of cultures—material, intellectual, and spiritual—which give ideologies and determine attitudes and actions.

The geographical background is also to be taken into consideration, because Man, in any area of the world, is a product as much of his geographical and economic environment as of his racial and cultural bearings and moorings.

No culture or civilisation has come into being in any country, and at any age, in a completed and a perfected form, like an Athena coming out full grown and fully-armed from the head of the Divinity, Zeus. There has always been an evolution in the development of Man and his surroundings—Man is for ever becoming; and like all things mundane, his affairs are ever in a state of flux.

INDIA—A UNITY IN DIVERSITY

India represents a remarkable diversity out of which a unity has developed. Some would prefer to describe it in the other way, as the expression of a basic and original Unity in its various manifestations. This other way of looking at the matter has something attractive in it for those who believe in a progressive degeneration from a Golden Age of their imagination, rather than in a sequential evolution through the ages.

But, in the face of observed facts, it is a case of a unity gradually becoming established out of diverse, and often contending, elements. It began, of course, with diversity, considering that the country presents a most remarkable array of geographical and climatic and attendant economic features, and that the first human habitants of India represented various different races whose origins and whose languages and basic cultures, to start with, were distinct from each other.

GEOGRAPHICAL VARIETY

In India we have in the Himalayan regions a climate which is as temperate as that of the greater part of Europe. There are dry sandy deserts which rival the deserts of Arabia. There are areas which display extremes of cold and heat in some of the seasons of the year and do not have any appreciable rainfall. And these areas breed a type of people who would naturally be quite different from those who live in the moister areas where there is more frequent rain than elsewhere.

There are mighty alluvial plains and riverain tracts stretching for hundreds and hundreds of miles which are exceedingly fertile and which have largely made for the wealth of the country that is based on agriculture.

There are high plateaus and wooded hills which also nurture other types of people. There are coastlands which have attracted people to maritime adventuring.

All these variations in climate and land-structure also help to bring about a most remarkable variation in the background of life, and in the life itself. Food and dress habits, as well as use of materials, styles of house-building, and ways of living, both domestic and social, have to be different, according to the background presented by Nature.

RACIAL DIVERSITY

Then the peoples who came to India represented various racial types; and with the material at our command, it has been attempted to appraise the different types of Humanity which came to be established on the soil of India, and how they reacted towards one another. The present work is concerned more with the mind and the spirit than with the body and the physical environment of the people of India—how they were enabled to think and act and find out for themselves a consistent world of ideas and of behaviour which have their value not only for the Indian Man, but also for the whole of Humanity. Consequntly, it is not so necessary to dilate upon the physical bases and aspects which came to characterise Indian life and civilisation in the different areas within the country. The great fact remains that peoples of diverse origin came to the country at different times, and they settled down beside one another; and entering into a short of great understanding or comprehension amongst themselves, they jointly built up the culture we are accustomed to associate with India: they build up 'the Wonder that is India.'

EVOLUTION OF INDIAN WAY OF LIFE

The articles mentioned above do not give the whole picture; as a matter of fact, considering the vast amount of lacunae in our knowledge of India in the formative period of her culture. It will not be possible for us to obtain the full picture. Out of a welter of race-movements and of ideological exchanges, ferments, and equillibria, we can only see dimly the gradual establishment of a way of thought and a way of life that became associated with India as a distinct entity among geographic units and human enoses. The various races follow each other as a phased sequence, or sometimes they tumble upon each other's heels throughout the centuries and millennia, making ultimately for that richness of life and experience and thought and spiritual perspective that are in the civilisation of India: the colithic Negroids from Africa; the Proto-Australoids and the Austric peoples, probably from Western Asia; the Mongoloids from the Far East, in their various ramifications; the congeries of the Asian peoples who appear to have brought the Dravidian language and culture into India; the Indo-Europeans in their various elements, racial and linguistic—not only Nordic, but also Mediterranean, Alpine, and Dimaric in race as well as language; Aryan—both as Indo-Aryan and Iranian—as well as Proto-Hellenic and historical Hellenic; and other various races and people, too numerous to mention even for the prehistoric period only.

History has forgotten, or there is want of recorded history, about at least some of these ancient races who have merged into the Indian people without leaving much trace. In historical times, other people also came, to whom we have plentiful records: the Assyrio-Babylonians, the Ancient Persians, the Greeks, the Scythians, the Parthians and other Iranians, the Turks, the Muslim Persians, the Armenians, and the modern West European peoples like the Portuguese, the French, the Dutch, and the English; possibly a backwash of the Polynesians; besides, Elamites, Finno-Ugrians, and some others. Sometimes they were quietly absorbed into the basic racial and cultural mixture that was going on—it was becoming a chemical compound and not a mechanical mixture. But there might have been, and as a matter of fact there have been, others who had already formed their own spirit of resistance, and so could give their impress, and added new elements to the culture that was being built up through unresisting co-operation; and in this way they strengthened or enriched the basic culture of India. Sometimes a kind of intransigence was noticeable; and this has given rise to problems due to mutual exclusiveness, which has still to harmonise itself with the general spirit of India—with an Indianism, or common Indian way of life and way of thinking, which has grown up.

ANTIQUITY OF INDO-ARYAN CULTURE

The Indian way of life, as it emerged with the birth of the Indian Man, which took place as the result of miscegination of Niṣāda and and Kirāta, and Dāsa-Dasyu and Ārya, i.e. of the Mongloid and the Austric, the Dravidian and the Indo-Aryan or Indo-European (possibly with other ethic groups about which we have no sure or positive evidence now), was a comparatively late thing in the history of Man. We have to bid good-bye to the theories of hoary antiquity for Indian Aryan culture, which we in India generally look upon as axiomatic. As it has been discussed in some of the papers in this volume, we might look upon the tenth century B.C., the last phase of the Vedic age, as the time when the Indian Man came into being. The beginnings of the Vedic Period may go back to the fourteenth or fifteenth century B.C., and outside India, in Iran and in Northern Mesopotamia, to a time when the pre-Vedic-Aryan or Indo-Iranian language was current. From the Mitannian and other documents, we have glimpses of the pre-Vedic and pre-Avestan language as it was in use round about 1500 B.C.

INFLUENCES FROM THE NEAR EAST

The second half of the second millennium B.C. was a period of large-scale tribal movements and racial disturbances throughout the whole of the Near East, touching also the fringes and sometimes the heart of India. In Vedic India of before the tenth century B.C., we have, it is exceedingly likely, some echoes of these racial movements. Harit Krishna Deb has shown in significant articles, which he contributed to the *Festschrift W. Geiger,*[1] that certain Mediterranean and Asia Minor peoples, who were Indo-Europeans, appear to have come to India and participated in local politics and local wars, as much as peoples like the Greeks (and with them a few other Europeans like Germanic Goths) appear to have come to India in the centuries round about Christ. The Egyptian documents of about 1200 B.C. mention a number of tribes who had come from beyond the seas into Lower Egypt, and their names are given in Egyptian documents as *śklś, 'kwś, Trś* and *Wśś,* and these names with the vowels added have been read respectively as *Shakalsha* or *Shakarsha, Akawasha, Tursha,* and *Washasha.* Three of these names are those of tribes well known in the Near East a thousand years before Christ—the Sikeloi or Siculi, i.e. the Sicilians; the Akhaiwoi or Akhaioi or Achivi, i.e. the Achaeans or Greeks; and the Tyrrhenoi or Tursci, i.e. the Tuscans, who have been often mentioned by Greek and Latin authors. Of these, the Tuscans were not, of course, Indo-European.

In the well-known Ṛg-Vedic hymn (VII. 18), describing the battle fought by the Indo-Aryan king Sudās with a confederacy of 'Ten Kings' who attacked him, we find the following tribes mentioned in the same context as being with the enemies of Sudās. They were the *Śigru,* the *Yakṣu,* and the *Turvaśa.* Harit Krishna Deb has suggested with great plausibility that the tribes mentioned in the *Ṛg-Veda* were the same as those mentioned in the Egyptian documents; only the Tursha and the *Washasha* from the Egyptian documents appear to have been combined into one tribe, probably confederated or united, as *Tur-vaśa.* This would suggest that extraneous influences from the Near East were not absent even in the initial period of India's emergence as a characterised cultural unit. Harit Krishna Deb had also suggested that there were, similarly, other groups of people—at least two of them—who might have come from the Near East, like the *Pulastis* and the *Kapardins.* Deb would identify the former with the people known to the Egyptians as the *Purasati* (who were the same as the Philistines of Palestine) and the latter with *Keftiu,* a people from Crete (the ancient Egyptian name being modified by the Jews as Kaphtors).

Less convincing, but nevertheless noteworthy, is Deb's proposal to identify some kings mentioned in the *Śatapatha Brāhmaṇa* (XIII.4.3.9) with rulers who lived and flourished in the seventh century B.C. in the lands of the Near East. A king named Arbuda Kādraveya is sought to be identified with the ruler of some peoples of ancient Iran like the Arbitai in Gedrosia-Arbuda being connected with Arbitai and Kadru (the source of the metronymic Kādraveya) with 'Gedro' in Gedrosia—and with peoples further to the west like the Elaunites. A king Asita-dhanva has been equated with Esarhaddon, the Hebrew form of the Assyrian name Ashur-akhi-iddina, who ruled over Assyria from 680 to 668 B.C. The name Matsya-Ṣammada is connected with a name like Mushezib-Marduk, a king of Babylon known to the Greek geographer Ptolemy as Mesesimordakos, who ruled in Babylon about 692 B.C. And a king Tārkṣya Vaipaścita, i.e. 'Tārkṣya the son of the Wise One' is suggested to be the same as Tarku in ancient Egyptian (or Tirhaka in Hebrew, and Tearkon in Greek), who was the king of Egypt and Ethiopia in the early seventh century B.C., whose immediate predecessor—possibly his father—was known as 'the Wise One' in Egyptian documents. These identifications may not be wholly tenable;

but they are very suggestive, and would go to show, if they at all are admissible, that the Indians, at least in North India, knew something about the names of the more important sovereigns of the Near East in the seventh century B.C.

ANTIQUITY OF VEDIC SANSKRIT

Until recently it was generally admitted that Vedic Sanskrit was the oldest Indo-Aryan language. Then came the Boghaz-köi documents which gave us some inklings of the pre-Vedic age of Aryan migrations in Northern Mesopotamia in the fourteenth century B.C. Finally, the Hittite question came before us, and it is now admitted that the discovery and reading (by the Czech scholar, the late B. Hrozny) of the language of the Hittites (the Kanisian speech) had brought for the history of Indo-European an earlier vista. The recent researches of two English scholars, Michael Ventris and John Chadwick (systematically published in their *magnum opus, Documents in Mycenean Greek*),[2] have thrown unexpected light upon the history of pre-Homeric Greek. Greek can now be taken back to several centuries before Homer, back to the fourteenth century B.C. In the Late Aegian inscriptions in linear writing, which have only recently been read by the above scholars, has been disclosed the flourishing state of Greek as a wtirren language—although with a very imperfect system of writing—as far back as 1400 B.C. This would make the ancient Greek language anterior to the Vedic by at least a couple of centuries. These are very intriguing facts which are coming to light, and they will have their repurcussions on our researches into the oldest phases of India's culture.

'AXIAL PERIOD' OF HUMAN CULTURE

But it does not matter at all that, if compared with ancient Sumer and ancient Egypt and possibly also ancient Asian Minor, our culture as a composite is not so old. But it has an ideology which is of universal appeal and value. In the history of Humanity as a whole, the first thousand years before Christ has been described as the 'Axial Period'. During these thousand years, the nations of antiquity which flourished at that time, or rather their intellectual and spiritual leaders, gave expression to certain ideas, certain intuitions with regard to the nature of the Unseen Reality, and also with regard to our relations with it, which are still vital for Humanity, and round which also the mind of modern man his gropings to grasp at the Unseen Reality is still revolving. It is the ideologies which developed in China, in India, in

Iran, in Mescpotamia, in Palestine, and in Greece that furnish the axis for modern thought-the living religions of the world.

Man, after he had become a civilised being and made life possible, and to some extent secure and comfortable, began to think seriously about the problems connected with life—particularly about the Great Guiding Force of Life and Being. It was arrived at by the deeper and the finer consciousness of Man when he had sufficiently advanced in civilisation; it was not merely the promptings of fear and wonder which lay at the root of primitive religion. Man made this great discovery for himself that behind life and existence there is a great Force, a great Presence, which has been viewed differently by different groups of men, conditioned as they were by their economic and cultural background. They discovered, as in India, the *EkṁSat*—'The One Single Existence That Is'; and the Indian sages also said that the wise men, evidently in the different societies, described it in a manifold way.

It was to be Axial Millennium with Humanity as soon as they had arrived at a postulation of this great Unseen Reality behind Life, and mankind as a whole become convinced of it. This was conceived as a unique Force which had to be obeyed without question and which would not tolerate man's homage to be paid to any other lesser conception: that was the Hebrew attitude—the attitude of the Old Testament prophets.

Behind this monistic idea of the Jewish prophets was the conception of *Aten* as arrived at by the philosopher-king of Egypt, Akhen-Aten (Amen-hotep), who saw in that Force the Lord of Light and of Guidance as manifested in the material sphere by the Sun.

In China, the conception of *Tao* or 'the Way', through which everything in this world is carried under an inevitable Law, was early arrived at, and it is the basis of all deeper religious thought in China, not only of Taoism, but also of Confucianism; and connected with the *Tao* concept is the great principle of *Yang* and *Yin,* i.e. of Light and Darkness, or the Positive and the Negative, or Heat and Cold or Sky and Earth or the Male and the Female—of Purusa and Prakṛti, in Indian parlance.

In India, possibly based on certain conceptions which worked already in the minds of pre-Aryan peoples, the great concept of Brahman or the Supreme Spirit, a kind of *Mana* (as the Polynesians named it), which is both transcendent and immanent (*kaṭa-v-ul,* as it has been called by the ancient Tamil sages of South India—'That which is beyond, and also within') in our mundane existence, was arrived at; and along with that went also the great concept of a Moral Order in the universe, which was analogous to the Chinese *Tao,* and came to be known to the Vedic people as *Rta* or the Supreme Truth, or as *Dharma* in later times, meaning 'that which holds things in itself, and represents their true nature'.

The conception of the Spirit as opposed to Matter (the latter being identical with Energy or Force—Prakṛti being the same as Śakti) also came to be developed in India, possibly before the Axial Period, or at its juncture. This had its bases in certain concepts like that of the Unseen Reality as the Great Mother of Universe which developed in the Near East before the Axial Period.

During this Axial Period, thinkers tried to rise above the imagination of Voodoo or Mumbo-Jumbo of sacrifice and religious ritual as the only means of appeasing or compelling the Ultimate Reality conceived in these and other forms. They tried to find out a rational and a civilised inter-pretation of all the ways of God with Man, i.e. of the relationship between the Ultimate Reality and mankind and also the world around. From their thoughts and concepts arose the great philosophies and the great religious—Taoism in China; the Vedānta in India, with its insistence upon knowledge or faith or good deeds or self-culture, rather than upon dry and barren ritual; the attitude of the Buddha that the Supreme Truth was to be attained by true wisdom going hand in hand with self-discipline and universal love and charity; the idea of Zarathushtra in Iran, which looked upon a conflict between Light and Darkness, between Good and Evil, as the vital drama in existence, and regarded the Unseen Reality as the Spirit of Good which for ever fights with the Spirit of Evil—Ahura Mazda versus Angra-Mainyu—, and held that it is the duty of Man to be a soldier in the cause of the good against evil. We have also the ideas of Socratic and Platonic philosophy which are essentially based on a faith in the Unseen Reality and in Man's duty to live a life of moderation and of wisdom. We have also at the other end the teaching of Christ, which, with certain Hebraic concepts in the background, is essentially that of love of God and Man; and this love for Man which has been proclaimed by Christ was already insisted upon the Buddha and by Mahāvīra (the founder of Jainism in its history form) five centuries earlier in a much more extensive and all-comprehensive manner by including all living creatures within the scope of man's loving solicitude.

II

Swami Vivekananda had great love for the propagation of the study of Sanskrit, especially the Vedas and the Upaniṣads. The present volume, with a section on Vedic Civilisation dealing with the Vedas and the Upanisads, may be deemed a partial realisation of Swamiji's cherished desire.

In the scheme of the multi-storeyed temple of learning exhibiting the numerous facts of the different aspects of the cultural heritage of India on its different storeys, the present volume, dealing with 'The Early Phases' of Indian culture, serves as the foundation on which the magnificent superstructure is reared up. And in it, Vedic civilisation occupies a respectable position. Written by acknowledged experts, the articles on the Vedic civilisation represent the quintessence of the long-standing study of the different aspects of the subject and will go a long way in creating and stimulating interest in Vedic study and research. The eleven articles comprising the section cover a wide field and throw a flood of light on the various facets of the Vedic civilisation, such as religion and philosophy, culture and society, rituals and other auxiliary sciences (Vedāṅgas), and meditation and mysticism.

It is too much to expert these articles to provide an open sesame' to all the problems with which the particular topic dealt with bristles, nor is it possible to do adequate justice to the vast and manifold scope of the subject in the space that could be provided in the volume. But there can be no two opinions about the utility and value of the present series of articles which will hold a place of honour in vedic studies.

MODERN VEDIC STUDIES

The modern period in the history of the Vedic studies be said to have been inaugurated nearly a century and a half ago when Colebrooke published his monograph 'On the Vedas, or Sacred Writings of the Hindus'. The field of Vedic research has since then been so enriched by a good collection of critical editions, translations, dictionaries, grammars, bibliographies, indices, concordances, lexicons, monographs, and several other works, besides innumerable articles in research journals, that perhaps no other branch of Indology offers such a vast and varied reference material and tools of research.Though much has been done there is still scope for further research in the domain of Vedism.

ṚG-VEDA AND THE INDUS VALLEY CIVILISATION

The *Ṛg-veda* was hitherto regarded as the fountainhead of everything India, the repository of the essence of Indian culture: the source of philosophical ideas and religious beliefs, of cultural life, of code of conduct, and of all the sciences was traced to the *Ṛg-Veda.* With the discovery of the protohistoric civilisation in the Indus valley thirty-six years ago, the pendulum has swung the other way. The discovery has affected the antiquity and prestige of the *Ṛg-veda.* Not only much of what is found in the religious practices as also in the meterial culture of India is now traced to the protohistoric people of the Indus valley, but the Vedic Aryans have been associated with the destruction of the civilization of the Indus valley. The Vedic deity or war lord Indra is said to be the commander of the invading Aryan forces, and his epithet *puraṁ-dara* (sacker of the city) is explained as having been applied to him on account of his wholesale destruction of the cities.

The dating of the Indus valley civilisation has been changing with the corresponding changes in Mesopotamian chronology. The 'carbon 14' tests at the pre-Harappan of Mundigak in Afghanistan tend to ascribe to the Harappā culture a period not earlier than 2500 B.C. The recent view is to place the Harappā culture between 2500 and 1500 B.C. The Aryan invasion of India is said to have occurred not before 1500 B.C. Thus a contact is sought to be established between the topmost layers or the last phase of the Indus valley civilisation and the entry of the Aryans into India.

There is, however, no positive or conclusive evidence to connect the Vedic Aryans with the excavated cultures subsequent to those of the Indus valley. The Painted Grey Ware Culture, which is found superimposed on the Harappā culture, is said to have been associated with the Aryans, and they are said to be the people of the cemetery H at Harappā. So far archaeological excavation has yielded nothing of the nature of sacrificial implements or other paraphernalia that can definitely be called Aryan and associated with the Vedic Aryans, though it must be admited that the Painted Grey Ware Culture has been found at all excavated sites connected with the Bhārata war. The recent archaeological excavations at Hastināpuṛa have corroborated the Paurāṇic statement about the desertion of the capital in the post-Bhārata war period on account of its being washed away by the Gaṅgā, by showing flood deposits on occupational layers at Hastināpura, and have thus enhanced the credibility of the other statements in the Purāṇas, The occupational levels of the Painted Grey Ware Culture at Hastināpura have been placed between *c.* 1100 B.C. (or earlier) and *c.* 800 B.C. Even if we assume some connection between the Painted Grey Ware Culture and the Aryan culture at the period of the Bhārata war, there is still uncertainty regarding the chronology of the Bhārata war and the *Ṛg-Veda,* and consequently in fixing the chronological position of the Indus valley civilisation and the *Ṛg-Veda.*

Another important factor to remember in connection with both the Indus valley civilization and the *Ṛg-Veda* is that in both cases we do not possess the entire material. It has not been possible to reach the lower-most strata in the valley and get particulars about the origin and antecedents of the Indus valley civilisation, nor are full details available of the topmost levels relating to the civilisation, much valuable material having been used in the construction of the track for the North-Western Railway in the last century. The extant Vedic literature represents but a part of the entire literary output of the period, and this should be borne in mind, especially when drawing conclusion from arguments *ex silentia*. Under these circumstances the last word in the matter cannot be said to have been pronounced. Unless excavations present strata containing antiquities definitely associated with Vedic culture, superimposed on layers of the Indus valley civilisation, or unless universally accepted decipherment of the Indus script furnishes some definite clue, the priority of the Indus valley civilisation to the *Ṛg-Veda* cannot be said to have definitely established.

Renou had stated that the Indus civilisation appears to owe nothing to the Veda, nor does the Veda appear to owe anything to it, and that 'the Aryan tribes may well have overrun it without in any way being influenced by it, settling on the ruins of decayed or decaying empire'.[3] On a comparison between certain *Ṛg-Vedic* hymns and some seal-designs and statuettes from the Indus valley, Ramachandran find the latter 'to be embodiments of the fancies of the Ṛig-Vedic poets'. In the portrayal of the three-headed bull, with its characteristic dewlap, he discovers the representation of the past, present, and furture stages of time. Ramachandran regards the *rhinoceros unicornis* to be the Vedic *varāha* or *yajna-varāha* which, he says, is not to be equated with the wild boar or pig. He identifies the statuette of the shaven-headed figure wearing trefoil-patterned garment with yajamāna (scrificer), and associates the toy cart with the carrying of *soma* plants into the scrificial hall during the course of sacrifices. According to Ramachandra, 'The minds of the *Rig-Vedic* people and the Indus valley people appear to have thought out on the same lines, as much in accepting animals, birds, and human beings as they are in realistic study as in integrating them into āveśas or "chimeras"....The *Rig-Vedic* poet and the Indus valley artist have fancied and fashioned alike'.[5] Without entering the controversy as to the chronological position of the *Rg-Veda,* it may be worth considering whether the culture of the *Rg-Veda* that of the Indus vailey are incompatible. It may be argued that the *Rg-Veda,* in some respects, represents an earlier phase of the culture found in the Indus valley, which shows a synthesis and fusion with non-Aryan elements. The Vedic culture, in its wake, was also influenced by the Indus valley civilisation and the mingling of these different cultures culminated in composite Hinduism.

ANTECEDENTS OF THE VEDIC ARYANS

In order to understand the cultural background of the Veda we should take note of the antecedentss of the Vedic Aryans. According to the view now commonly accepted the primary Urheimat of the common Indo-European stock was located in the Ural-Altai region. Leaving their original home some tribes migrated towards the south-east and settled down in the region around Balkh. During their long here, these Aryans, ancestors of the Vedic people and the ancient Iranians, developed the Aryan language, the parents of the Vedic and the ancient Iranian, and the Aryan religio-mythological thought, the source of the religion and mythology of the Veda and the Avesta, Later, during further migrations among these Aryans, peaceful tribes among them moved to the south-east and settled in what was later called Iran—Ārāmāṇ=(land) of Aryans—, while the warlike ones advanced towards the Sapta-Sindhu, and these were the immediate forefathers of the early Vedic people. The mythico-religious concepts of the Vedic Aryans covered the cosmic worship and the fire worship, which were shared by them in common with the Indo-Iranians, as also hero worship which they had evolved in course of their victorious advance. The *mantras* of the Vedic people thus revolved round these three aspects of their religion. These antecedents of the Vedic people also explain the peculiar attitude of the European scholars about the value of the traditional interpretation which they reject in favour of modern interpretation on the basis of comparative philology and other material.

PRESERVATION OF THE TEXTS OF THE VEDAS

The preservation of the entire text of the *Ṛg-Veda* intact by oral transmission throughout centuries is a unique phenomenon in the annals of world literature. This preservation of the text without corruption was ensured by introducing at least five modes of recitation of individual *mantras* from the *Ṛg-Veda:* (i) The *saṁhitā-pāṭha* (continuous recitation) was the normal text govrned by the rule of metre and rhythm. (ii) In the *pada-pāṭha* (word recitation) each word in the Saṁhitā-text was recited without *sandhi* (compound) in its own specific accent. (iii) The third was the krama-pāṭha (step recitation), where each world of the *pada-pāṭha* was recited twice, being connected both with what precedes and what follows, e,g. ab, bc, cd, etc. (iv) The *jaṭā-pāṭha* (woven recitation), which was based on the *krama-pāṭha,* recited each of its combinations twice, the second time in a reverse order, e.g.ab, ba, ab; bc, cb; etc. (v) In the *ghana-pāṭha* (compact recitation) the order was ab, ba, abc, cba, abc; bc, cb, bcd, dcb, bcd; etc. The significance of the complete means of success achieved by this system in preserving the text from interpolation, modification, or corruption will be realised when we find that in the entire text of the *Ṛg-Veda*, covering 1,028 hymns or about 10,560 *mantras* or about 74,000 words, there is only one variant reading, viz *maṁścatoḥ* for *māṁścatoḥ* in VII.44.3.

MANTRA OR PRE-SAMHITÀ PERIOD

During the centuries that elapsed between the composition of the mantras, which constitute the beginnings of what later came to be called the *Ṛg-Veda,* and their incorporation in the Saṁhitā-text or codification, the *mantras* were handed down in different families and employed at cermonies so that they were exposed to considerable change. The present text which is preserved through oral transmission represents a fairly late stage in the development of the *Ṛg-Veda;* the language is not homogeneous; several divergent forms, some archaic and some representing the language of the time, have crept in. Tradition has no doubt scrupulously preserved that text, and the. unchangeability of the *Ṛg-Veda* after its codification is a fact; but that the same cannot be said of the pre-Saṁhitā text can be demonstrated by the innumerable variations recorded in the *Vedic Variants* by Bloomfield and Edgerton.

THE RG-VEDA

Though tradition knows of several recensions of the *Ṛg-Veda,* only the Śākala recension, which is meant when we speak of the

Ṛg-Veda, has come down apparently in its entirety, and parts of the Bāṣkal and Vālakhilya recensions. This text, which represents but a late phase of the original *mantras*, as stated earlier, has been to a certain extent regularised and corresponds exactly to the rules given in the Prātiśākhyas. The texts constituting the *purorucas*, *nivids* and *praisas* pertain to the pre-Saṁhitā period.

TRAYI AND THE ATHARVA-VEDA

It is interesting to observe the views—sometimes conflicting — held by scholars with regard to the designation of the Vedas as trayī (triad, i.e. *Ṛg-Veda, Yajur-Veda,* and *Sāma-Veda* and the eligibility of the *Atharva-Veda* to be included among the Vedas, some of which have been referred to in the present work. The *Atharva-Veda,* in the point of antiquity, stands comparison with the *Ṛg-Veda,* some of its hymns going to the pre-Saṁhitā period as well. According to one view, the *Atharva-Veda* which related to magic, witch-craft, superstition, etc. represented the religious of the masses in contrast to the other Vedas relating to cosmic worship representing the religion of the classes. Another view explains the purpose of the three Vedas and the *Atharva-Veda* to be respectively the attainment of the desired objects and the warding off of the evils, and takes the omission of the *Atharva-Veda* at places where the trayī is mentioned as being due to want of necessity or propriety of reference, and not to its inferiority or supposed non-Vedic character, for a large number of highly philosophical hymns occur in this Veda and it shares many hymns in common with the *Ṛg-Veda.*

POST-VEDIC PERIODS

After the Mantra period, representing the beginning of the Vada nd Saṁhitā (collection of the *mantras*) period, come the Brāhmaṅa period, the Upaniṣad period, and the Sutra-Vedāṅga period, completing the whole range of Vedic literature, there being an interregnum, which witnessed the growth of Jainism and Buddhism, between the last two periods. The Brāhmaṇas, which, along with the *Yajur-Veda*, represent the earliest specimens of Sanskrit prose, were also the earliest commentaries on the Vedas and a repository of ancient legends. The Upaniṣadic period did not represent a spirit of revolt against ritualism, but as stated by Renou, a natural growth, a supplement to the Brāhmaṇas.

PHILOSOPHY

Beginning of philosophic speculations are traced right from the *Rg-Veda,* not merely in its Tenth Book, but even in the older *Ṛg-Veda,* for instance in III.54.9, where, in the words of Renou, 'we already have a full formation: the single original principle, and the realm of the gods lying between Man and the Supreme Being. Religion and speculation go hand in hand from the very outset'.[6] That the *Ṛg-Veda* anticipates the doctrime of *māyā* and *rūpa* by employing these terms precisely in their Vedāntic sense is shown by B.K. Ghosh, according to whom the *Ṛg-Vedic* significance of these terms is respectively 'that occult power by means of which the deceptive appearance can be assumed or discarded' and 'the transient and deceptive appearance'.He further wonders how this fact has not yet been properly emphasised by any modern investigator.[7]

The sacrificial system of the Brāhmaṇas has hitherto been excluded by the historians of Indian philosophy from the purview of consideration from the view-point of philosophy. In his Introduction to Upaniṣads,[8], Laxman Shastri Joshi has shown that the sacrificial worship in the Brāhmaṇas is responsible for the philosophic contempleation as envisaged in the Upaniṣads; that Ātman philosophy has evolved from the worship of several forms of Puruṣa that was in vogue; that 'the altar-construction was a source of some features of Śaivism'; that 'the sacrifice was the origin of the Bhāgavata faith called Pañcaratra'; and that 'we can show a direct connection of Vaiṣṇavism with the sacrifice....'

RELIGION AND MYTHOLOGY

It may be observed in connection with *Ṛg-Vedic* religion and mythology that the *Ṛg-Veda* faithfully reflects, and is deeply influenced by, contemporary life, so that any changes in the conceptions of mythology are to be viewed in the background of the prevailing conditions. The different concepts in the formulation of Varuṇa and Indra, the eclipse of Varuṇa and the rise of the Indra, the inclusion of Aśvins and of Rudra, the ambivalence of divinities and their association in pairs and groups—each of these has a social and cultural background.

Vedic mythology is the complex interweaving of several planes—naturalistic, mythical, and mystical; ritual, social, and historical; etc.—ranging between absence of any mythology and complicated symbolism.

Though it is contended that the naturalistic interpretation of Vedic mythology sponsored by Yāska and followed by the early school of modern Vedists is not quite adequate, Vedic Nature-worship is undeniable. The exploits and adventures of gods are in part transpositions of natural phenomena to the mythical plane. Some myths undoubtedly record historical facts, and ritualistic approach also cannot be excluded.

This uncertainty of approach, emphasis, and meaning, as also the complexity of the material, has led to several mutually contradictory interpretations of Vedic mythology. As a specimen of the results which modern interpreters obtain on the same set of facts along totally disconnected lines, that the different approach pursued by them leads to, reference may be made here to not less than different interpretation of Rudra, a minor deity, that have appeared during the last twenty years (since 1938) in a chronological order.

(i) On the theory that the conception of Vedic gods is based on constellatory configurations, Rudra is equated with Sagittarius (ii) Rudra is taken to be an agricultural deity or a cure deity. (iii) Interpreting the Rudra myth in the light of 'aurora boreaiis', Rudra becomes the god of the Arctic nocturnal sky of winter combined with the phenomena of storms. (iv) The Rudra conception is explained (a) on physical basis, (b) as *'pons Varolii'* on the cerebro-spinal nervous system, (c) as anticipating the conception of Śiva, and (d) as stom. (v) Rudra was an Aryan deity of solar origin. There is nothing Dravidian in the cult of the phallus, which is Aryan in ongin. There is nothing to support a non-Aryan origin for the Paurāṇic Śva. (vi) The lunar Soma cult in India is associated with ideas of manes, fertility, phallus,...stoms (of Rudra), priestcraft,...(vii) Rudra and Agni represent the same divinity. At least in the *Kṛṣṇa Yajur-Veda*, the word 'Rudra' is used with reference to Agni, or faiiing it, to some cruel god. (iii) Rudra, properly speaking, is the god of death in Veda. (ix) Rudra may be an approximation to the Aryan god Rudra (Roarer, Father of Maruts, etc.) from an original translation of Rudhra, the name of a Dravidian divinity meaning 'red god'. (x) Rudra is identified with Apollo.

This diversity of interpretation brings us to the important question of Vedic exegesis.

VEDIC EXEGESIS

The Brāhmaṇas constitute, as already stated, the earliest commentaries on the Saṁhitās. The problem of interpretation gradually continued to assume complexities and by the time of the Nirukta several schools of Vedic exegesis had arisen to which reference has been made in the following pages of this volume. The tradition of interpretation, about which till lately the prevailing impression was that Sāyaṇa was the only commentator of the *Ṛg-Veda* after Yāska, has now been found to be unbroken, uniform, and continuous, right from the Brāhmaṇas up to the present day, throug Yāska, Pāṇini, Sāyaṇa, and pre-Sāyaṇa and post-Sāyaṇa commentators. The force of continuity in the tradition can now be maintained; but the multiplicity of methods of interpretation detracts from the value of tradition as the sole repository of the authentic interpretation of the Saṁhitās.

The modern period of Vedic studies, in the early part, had two distinct schools of Vedic exegesis, represented by Roth, Benfey, Grassmann, and Kaegi, on the one hand and by Pischel, Geldner, and Sieg, on the other. The former regarded the *Ṛg-Veda* as predominatly an Indo-European document, so that its interpretation demand the basis of comparative philology and comparative mythology and consequently traditional commentators were kept in the background as of little or no help. The other school, however, preferred the orthodox Indian tradition represented by Yāska and Sāyaṇa to the modern philological methods as, in their opinion, the Veda is pre-eminently Indian in character and indigenous tradition would enable us to understand the spirit behind the world, linguistics being able to give us the bare meaning alone. At present due importance is attached to traditions of ritual; internal evidence serves as a powerful tool in Vedic interpretation in several ways, e.g. ascertaining meanings of words, supplying lacunae, etc.

In recent times, beginning from Swami Dayananda Saraswati of the Ārya Samāj, there have been several attempts in India at Vedic exegesis, and reference may be made here only to a few. The attitude of the Ārya Samāj, which claims for the Veda a most scientific character by seeking to establish origins of modern scientific inventions therein, was the result of a reaction to the uncritical and unjust attacks on the Vedas by ill-informed foreigners of the early nineteenth century. According to Sri Aurobindo, the Veda is a mystic and symbolic poetry. The Veda is not full of silly and childish conceptions, nor is it a barbarous and unintelligible hymnery, tedious and commonplace, representing human nature on a low level of selfishness, which amounts to putting our own conceptions into the words of the ṛṣis. The Veda symbolises the passions of the soul and its striving after higher spiritual planes. Coomaraswamy finds the Veda devoid of any historical content and as containing an original metaphysical tradition. Aryans are pioneers not of conquest, but of law and order. Sarasvatī is the mythical river over which a bridge is constructed by pañcajanāḥ, joining 'dark world' with 'light world'. R. Samasastry favours astronomical nterpretation of Vedic history and mythology.

Needless to add that in the above cases the approach of scholars to Vedic exegesis, whether naturalistic (*ādhibhautika*), mythical (*ādhidaivika*), mystical or metaphysical (*ādhyātmika*), has been influenced by their views regarding the origin and nature of the Veda, which has also largely determined the particular method adopted by them—evolutionary, philological, or tıaditional.

A few observations seem to be called for in connection with tradition.*Ṛṣis* are said to have received their wisdom directly through intuitive insight. Those that derived their knowledge from others were known as śrutarṣis, and with them started the tradition since they had direct connection with the composers or-authors. These śrutarṣis later instructed others, and thus arose the tradition of interpretation of the Vedas. Now, direct connection with the author does not necessarily invest the interpretation, with the receiver may put, with authority. Matters were further complicated by there being different traditions for different branches or families, which gave rise to the schools of *Yājñikas*, Vaiyākaras, Nairuktas, *Aitihāsikas,* etc. to which reference is made in the Nirukta.With these various interpretations, sometimes contradictory, all claiming to have descended from tradition, the question arises as to which of them correctly represents the meaning of the Veda, as all of them cannot be equally true.Traditional interpretation further requires to be strengthened by the evidence of the Vedāṅgas.

Some western interpreters who rely on linguistics, to the exclusion of the information supplied by tradition, run the risk of indulging in unsound and insecure linguistic speculation. The meanings of words are not invariably to be settled on the basis of grammatical rules alone, but the conventional sense of words has to be accepted in several places when the word has been in vogue pretty long and has acquired a peculiarly distinct sense. On the other hand, it is also equally unsound to ignore comparative philology altogether. The proper course would be to proceed on the joint testimony of tradition and comparative philology and treat them as mutual correctives.

It is somewhat difficult to state what one means by the correct interpretation of the Veda. Naturally, it would be the interpretation which was intended by the seer to whom the *mantra* was revealed. But how are we to know was the interpretation intended by the author, and who is to judge what the intended interpretation? The general experience, especially with regard to creative works, is that the correct interpretation is known to the author only at the moment of composition when the inspiration was there. The author himself cannot be always said to supply the correct interpretation at a later period. Not to speak of the Veda, in the case of the Upaniṣads the *Mahābhārata*, some medieval works, or even some modern works, it is found that several interpretations have been offered. In literacy works commentators try to interpret the works by giving various alternative meanings. At times, in order to get over conflicting interpretations, recourse is had to *samanvaya* or reconciliation. That can hardly be said to have been intended by the original author. The aim in interpretation should be go get as near to the intention of the original author as possible.

The widening of the scope and fields of modern knowledge makes severe demands on the equipment of the interpreter of the Veda. He should not only be conversant with the Veda and Vedāṅga in the traditional way, but also possess an expert knowledge of text-criticism; comparative philology; comparative mythology, religion, and philosophy; ancient history; anthropology; archaeology; Assvriology; and several other relevant sciences.

References

1. Leipzig, 1931.
2. Cambridge University Press, 1956.
3. Religions of Ancient India, p. 3.
4. Presidential Address, Section I, Indian History Congress, Agra, 1956, p. 9.
5. Ibid.
6. *Op. Cit.*, p. 8.
7. *Vedic Age*, pp. 549, 551, f.n. 31.
8. pp. 9, 21, 22, 23.

4. Mother Earth

The nearest and dearest. The Mother Land. Earth is called 'Dharitee', meaning one that bears and holds us all. We are born, living and dying on her lap. The first thing to know and depend upon, for all that life means, like food and drink, movement in work and play, multiplication and consciousness.

We come from this mother Earth. But how? Keeping the spark of life aside, our body which has undergone birth, growth and decay, is composed of protoplasm, constituting ribo-nucleic and de-oxyribonucleic acids forming proteins, out of the elements, Hydrogen, Oxygen, Nitrogen and Carbon, chiefly derived from the earth.

Thus came, on the extensive lap of mother Earth, diversified by various forms of rock, soils and waters, different kinds of lives, algas and plants, microbial organisms, such as fungi, someba and bacteria, fishes and reptiles, aqueous and amphibious, bipeds like birds and men and quadruped animals.

Once the lives were born, they multiplied with great speed, (simulated in the 57th Hymn of *Prithivee sukta of the Atharvaveda*), "like the blowing of dust from the hoofs of fleet-footed horses spread all over the earth"—अश्व इव रजो दुभुवे वि ता जनान् य आक्षियन् पृथिवी यादजायत।

Of these lives, man, endowed with superior intelligence and mobility, has ruled over others.

Where from came this earth with such immense potentiality? As far as modern science has penetrated into the endless pace, the nebula, known to be composed of extremely hot gases, whirling constantly, is supposed to be flinging parts of it centrifugally, one of which is our solar system, wherein the earth, similarly flung out of the central sun, but fastened by gravitation, was set to revolve round it. So earth derived and continues to derive all her potentials from the sun including all the lives and beauties of nature through the variations of day and night and the seasons.

Our scriptures which are in no way less scientific, however, spell the advent of earth in a different manner.

In the beginning, there was Space alone with the function of sound. From Space was born Air with the functions of Sound and touch. Air gave rise to Energy with functions of Sound, Touch and Form. Energy, on its turn, created Water with Sound, Touch, Form and Taste. Lastly Earth was born from Water with all the above functions plus Flavour. These are called 'Pancha Tanmatras' or the five subtle elements which, however, had no physical existence or use. Later, half of Space with an eighth part of the rest four, formed the palpable Space. Similarly, half of Air combined with the eighth of other four formed tangible Air. In similar fashion, the tangible Energy, Water and Earth were born. So the earth has been the most favoured of the elements. This is indicated in the 7th, 9th, 10th and 43rd hymns of *'Prithivee sukta'*, where it speaks of the "Mother Earth whom the gods ruling over the elements rear with sleepless care" and "whose vital element remained immortal in space, involved by truth" etc.

यां रक्षन्तयस्वप्ना विश्वदानी देवा:।। 7 ।।
यस्यामापः परिचराः समानीरहोरात्रे अप्रामादं क्षरन्ति।। 9 ।।
यामश्विनावृमिमाता विष्णुर्मस्यां विचक्रमे।। 10।।
यस्या: पुरो देवकृता:।। 43 ।।

What holds the earth? Beyond the physical bond of gravitation the *'Prithivee Sukta'* opens in its first hymn with the mention of subtler bonds.

सत्यं वृहद्रु तमुग्र दीक्षां तपो ब्रह्म प्रथिवी धारयन्ति
सा नो भूतस्य भव्यस्य पन्त्पुरू लोकः प्रथिवी नः कृणोतु।। 11 ।।

"Truth, greatness, rectitude, vigour, consecration, austerity, knowledge and sacrifice hold the earth state" It sounds esoteric. The earth is taken with all her conscious elements lorded over by the superior life of man. This obviously means that human society is not only bound by these qualities for healthy living among themselves, but also, beyond ruling over the other lives, to look after them and not to cause damage to the wholesome abode in any way. In this context, let us quote from hymns 28 & 35 of 'Prithvee Sukta'.

उदीराणा उतासीनासित्ष्ठन्त: प्रक्रामन्त।
पद्भ्या दक्षिणसव्याभ्यां मा व्यथिष्महि भूम्याम्।। 28 ।।
यत्ते भूमे विश्वनाभि क्षिप्रं तदत्ति रोहत्तु।
मा ते मर्म विमूव्वरि मा ते हृदयमपित्तम्।। 35 ।।

"The land on which we freely stand, sit or walk with our feet, let us not do anything to damage." "May we never cause harm to you etc."

It is sad, how these ideas of the hymns have been flouted by men in this industrial age, who jeer at the idea of reverence to earth which to them means nothing but inert dirt. The rivers are disrupted and polluted by their fifth, atmosphere with poisonous gases, the cites through congestion and resulting diseases, forests have been denuded, with drought and flood as consequences. Hills and dales are dug up, perforated, blasted indiscriminately. Atomic explosions poison the land irredeemably.

The hymns 15, 16 and 17 state—

"From your soil lives were born, lives move about on you. All mortals, including bipeds and quadrupeds are reared by you and nourished by the life-giving radiance of the rising sun. All such five kinds of lives or *Manavas* are all yours, oh, Earth.

"These comprise the inhabitants of our land. Give me, oh, Earth, enough sweetness of expressions, so that all the population may be led to enjoy united lives.

"The mother of all, including plant life, the immutable and great earth, held in scrupulous law and order, benign and blissful, the land of ours, must be ceaselessly served by us all."

In the vernaculars of the Eastern region of India, the soil of land is called "MA-TI" which in split syllables means 'The Mother'. Many, many patriotic men have sung the song of this 'Ma-ti', some even while ascending the gallows gleefully—to mention just one immortal young man, 'Khudiram'. The great writer Bankimchandra produced the national song '*Bande matarm*' and D.L. Roy sang the ever-famous song *'Janmabhoomi'*, besides many other famous poets like Rabindranath, Subramaniam Bharati, Iqbal and others.

It has been quoted earlier from the text of *'Prithivee sukta'* of earth's vital elements which remained immortal high in space, enveloped by truth" and in the opening hymns Earth clearly means a whole entity, including all conscious lives whom she bears and rears. This precious creation is synonymous with 'Sansara' which is esoterically simulated in the 'Upanishads' and 'Geeta' to a Peepal tree which has its roots either grow upward with high ideals or low according to the virtues attained and trends towards sense object. The leaves represent knowledge (Chandans-Vedas), gathered from the environments, which sustain and modify the lives and the world. The power of intellect and hence knowledge are collected from the elements, as mentioned in the 53rd hymns.

द्यौश्च म इदं पृथिवी चान्तरिक्षं च मे व्यचः।
अग्निः सूर्य आपो मेघा विश्वे देवाश्च स ददुः ।। 53।।

"The earth with the radiant sphere above and the endless space all around is ours. The Fire, the Sun, the Water and all other gods of elemental power, have joined together to give us the power of intellect".

Knowledge was developed by man through devoted culture at the altars of 'Yagnas' (Endeavours of self-dedication for community), as indicated in the hymn 38 & 39.

"At your assembly for worship, altars are made for making sacrifice. There the worshippers, wise in the eternal knowledge of Vedas offer prayers with recital in poetry and songs and the presiding priests prepare for invoking the Supreme Power with the choicest intoxication of self-dedication (*like that of Soma-rasa*).

"Where the ancient seven Rishis (sages) with far-penetrating intellect had in such assemblies of devotion and sacrifice zealously uttered messages of the new horizons of creation".

Men not only gathered and cultivated knowledge from the elemental richness of the earth, but enjoyed with their heart's content, the beauties of nature manifest in the glorious earth and enriched their mind and life.

Hymn 23—"Oh, Earth, the wealth of fragrance that came upto you and held by the plants reared with water, which inspired the singing and dancing once may that fragrance bring us sweetness too. Let not any envy us".

Hymns 24—"What fragrance of yours got into the blue lotus, the sweet heat of the Dawn, when sun shine got united with it, its cherished sweet flavour was swept off high into the heavens. May that fragrance being sweetness to us".

The flavour of mother Earth is not only sweet in fragrance, but is the source of energy that plants, animals and men equally derived.

"The energy of Fire exists in the land, in the plants, even in water and rock. It is present also in men and beasts." This wonderful concept revealed in the text of the *Atharva Veda* vies with the most modern science. Fire *(Agni)* is only the manifestation of energy as heat and light. But energy exists in chemical and biochemical form in the land, in biological form in the plants, in mechanical and physiological form in water and latently in atomic form in rock and so on. Man and animal contain and are able to produce multiple forms of energy.

Hymn 21—

अग्निवाज्ञा पृथिव्यसितज्ञूस्त्विषीमन्त संशितं मा कृणोतु।। 21 ।।

"Wearing the apparel of Fire, on, black-bottomed Earth, pray, keep us equipped with power and consciousness".

Earth is indicated here, as covered all round with ingredients of energy. The subterranean region is mentioned as black obviously with coal and fuel oil.

It is only at this present juncture of world's paucity in sources of energy, that the scientists are trying to explore and utilise the unconventional sources anumerated in this text.

In this context, hymn 25 speaks,-"The rich and delightful flavour of yours invigorates men and wedded couples, horses and horsemen heroes, antelopes, elephants and the virgin girls. May the same bring me up. But let none envy me".

Alas, how the abundant resources of energy resting in the black bottom of mother Earth, treasured for aiding all dedicated enterprises of mankind for raising food and other necessities of life, are being misused today, in making the instruments of destruction in fratricidal warfare and plundering the innocents, for heightening the fast lives of people with *Asuric* (demoniacal) propensities. Hobel invented

'Dynamite' for noble purposes, but later found it, to this dismay, being used for monstrous activities.

The prime necessities of life in the days of the Vedas, as well as today, are food, drink, shelter and a peaceful society, free from enemies and diseases. In the texts of the *Prithivee sukta,* man has begged of mother Earth to fetch help from the elemental Powers for profuse rain, so that rivers may run full and pure, the crops may be grown in abundance, the forests may be rich with delicious fruits, fuel and beneficial herbs and cattle may thrive, to provide milk and butter. He has sought safe and suitable shelter and habitation, free from storm and floods, wild animals and marauders, venomous creatures and fatal diseases. Besides, there are the ideas of gathering knowledge, through dedicated austerities at altare of *Yagnas*, assemblies of wise men and from natural environments. It is also said, that, to acquire power, the sources of power have to be kept alive and cultivated through their own contribution, in ingredient material (*Habih*) and labour.

There is also the desire of man for a brotherhood of all human beings, irrespective of languages, faiths and place, to live in peace and plenty, without jealousy.

Hymns 45—

जनं विभ्रती बहुधाा विवाचसं नानाधार्माण पृथिवी यथौकसम्।
सहत्र घारा द्रविणस्य में दुहां ध्रुवेव धोनुरनपस्फुरन्ती।। 45।।

"The earth that holds people, speaking divers languages and following several faiths, in their respective places, ungrumblingly and undisturbed, may she, like the mother cow, shower favours in thousand streams."

Hymns 38 to 62 purport as follows.

Let our places of worship be for self-dedication, so that we may look forward to new horizons of creation, as the wisest among us have visualised, May we be strong enough to drive away our enemies, grow plentiful of crops, carry out industries, utilise the riches of this earth, be free from venomous creatures, swindlers, robbers, ferocious animals and tribes. May we make comfortable homes, free from the inclemency of nature and live long and healthy life.

The assemblies for worship and gathering knowledge with self-dedication, as mentioned in the hymns 38 & 39, have now ceased to be. Their places have been taken by assemblies of self-centred men, by virtue of wealth and power, to promote dissensions among men, between different languages, different faiths and different places, completing upsetting the ideals.

Though mother Earth has remained immutable, rich and banning through the ages that separate the present man from the man who sang the 'Song Mundance' (*Prithivee sukta*) there has occurred very large departure in the life, activity, thoughts and ideals of man today.

There has been immense development of his knowledge and activity in material science, so much so, that having put one foot down on the moon, he has stretched out his hand towards the galaxy. He can make and unmake umpteen changes in matter, has invaded space in noval crafts and has built up monstrous power out of nuclear elements, which may destroy even the mother Earth, the very source of all energy and inspiration.

Money which was devised for convenient sharing of the produces of agriculture and industries, has assumed demoniacal authority over ethics, brotherhood and the fragrance of love which once enriched the '*Sansara*' that is, mother Earth.

Hymns 5—

यस्यां पूर्वे पूर्वजना विचक्रिरे यस्यां देवा असुरानभ्यवर्तयन्।
गवामश्वानां वयश्च विष्ठा भगं वर्चः पृथ्वी नो दधातु।। 5।।

"Where our fore-runners, in days gone by, did various deeds where the *Devas* (godly ones) overran the *Asuras* (ungodlies), may the same Earth, sheltering animals, like cattle, horses and birds, grant us wealth and power."

The wealth and power were granted all right, but they have now been snatched by the *Asuras* (demons) born in human society, by running down the godly elements of society.

Where the early man sought consciousness and knowledge at the altars of dedication, where the wise *Rishis* (sages) spoke[1] of the new horizons, now knowledge is sought with the sole objective of money and power from masters who evolve processes of plunder and lewd pleasure in sex and liquor.

Man has forgotten, that the same blood runs in the veins of all mankind. He has forgotten, that 'anything that exists, any where, in this moving universe, belongs to God. For whatever has come to us to enjoy we have not the least credit, nor right and has to be enjoyed by sharing it with others' (*Eesopanishad*)

Not only are we now consuming the unearned gifts, by grabbing other's shares like thieves, but men savage power, are enlarging their authority and plundering all over the world. Discontent, hatred and murderous propensity, have blackened the beautiful face of Mother Earth.

—*Govind Gupta & Priyabrata Das*

References

1. A Vedic sage stood up before the world and in trumpet voice proclaimed the glad tidings. "Hear ye, children of immortal bliss, even ye that reside in higher spheres, I have fond the ancient one who is beyond all darkness, all delusion, knowing Him alone, you shall be save from death over again."

(Śvetāśvatara Upanishad)

5. Mythical Tradition

The mythical tradition runs right through the religious history of this country from the days of the Vedic rśis. This tradition may sometimes have been overcome by a ceremonial piety or by a rationalise dogma. Yet it always reappears faithful to its original pattern. Its characteristic tendencies are those set forth in the Upanisads.

RELIGIOUS EXPERIENCE

Religion is a matter of experience. It is not an awakening from a swoon, but a transformation of one's being. It is not an addition to one's intellectual furniture, but an exaltation of one's personality into the plane of the universal Spirit. It is *Brahmadarśana*—insight into Reality, a direct awareness of the world of values.

Religious experience is not to be confused with the pursuit of truth, beauty, or goodness. It is a life of adoring love transcending these. The Divine is not a mere sum of knowledge, love, and beauty. The ultimate Reality which responds to our demands is more than rational. Religion means awe more than service, holiness more than virtue. We worship not what we can, but what we cannot understand. There is the Unknown, the reserve of truth, which the intellect cannot reach and yet feels to lie behind. There is an element of mystery in all religion, an incomprehensible certainty which is not to be explained by grammar or logic. Life is open only to life. Religious experience, when genuine, is characterised by vividness, directness, freshness, and joy. In it we feel the impact of Reality. It is spiritual discovery, not creation. The men of experience feel the presence of God and do not argue about it. The shoals and shallows of existence are submerged in a flood-tide of joy.

GOD AND THE UNIVERSE

We do not infer God from our feeling of dependence or an analysis of the self. The reality of God is revealed in an immediate intuition of the essential dependence of all finite things, of the priority of absolute to relative being.

Though the experience is beyond reason, it is not opposed to reason. While the Upanishads emphasise the direct awareness of the world of Spirit, they also adduce reasons support of the reality of Spirit. Their approach is both objective and subjective.

Each order of reality known to us is only truly apprehended from a standpoint higher than itself. The significance of the physical world (*anna*) is disclosed in the biological (*prāna*); that of the biological in the psychological (*manas*); that of the psychological in the logical and ethical (*vijnāna*). The logical finds its meaning in the spiritual (*ananda*). The drift of the world has an underlying tendency, a verifiable direction towards some implied fulfillment. If the vast process of the world leads up to the spiritual, we are justified in finding in the spiritual the best clue to the understanding of the world.

It is now admitted that the forms and properties of mature animals and plants, in their varied classes and orders; and human beings, with their power of choice between good and evil, did not come into existence in their present form by a direct act of Almighty God, but assumed their present forms in slow obedience to a general law of change. The higher exerts a curious pressure on the happenings of the lower and moulds it. This fact requires explanation, and modern philosophers confirm the suggestions of the Upanisads on this question.

Professor Lloyd Morgan, who studies the problem from the biological side, affirms that while resultants can be explained as the results of already existing conditions, emergents like the advent of life, mind, and reflective personality cannot be explained without the assumption of divine activity. The progressive emergence, in the course of evolution, of life, mind, and personality, requires us to assume a creative Principle operative in nature, a timeless reality in the temporal.

Professor A. N. Whitehead argues, after Plato, that there are eternal objects, answering to the eternal forms or patterns of Plato, and makes God transcend both the eternal objects and the concrete occasions. He is the active source of limitation or determination. For

Plato also, the ideal world ruled by the supreme Idea of the Good is different from the creative God. The Supreme Being is the Ideal world, and the Demiurge contemplates the Ideas and their unity in relation to the Idea of the Good and reproduces this heavenly pattern as far as is possible in time and space. Plato does not tell us what exactly the relation of form to sensible fact is; nor does Whitehead tell us what exactly the relation of eternal object to concrete occasion is. Is a sensible thing a mere assemblage of forms or eternal objects or universals or is it more?

Aristotle felt that Plato's mistake lay in separating the universal characters from sensible things and setting up these supersensible abstractions as the source of the things we see. Aristotle believes that he gets over the difficulty by affirming that the form exists only in the individual thing and is just its essential character. The solution is not quite so simple. We still ask, what is the status of eternal objects and how are they related to the things we perceive? What is the position of moral ideas and how are they related to moral facts? Whatever these difficulties may be, it is agreed that the universe is not self-explanatory.

When we consider the nature of cosmic process with its ascent from matter to spirit, we are led to the conception of a supreme Being who is the substantiation of all values. These values are not only the revealed attributes of God but the active cause of the world. Till these values are realised, God is transcendent to the process, though He inspires it. God is the creator, destroyer, and sustainer of this universe. He transcends all creatures as the active power in which they take their rise.

GOD AND THE SELF

An analysis of the self yields the same result. The Upanisads undertake an analysis of the self and make out that the reality of the self is the divine universal consciousness. It is needless to repeat here the careful accounts which the *Chādogya* and the *Māndūkya Upanisads* relate.[1] Some modern thinkers arrive at similar results. The Jivātma is not a *substance*, but an *activity*, what Aristotle calls *energeia* or self-maintaining activity.

We have to distinguish the logical subject from the substratum of qualities. The former is a logical problem, while the latter is an ontological one. So long as we adopt the 'substance' theory of the self, difficulties arise. Locke was obliged to reduce substance to an unknowable substratum, a something he knows not what, which supports its attributes, he knows not how. It becomes a superfluous entitle and rightly did Berkeley abolish material substance altogether. Its attributes, which he called ideas, could just as well be said to inhere in one divine mind as in a multitude of unknowable substrata. But Berkeley retained spiritual substance, for, according to him, the essence of any existent thing is to be perceived by a mind.

Hume applied a more rigorous analysis. He breaks up the self into a succession of impressions and ideas. He would recognise nothing in the mind except these: "when I enter most intimately into what I call myself,' he said. 'I always stumble on some particular perception or other of heat or cold, light or shade, love or hatred, pain or pleasure. I never can catch *myself* at any time without a perception, and never can observe anything but the perception.' He infers that 'were all my perceptions removed by death, I should be entirely annihilated'. For him there is nothing 'simple and continued'. The successive perceptions only constitute the mind." But Hume's analysis does not account of the continuity of self and the feeling of identity. How can a series of feelings be aware of itself as a series? Hume has no answer to this question but takes shelter under 'the privilege of a sceptic'.

Kant, however, was greatly disturbed by the precarious position in which Hume left the problem of knowledge. He started with Hume's analysis and tried to cure its defects by the use of a priori principles. But he conceived the self on the analogy of material substance, as the permanent in change, which is necessary for the perception of change. He did not raise the question of the relation of changing attributes to the unchanging substance. Does the substance itself change when the attributes do?

We must seek for the source of substance not in the external persistence in space, but in the internal continuity of memory. The question, why do the contents of the mind hang together, how are they unified, Kant answers by referring us to the transcendental subject, to which all experiences are finally to be referred. It is the subject which is the correlate of all objects. But it is only the logical subject, and is not to be confused with the metaphysical soul or a spiritual substance which is simple and indissoluble and therefore immortal. Even McTaggart, in the second chapter of his *Studies in Hegelian Cosmology,* attempts to establish the immortality of the self on the ground of its immutability. But that which is immutable and therefore immortal is not the empirical self. This transcendental Self is the Paramātman, functioning in all minds. It is not capable of existing in the plural. There is only one transcendental Self and our empirical selves are psychical facts, streams of change. The Jivātman is not a substance, but an activity, whose nature is to change continuously. Whether we look at the real from the objective or the subjective point of view, the real can be defined only as Spirit.

Though the being of man is Spirit, his nature is complex and unstable. Thee are other grades and kinds of life in the human individual. That is why he has the creaturely sense over against the transcendent majesty of God, the spaceless Spirit of all individual spirits.

GOD AND MAN

Those who live in God do not care to define. They have a peculiar confidence in the universe, a profound and peaceful acceptance of life in all its sides. Their response to ultimate Reality is not capable of a clearcut, easily intelligible formulation. The mystery of God's being cannot be rationally determined. It remains outside the scope of logical concepts. Its form does not lie in the field of vision, none can see it with the eye. There is no equal to it. An austere silence is more adequate to the experience of God than elaborate descriptions.

The Upanisads often give negative accounts of the supreme Reality. God is nothing that *is*. He is non-being, Pagans like Plotinus and Christians like Nicholas of Cusa support the negative theology of the Upanisads. This negative theology also gives us a knowledge of Divinity. It affirms that Divinity is not perceived by the categories of reason. It is grasped by the revelation of spiritual life.

When positive accounts are given, we abandon concepts in favour of symbols and myths. They are better suited to life which is inexhaustible and unfathomable. God is regarded as father, friend, lover. Infinite power and infinite love are both revelations of God. God is infinite love that pours forth at every time and every place its illimitable grace on all that ardently seek for it. The divine solicitude for man is easy of comprehension when we look upon the Divine as Mother. She wishes to possess us and so will pursue and track us down in our hiding places. God is in search of us. This conception has been made familiar to us by Francis Thomson's *The Hound of Heaven*.[3] Among the worshippers of the Divine as Mother, Ramakrishna holds a high place.[4] In polytheistic religions, the nature of the Divine becomes as it were divided into fragments.

GOD AND THE ABSOLUTE

The positive descriptions are variations of the central theme that God is a person. The negative theology makes out that even personality is a symbol. In later Vedānta, a distinction is drawn between the Absolute Brahman and the Personal Iśvara. Śankara says: 'Brahman is realised in its twofold aspect: In one aspect it is endowed with the *upādhis* (adjuncts) of name and form, that are subject to modification and cause differentiation; and in the other it is just the opposite (bereft of all *upādhis*), i.e. the transcendental Reality.'

The Absolute answers to the essential deity, of which Eckhart speaks, deeper than God Himself and the groundlessness of Bochme, Brahman and Iśvara. Absolute and God, are not contradictory, but complementary to each other. Each is the perspective offered to the mental standpoint of the seeker. Religious experience also lends support to this dual conception. It has normally two sides, an experience of personal intercourse with a Personal God as well as a sense of rest and completeness in an absolute Spirit which is more than personal. If the latter alone were experienced, we should not lapse from the condition of absolute freedom. It is because our natures are rooted in the world of space-time as well that we look up to the Absolute as something different from us, with whom it is possible for us to have personal relations. There are experiences of men who are convinced that they are working with God, thinking and striving under pressure from Him. For them God is not an unchanging Absolute, a Being perfect in nature and realisation. God is aiming at something through the medium of the human. There is a sense in which God has real need of us and calls us to share in his increasing victories and another in which God is timeless, and completes our being. When we emphasise the former aspect, we call it the Supreme God: When we lay stress on the latter, we call it the Absolute.

BRAHMAN, ATMAN, AND ISVARA

There are three terms in constant use in the Indian religious vocabulary, which bring out different aspects of the Supreme: Brahman, ātman, and Iśvara. These words are used with little appreciation of the distinctions implied by them. Brahman is the Immense, the Vast, the Ultimate, permeating all the universe and yet eluding and conceptual definition. We experience its living reality, its otherness, its unconditionedness by all that is of this world. To the logical mind its character is not clear and yet its reality is apprehended as something which contrasts with the time-series. We have direct relationship with it. Brahman is the name we give to that substantial and eternal Being. It is the object of our metaphysical quest. It is the transcendent and abiding Reality which is far beyond the world of succession, though it gives meaning to the process and supports it all through.

Since it is apprehended by us it is clear that we have in us a quality which apprehends it. It is we that possess the ineffable consciousness of the Eternal. The soul it is that becomes aware of Brahman. The Absolute is Spirit. Though unspeakable in its transcendence, the Supreme is yet the most inward part of our being. Though Brahman in one sense entirely transcends us, in another sense it is intimately present in us. The Eternal Being, Brahman, is Spirit, Ātman. That which we indicate with awe as the Absolute, is also our own transcendental essence. It is the ground of our being, that in which our reality consists.

Off and on, in some rare moments of our spiritual life, the soul becomes aware of the presence of the Divine. A strange awe and delight invade the life of the soul and it becomes convinced of the absoluteness of the Divine, which inspires and moulds every detail of our life. To bring out that God is both transcendent and immanent, that He is a presence as well as a purpose, the conception of Iśvara is used. It affirms the ever-present pressure of God on the here and now. He is the lord and giver of life, in this world and yet distinct from it, penetrating all, yet other than all. Iśvara is the Absolute entering into the world of events and persons, operating at various levels but most freely in the world of souls. Iśvara as the divine Presence is maintaining, helping, and preserving the whole world to move up, at every plane, in every person, and at every point, to reach towards greater perfection, to get into conformity with its own thought for the world. It is the pure, Absolute Brahman acting. The religious sense that spiritual energy breaks through from another plane of being, modifying or transforming the chain of cause and effect, finds its fulfillment in the concept of Iśvara. As the Upanisad has it: 'The divine Intelligence is the lord of all, the all-knower, the indwelling Spirit, the source of all, the origin and end of all creation.'

CATHOLICITY OF HINDUISM

In Hinduism the descriptions of the Supreme are many-sided and comprehensive. A catholic religion expresses itself in a variety of forms and comprehends all the relations which exist between man and God. Some of the great religions of the world select one or the other of the great relations, exalt it to the highest rank, make it the centre and relate all else to it. They become so intolerant as to ignore the possibility of other relations and insist on one's acceptance of their own point of view as giving the sole right of citizenship in the spiritual world. But Hinduism provides enough freedom for a man to go forward and develop along his own characteristic lines. It recognises that the divine light penetrates only by degrees and is distorted by the obscurity of the medium which receives it. Our conception of God answers to the level of our mind and interest. Hinduism admits that religion cannot be compressed within any juridical system or reduced to any one single doctrine.

The different creeds mark out the way of the spirit. Religious life has to be built through their aid. Ramakrishna practised forms of worship not only of the different Hindu sects but also those of Islam and Christianity. From actual experience, he established that the goal of all religious is the same. 'As the same sugar is made into various figures of birds and beasts,' Ramakrishna used to say, 'so one sweet Mother Divine is worshipped in various climes and ages under various names and forms. Different creeds are but different paths to reach the Almighty. As with one gold various ornaments are made, having different forms and names, so one God is worshipped in different countries and ages, and has different forms and names'[5] Real contradictions are found more often in mediocre minds, but the vastness of soul of the spiritually profound gathers within itself opinions and tendencies profoundly contradictory.

SYMBOLISM IN RELIGION

Idolatry is a much abused term. Even those who oppose it are unable to escape from it. The very word brings up to our to mind thoughts of graven images, strange figures of frightful countenances, horrid animals, and shapes, and so long as the worshippers confuse these outer symbols with the deeper divine Reality, they are victims of idolatry.

But, as a matter of fact, religion cannot escape from symbolism, from icons and crucifixes, from rites and dogmas. These forms are employed by religion to focus its faith, but when they become more important than the faith itself, we have idolatry. A symbol does not subject the finite, but renders the finite transparent. It aids us to see the Infinite through it. When, however, we confuse the symbol with the Reality, exalt the relative into the Absolute, difficultiešs arise and an unjustified idolatry develops.

It is this idolatry that stands in the way of religious fellowship and understanding today. Every dogmatic religion overlooks the spiritual facts and worships the theological opinions. It is more anxious for the spread of its dogmas than for the spiritual education of human race. If we realise the true place of symbolism, then we shall not bother about how men reach the knowledge of spiritual Reality.

The different religious groups bound within themselves by means of rites and ceremonies militate against the formation of a human society. Intuitive religion rebels against these communal and national gods, confident in the strength of the one Spirit whose presence works and illuminates the whole of mankind.

ABSOLUTE AND THE UNIVERSE

The Absolute which is timeless is reflected in some fashion in our world of space and time. The world is the appearance of the Absolute. It is the *vavarta* of the Absolute. The unity of the Absolute is not affected by the plurality of existent worlds, though the world is an expression of the Absolute. Of course, the nature of the Absolute is by no means exhausted by this world or for that matter by any number of such worlds, and the changes of the varied worlds do not in any way affect the unity of the Absolute. We cannot, however, say that the empirical universe is the result of the apprehending consciousness, for that would mean the Absolute is a thing in itself and the world a mere appearance, and there is nothing to tell us whether it is an appearance or whether there is a thing in itself at the back of it. Much the best solution is to admit that the world expresses the Absolute without in any way interfering with its unity and integrity. Such a kind of relationship is what is called *vivarta* by Indian thinkers.

Without being content with such a view, we sometimes make out that the real is not pure Being which excludes all negation, but a self-conscious Principle which involves a certain negation of absolute Reality. God is a form of absolute Being. Even as the world is distinct from, and is in a sense a negation of the absolute Being. God is limited expression of the Absolute. So far as God is concerned, the world is as necessary to God as God is to the world. God would not be God but for the world which expresses Him. The world is an expression or *parināma* of God, though a *vivarta* of the Absolute.

KARMA AND MUKTI

The idea of *karma* has been with us from the beginning of philosophic reflection. The self is a composite of mind, body, and activities.[6] Surely 'one becomes good by good action, and bad by bad action',[7] When a man dies, the two things that accompany him are *vidyā* and *karma*[8]. According as one acts, according as one conducts, so does one become,;[10] Desire becomes action, and actions determine the course of life. Evolution of life goes on until salvation is attained.

Salvation or *mukti* is life eternal and has nothing to do with continuance in endless time. No adequate account of *mukti* can be given since it transcends the limitations with which human life is bound up. So the question of the nature of salvation, whether it is individual or universal, has no relevance or meaning when applied to life eternal, which is altogether a different life.

The question becomes important when we attempt to describe the state of salvation from the standpoint of the empirical world. Whether salvation is individual or universal has significance only on the basis of the plurality of individual souls on the empirical plane. If in this universe we have only one soul, then salvation of that soul means the redemption of the whole universe. In the Ekajivavāda, universal salvation and individual salvation are identical.

Though some later Advaitins adopt this position, Śankara is opposed to it. If all the different souls are only one Jiva, then, when, for the first time, any soul attains liberation, bondage should have terminated for all, which is not the case. He says: 'No man can actually annihilate this whole existing world...And if it actually could be done, the first released person would have done it once for all, so that at present the whole world would be empty, earth and all other substances having been finally annihilated.'[10]

From the empirical standpoint, a plurality of individuals is assumed by Śankara and many of his followers. On this view, salvation does not involve the destruction of the world. It implies the disappearance of a false view of the world. The idea is further elucidated by *Śankara* in the *Sūtra-bhāsya*: 'Of what nature is that so -called annihilation of the apparent world? Is it analogous to the annihilation of hardness in congealed clarified butter (*ghee*), which is effected by bringing it into contact with fire? Or is the apparent world of names and forms which is superimposed upon Brahman by nescience to be dissolved by knowledge, just as the phenomenon of a double moon which is due to a disease of the eyes is removed by the application of medicine?'[11]

TYPES OF MUKTI AND THE STATE OF THE RELEASED

Śaṅkara admits that the world-appearance persists for the *jivanmukta* or the *sthitaprajna* of the *Bhagavad-Gitā*. The *jivanmukta* though he realises *mokṣa* or *Brahmabhāva*, still lives in the world. The appearance of multiplicity is not superseded. It is with him as with a patient suffering from *timira* that, though he knows there is only one moon, sees two. Only it does not deceive the freed soul, even as the mirage does not tempt one who has detected its unreal character. Freedom consists in the attainment of a universality of spirit or *sarvātmabhāva*. Embodiment continues after the rise of the saving knowledge. Though the spirit is released, the body persists. While the individual has attained inner harmony and freedom, the world-appearance still persists and engages his energies. Full freedom demands the destruction of the world-appearance as well. Śankara's view of the *jivanmukta* condition makes out that inner perfection and work in the finite universe can go together.

It is usually thought that at death the soul attains final liberation or *videhamukti*. It is not easy to reconcile this view with Śankara other statement that Apāntaratamas, Bhaṛgu, and Nārada even after death work for the saving of the world.[12] These are said to be the 'possessors of the complete knowledge of the Vedas'. Śaṅkara writes: 'The continuance of the bodily existence of Apāntaratamas and others depends on the offices which they discharge for the sake of the world. As the sun, who after having for thousands of ages performed the office of watching over these worlds, at the end of that period, enjoys the condition of release in which he neither rises nor sets, so Apāntaratamas and others continue as individuals, although they possess complete knowledge, which is the cause of release, and obtain release only when their office comes to an end.' So long as their offices last their *karmas* cannot be said to be exhausted. Śaṅkara here admits that *samyagdarśana,* though it is the cause of release, does not bring about final release, and the liberated individuals are expected to contribute to *lokasthiti* or world-maintenance. Their *karma* can never be fully exhausted, so long as the world demands their services.

This view is not to be confused with *karmamukti* or gradual release which is the aim of those who are devoted to Kārya-Brahman or Hiranyagarbha.[13] Śankara is discussing not gradual release, but release consequent on *Brahmajnāna* which is attainable here and now. And for even such released souls, persistence of individuality is held not only as possible by Śankara, but necessary in the interests of what is called *lokasthiti.* In other words, the world will persist as long as there are souls subject to bondage. It terminates only when all are released, i.e. absolute salvation is possible with world redemption.

Such a view of Śaṅkara's philosophy is by no means new. Appaya Diksita, for example, takes his stand on those passage in Śaṅkara where the Jīva is said to be of the nature of Iśvara and not Brahman, and holds that the liberated individuals attain communion with Iśvara and not union with Brahman. 'The Self of the Highest Lord is the real nature of the embodied self' (*B.S.,* III.4.8), and so he contends that Śaṅkara supports the view of *mokśa* as attaining the nature of Iśvara. He also suggests that when all the Jivas attain liberation the world, with the liberated souls and Iśvara, lapses into the Absolute where there is neither subject not object, neither world nor God. But so long as some souls are unredeemed, even the liberated are in the world, which is governed by Iśvara, though filled by the spirit of oneness of all, and fulfill their redemptive functions.

That the individual does not become identical with Brahman but only with Iśvara comes out from what is called the theory of reflection or Bimba-pratibimbavāda. When a face is reflected in a number of mirrors, the destruction of a particular mirror means only the lapse of the image into the reflecting face and not the face in itself. It is only when all reflection ceases, i.e. when all mirrors are destroyed, that the reflecting face disappears and the face in itself appears. The full release or the attainment of Brahman is possible only when all *avidyās* are destroyed. Until then, release means only identity with Iśvara.

If such a vies is adopted two conditions are essential for final salvation: (1) inward perfection attained by intuition of self; and (2) outer perfection possible only with the liberation of all. The liberated souls which obtain the first condition continue to work for the second and will attain final release when the world as such is redeemed. To be saved in the former sense is to see the Self all in all, to see all things in the Self and to live in the Self with all things. To be perfect is to be oneself and all else; it is to be the universe. It is to give onself, so that all might be saved. Commenting on the *Mundaka Upanisad* text (III.2.5), Śankara says: 'He who has reached the all-penetrating ātman 'enters into the all.' Kumārila in his *Tantravārttika* quotes Buddha as saying: 'Let all the sins of the world fall on me and let the world be saved.'[14]

THE LIBERATED INDIVIDUAL

The liberated individual has the consciousness of the timeless Infinite and, with that as his background, takes his place in the temporal world. He has what the seers called *Trikāla-drśti,* an intuition of time in which past, present, and future, exist together for ever in the self-knowledge and self-power of the Eternal. He is no more swept helplessly on the stress of the moments. He lives in the consciousness of the universal mind and works for the welfare of the world in an unselfish spirit. True renunciation is not abandonment of action, but unselfish conduct.

REFERENCES

1. See the writer's *Philosophy of the Upanishads* (George Allen & Unwin, London Revised Second Edition, 1935).
2. *Treatise of Human Nature* (Ed. by Selby Bigge) pp. 252-53.
3. Cf. Pascal, *Mystere de Jesus*: 'I have loved thee', said Christ to Pascal, 'more ardently than thou hast loved the defilements.'
4. Compare the lines of *Any Mother* by Katharine Tynan:

   There is no height, no depth, my own, could set us apart
   Body of mine and soul of mine; heart of my heart'.

   If some day you came to me heavy with sin.
   I, your mother, would run to the door and let you in,
   I would wash you white again with my tears and grief,
   Body of mine and soul of mine, till you found relief.
   Though you had sinned all sins there are 'twixt east and west,
   You should find my arms wide for you, your head on my breast,
   Child, if I were in Heaven one day and you were in Hell—
   Angels white as my spotless one stumbled and fell—

I would leave for you the fields of God and Queen May's feet,
Straight to the heart of Hell would go seeking my sweet,
God may hap would turn him round at sound of the door,
Who is it goes out from me to come back no more?
Then the blessed Mother of God would say from her throne:
Son, 'tis a mother goes to Hell seeking her own.'

5. Max Muller: *Rāmakrishna: His Life and Sayings* (Advaita Ashrama, Calcutta, 1951). P. 100.

6. *Brhadāranyaka*, I.6.1.

7. *Ibid.*, III. 2.13.

8. *Ibid.*, IV. 4.2.

9. *Ibid.*, IV. 4.5.

10. *Brahma Sūtra-bhāsya*, III.2.21.

11. *Ibid.*, III.2.21.

12. *Ibid.*, III.3.32.

13. These attain liberation when the office of Hiranyagarbha terminates.

14. See the writer's *An Idealist View of Life* (George Allen & Unwin, London). Ch. VII.

6. Mystical Discipline A Psychological Approach

INTRODUCTORY

A long process of concentration on the object of spiritual quest is deemed essential for spiritual adjustment in many patterns of religious culture. The practice of concentration has also been regarded as an important phase of mystic discipline that often overreaches the schemes of social religion. In fact, the mind which cannot concentrate is sometimes said to be totally unfit to attain the higher reaches of spiritual life. The first *Jhāna* of Buddhism, for instance, is described as a state in which "attention is applied and sustained, which is born of solitude and filled with zest and pleasurable feeling." And this is the avenue of further progress on the way of wisdom. In the *Yoga* scheme, again, the capacity for concentration is the indispensable condition of mystical ecstasy.[1] The mind must be one-pointed in order to penetrate into the life of the spirit.

The phenomenon of attention adjustment seems to be both a test and a technic. A mind that cannot concentrate would also be found wanting in certain essential qualities necessary for progress on the mystic way. Concentration is a technic; for it is cultivated by a long course of psycho-physiological discipline that aims at achieving quiescence of turbulent desires and proliferation of favourable emotions and attitudes. A mind practised in concentration can use all its innate and acquired tendencies as urges to spiritual advance.

---

* The editors very much regret that Prof. N. N. Sen Gupta who was associated with the Volume from the very beginning, has now passed away.

Concentration as a phase of mystic discipline is always undertaken in the setting of a particular religious ideology and myth. The Buddhist attempts to subdue the carnal desires by a contemplation of the foulness of the body. Hence, he seeks to direct his attention upon the loathsome aspect of the body and its organs. "Just as a clever butcher", says the text, ... "when he has slain an ox, displays the carcase piecemeal at the cross ways as he sits, even so does a monk reflect upon this very body." There are other practices of concentration which bring about many transformations of consciousness in consonance with the Buddhistic outlook and ideology. Hence the author concludes:

"Therefore the wise should not be negligent
In constant application to this mode
Of concentration-culture, which has such
Advantages, and purges passion-taints."[2]

The Vaishnava, on the other hand, prescribes other objects that fit in with its special aim, method and outlook. The devotee is asked to concentrate, for instance, upon the episodes presented in the Krishna-mythology. A Vaishnava text, suggests the following among others as a fit topic for concentration: "Concentrate on Krishṇa, whose body is aglow with the rays of millions of suns which are, at the same time, soothing as the beams of as many moons. Think of the divine form as pervading the whole universe and recite the mystic syllables." The devotee is again asked to concentrate on the scene depicted in the Gītā where Kishṇa is discoursing to Arjuna on the vital truths of the life of the spirit. Each task of concentration is intended to place the mind in a well-defined context of theories, images, myths and emotions.

In the beginning, the mind moves from the one plane to the other: from the plane of normal life to that built up by religious concentration. These, however, slowly blend into each other in the course of religious life. A new field comprising all the diverse orders of facts that mind takes account of, takes shape sometimes gradually, and sometimes with dramatic suddenness. This new scheme of things eventually secures control over both body and mind determining the direction of sentiments and interests and the course of behaviour. An integral personality emerges in this manner as the fruition of the discipline of concentration.

I.—In the Upanishadic Tradition:

(i) The concept of *Dhyāna* is well-known as a technique of spiritual orientation in the early Aryan tradition. *"Dhyāna"*,

says Śaṅkara in his commentary to an Upanishad text, "is the one-pointedness of mind directed to gods, etc., as described in the traditional texts or *Śāstras*. The process of *Dhyāna* maintains its object in an unchanging condition and gives rise to a continuous succession of mental states possessing a specified common character and determined by a well-defined *set*," Attainment of every kind of wealth, position, or learning, represents at least partial success in concentration. Quarrelsome people, scandal-mongers, and people who are ever ready to point out other peoples' faults to them are far from the path of concentration and remain small men.[3] The way to life of the spirit, then, lies through concentration.

Another Upanishad text defines the role of concentration after the analogy of striking fire by friction. "One's own body is the piece of wood to be lighted. *Praṇava* is the piece to be rubbed against it. Concentration is the process of friction. It is in this way that the latent spiritual reality can be discerned." The task of concentration, then, must have a two-fold support in the mystic formula, the *Praṇava,* and in the psycho-physical changes that it induces, in the course of recital of the *Praṇava*.

The same text proceeds to describe the technic. "May the Sun", says the text, "direct and fixate my mind to the Brahman; may it fill my body and its senses with heavenly illumination that makes all truth and reality manifest." The concept of the Sun is very important in this context. It seems, as the Upanisad proceeds to describe in the same chapter, that various *sensory experience* arise in the course of the *Yoga* practice. One of these is called the 'Sun'. If we understand the prayer cited above in the reality through the meditation of the *experience* called 'Sun'. It appears that there are facts in Christian mysticism that conform to this interpretation. Jacob Boehme, for instance, speaks of waiting for and attending the *supernatural and divine light as the superior light appointed to govern the day, rising in the true east which is paradise.* This "light" is said to break forth "as out of the darkness within thee through a pillar of thunder-clouds". Even the technic in the two cases has some resemblance. "Cease from thine own activity", says Boehme, "steadfastly fixing thine eye upon one point, and with a strong purpose relying upon the promised grace of God in Christ." Such orientation of the mind and of the entire personality to God will, as the practice consummates itself, reveal a new order of experience. "So shall thy light break forth as the morning; and after the redness thereof is passed, the Sun himself, which thou waitest for, shall arise unto thee." This new light should prevail over the 'light of nature': the human reason and the senses. It is only thus that man's mind approaches God.[4]

(ii) Contemplate the Self as the *Hamsa,* the Swan, the symbol of identity of the ego and the reality, suggests a text. It should be thought of as resting on a lotus with eight petals; particular parts of its body should be imagined to represent the Fire, Moon, Rudra and Rudrāṇī, and to the aglow with the rays of millions of suns. Various mental changes seem to arise in the course of such concentration on the petals of the lotus. In one case, it is an inclination to good deeds; in another, it is a disposition to sloth and sleep; in a third, we have the growth of mental crookedness; and in a fourth, there develops a tendency towards sin. A condition of intellectual lucidity, a desire to play games and to move about, an inclination to amorousness and to acquisition of things also arise. There also develops an attitude of disinclination to all material things and enjoyments, a life of conscious harmony and intellectual lucidity. And finally the supreme state of non-relational consciousness, free from all material images, slowly grows entirely dissolving the mind in the sound and the symbolic meaning of *Om*[5]. The account reads like one of the oscillation of two planes of experience ultimately reaching its consummation in integration.

(iii) The five types of *'vital air'* were also used as objects of fixation of attention. It is supposed that there are five kinds of 'air' circulating in the body, each kind being defined by the manner and direction of its circulation. Man concentrates on each of these processes of circulation in order to attain a state of bliss. Such fixation, considered as a psycho-physical process, involves tension in certain mechanisms of adjustment and relation in others. It is likely that there would be a state of relaxation of the psycho-physical system with respect to certain *organic sets* representing desire and

emotional fixations. This is likely to ensure a sense of relief and even of joy. The field of attention comprising, as it would, of mere breathing processes or sometimes points of fixation on imaginary processes resembles the contracted field of attention in hypnosis. Two consequences ensure from this: (a) partial relaxation and relief from organic tension give rise to a sense of pleasure: (b) it becomes possible, in the absence of rival contents in the field, to induce an ideology of the scheme of religious life more easily.

(iv) The Upanishad texts often speak of three different phases in the process of 'holding' of the mind—of arresting its tendency to oscillate. These are placidity of mind *(Prasāda)*, immobility of attention (*Niśchālya*) and concentration (*Nivesha, Niyoga*). The three appear to be inter-dependent and represent the nuances of attentional process. Concentration is the process of fixation of mind to a process, object or part of the body. It is a phenomenon in which the range of oscillation of mental operations is restricted within narrow limits. "As a tortoise withdraws its limbs within its shell, withdraw the mental operations in the same way within the region of the heart. Limit the mental functions to the process of recital of the *Praṇava*, Om." Such limitation finally leads to a state of immobility of the mind; and this condition in its turn induces a sense of joy. The technics for this type of practice are many.

Another text suggests the following: Withdraw the mind from its normal objects. Fixate it on the notion that there is a unison of consciousness pervading all parts of the body. Fixate upon this as pure consciousness. This is *Dhāranā*. When the awareness of the attentional process itself no longer figures in the field of consciousness there is a state of *entire absorption of the mind*, the state of *Samādhi*. The end of these operations seems to be to induce a condition in which there is consciousness but no mental activity or perception of change. It is an object less *pure consciousness* and sometimes described as the re-absorption (*Laya*) of the mind in its base or the non-mental [6]

The technic of attention considered in this section aims at two types of transformation which commence when the mind is disoriented from its normal setting. The mental operations break away from their objects; their changes are controlled within narrow limits; a condition of relative tranquility develops. Two lines of progress are suggested from this point. (i) The mind may orient itself to a new ideology which builds up a new field of attention. It competes with the normal contents of consciousness, interpenetrates with them and thus brings about a new personality-synthesis. A new range of ideas and feelings, a new scheme of values and conduct and finally, a new outlook gradually emerges, (ii) Or, the quiescent mind finally loses itself in an undifferentiated expanse of pure consciousness. It is an objectless awareness interwoven with subtle strands of joy and peace. Nothing but this exists for the mind, and it becomes the sole reality. Both of these courses of discipline have their adherents in the later history of Indian thought.

II—In Buddhism:

We find in Buddhism an elaborate consideration of attention under two main heads. On the one side, we find an analysis of forms and functions of concentration in the context of spiritual life. On the other side, we find descriptions of the different objects to which attention could profitably be directed for spiritual purposes. We shall discuss these two topics separately.

A General Analysis of Attention in Early Buddhism:

(i) Various Types of Attentional Phenomena:

Several different terms are employed in Buddhism to indicate the different phases of the attentional process. *Manakkāra, Manasikāra, Ekaggatā, Vitakka and Vichāra* are some of the important concepts. The first of these indicates a process of conscious selection that arises with a specified object-reference. This signifies that the process in a question is a *specific attentional act* rather than the *attentional set*. As the text says: "It does not go anywhere and everywhere,"[7] The term *Manasikara* seems to connote the general *attentional attitude* in entertaining any thought. The state of one-pointedness concentration or *Ekaggata*- seems to signify a condition of fixation. This is evident from the theory that 'concentration lasts as long as a desire lasts.' *Vitakka* is defined as adaptation of attention and *Vichāra* its persistence.[8] All of these operations are essential for the adjustments demanded in the course of spiritual discipline.

(ii) Contemplation or Jhāna as Application of Attention.

Concentration is defined in the context of spiritual discipline as "collectedness of moral thought." It is defined in the *Vibhaṅga* as "Indifference, mindfulness, awareness, ease, as well as collectedness of mind." The stage of supreme exaltation, *Ekodibhāva,* which arises in the course of contemplation is said to be a "synonym for concentration." It seems to possess, as a psychological process, two principal features. (a) The mental states should be "well-placed" or mutually adjusted in reference to an object-situation in such a manner that they can remain in this specific configuration for the desired length of time. This phase is called *Samādhāna.* (b) Secondly, there should be no change in the character of the configuration itself; nor should there be any 'wavering' from fixation. This is called *Avikkhepa.*

Concentration may be viewed as of two kinds: *Access concentration* and *Ecstasy concentration.* The former prepares for the higher reaches of spiritual life and the latter sustains the ecstasy-experience that finally emerges. The preparation for the first *Jhāna* itself brings in its wake the subsequent adjustments needed for its practice. Finally, the way is made easy for the rise and maintenance of ecstasy. The first state is *Access-concentration* and the second, the *Ecstasy-concentration.* The Buddhist writers have employed several other principles of classification. These are: (i) presence or absence of 'rapture' in concentration, (ii) ease or indifference associated with the process, (iii) direction of concentration to spiritual or to material objects. The practice of *Jhāna,* then, is the culture of various patterns of concentration. It is, as the text says, "applied thinking, sustained thinking, rapture, bliss, and collectedness of mind."[9] The varieties of contemplative life are defined probably with greater clearness mainly in terms of attention in another manual. It is said that there are five types of *Jhāna,* the first of which is associated with (i) *vitakka,* (ii) *vichara,* (iii) *pīti* (friendliness, (iv) *sukha* (joy), and (v) *ekaggatā* (one-pointedness).[10]

(iii) The Effect of Concentration

Success in concentration appears to possess in this context several esoteric properties such as causing rebirth in a better world. It possesses several other properties as well. It is said that concentration is the avenue through which reality can be known in its true nature. "Monks, practise concentration. A monk who practises concentration knows a thing as it really is." The practice of concentration is said to favour "the attainment of cessation from perception." Since the end of the mystic quest is often the denial of the world, the perceptual processes must cease in order that the final consummation may be reached.[11]

B. Special Applications of Attention

Attention must be sustained on objects. The character of object on which mind concentrates would naturally determine the course of transformation that takes place in the mind. Fixation of attention on specified topics and things brings in its wake particular sets of attitudes and feelings. The process of concentration, therefore, induces in the mind a specific object-situation and a particular order of feelings and attitudes; it also inhibits all other processes that do not fit in with this pattern. A new configuration of states and functions instals itself in this way as the dominant principle of mental life.

(i) The Phenomenon of "Intent Contemplation"

(a) One of the objects of intent contemplation is the human body itself. The seeker after realisation is enjoined on fixation on the body as a collection of limbs. The body is, again, viewed as "sprung from parents' blood and seed, in nature impure, putrid and ill-smelling, disturbed by passion, hatred, delusion ... full of a hundred thousand diseases." The body is also thought of as impermanent and changing. it grows and decays by regular stages, according to laws which no one can alter.

"The Bodhisatva must regard the body as a running from nine apertures. He must regard the body as a dwelling place for eighty-thousand broods of worms ...The Bodhisatva must regard the body as the food for others, of wolves and jackals; as an excellent machine, a collection of tools fastened together by bones and sinews."

Finally, the body is thought of as mere matter; and matter tends to be viewed as extension. "This body is like space." Thus he contemplates the body like space. 'That is all space', he thinks. For the full understanding of the body his intellect does not direct itself to anything else, does not divert itself thither or fix :tself there."

(b) A similar analysis is carried through with respect to feelings. "Whatever feeling he (the seeker) has, he understands that it is impermanent . . . What is pleasant is impermanent, what

is painful is unpleasant, and what is indifferent is unsubstantial." But the procedure is not intended to annihilate feeling. The aim of the technique seems to be to develop an affective *Anlage* as the context of all orders of feeling. "For himself" says the text, "he does not aim at the destruction of feelings. Whatever feeling he has, it is permeated with great compassion."

(c) The sensory phenomenon is another object towards which attention is directed. "Sensation has been defined as experience. But by whom is that sensation felt? There is no experience other than Sensation." Memory and intelligence and other functions are to be retranslated into the sensation and realised as such, so that thee remains nothing in the operations of mind other than a flux of sensations. "As Wisdom" says the text, "so this Sensation is calm, pure and bright."

There are two important points in this procedure of concentration. (i) It has been experimentally verified that attention directed to complex mental operations leads to their disintegration. Each phase of a mental function appears as a sensory-experience without any background of meaning. It is, thus, possible to understand how consciousness becomes merely a plane of sensory-experience through the operation of attention.[12] (ii) A sensory plane of mental life, which leaves no residue of meanings and settings in the unconscious, would naturally be 'pure bright and calm.' Empiricism and sensationalism acquire, in this manner, a new meaning in the context of the Buddhist discipline.

(d) A similar introspective and attention operation is directed to thought processes. Phenomenally described, thought is "formless", unseen, not solid, unknowable, unstable, homeless." In regard to its location in the world of experience, thought is not internal, "not outside him (the observer), nor in the conformations, nor in the elements, nor in the organs of sense." Yet, the object of thought and the thought itself are the same. It is finally concluded that thought cannot observe itself. "As the same sword blade cannot cut the same sword blade, as the same finger tip cannot touch the same finger tip, so the same thought cannot see the same thought." Buddhism does not accept James' view that the passing thought is the thinker.

What is the significance of the life of thought? Thought is ever restless, "like a monkey or like the wind." It is "lightly turning, sensual, moving amid the six objects of sense, one thing after another." Thought can, however, be utilised when it is intent, immobile and concentrated. The real nature of thought is "like illusion." It arises and passes away, like a flash of lightning. Yet, we can speak of a process of "edification" of thought in which it is directed towards renunication for the purpose of inculcating in the personality the principles of spiritual life.

(e) Attention, again, is directed in the course of Buddhist discipline, to the nature and constitution of the universe. All things dissolve into elements. But these are mere abstractions. "In them there is no substance, there is no being, or living being, or creature of human being." They are the products of conceptual construction. "If they are brought about, they arise; if they are not brought about, they do not arise."

The elements build up things and events when they form aggregates. The phenomenon of aggregation depends upon primary and secondary causes. These causes, according to Buddhism, link themselves into a chain, the chain of twelve causes, the *Paticcasamuppāda,* which is the one fixed point of reference in the Buddhistic universe. The process of concentration, then, transforms things and events into aggregations. Further attentional practice dissembles these into elements. These in their turn are seen as work of the mind. Mental life, as we have seen in the previous section, sheds its certainty and sense of reality under the scrutiny of attention. The universe thus dissolves into a series of names. But "Name is a matter of habit." Everywhere reigns "emptiness: nowhere are gods, Nāgas or Rākshasas. Men or no men, all are known as that." When the world to which the desires are fastened becomes a mere cipher of experience, man's spirit achieves true freedom and purity. It is under such conditions can the true meaning and values of spiritual life infuse themselves upon the mind. This seems to be the end of the Buddhist technic of attention.[13]

(ii) ***The Kasiṇas. The Practice of Concentration with Material Aids***

Buddhism prescribes several types of contemplative devices as aids to the process of transformation that spiritual discipline aims at. There is a definite method of employing material aids for ensuring concentration and inducing a specific order of psychic change. These aids are called *Kasiṅas* and are ten in number. They are earth, water, heat, air, blue-green, yellow, red white light, and the separated spaces. Each of these is fixated through a particular type of mental operation. The earth-device, of all of these, is considered in one of the authoritative texts in great detail. The rest repeat the same technic. We shall, therefore, follow mainly the procedure of the earth-device, the *Paṭhavī-kasiṇa,* in our exposition of the method.

The earth-device is intended to secure a durable and progressive concentration of attention as a preparation for the *Jhānas* or contemplative life. These arise from "sustained thinking, rapture, bliss, collectedness of mind." It is necessary to alienate the mental operations from their normal objects in order that the desired consummation may be reached. The *Kasinas* are the technics that serve to detach the mind and also to develop "sustained thinking."

(a) The General Conditions of Kasina

The *Kasiṅas* involve several preliminary steps. (1) The practice needs a specific attitude or mental set which defines the aim of the practice and engenders confidence in its success. Thus, it is enjoined that the monk should inculcate the following idea: "By means of this practice I shall be freed from old age and death." (2) The culture of a favourable emotional disposition is also regarded as an essential for the process. The spiritual aspirant thus adopts a "reverential attitude of mind and in a loving mood binds his heart to the object," that is to say, to the object of attention. (3) The body should be freed from all that may operate as impediments. Thus, the long hairs should be cropped short, nails etc., should be cut and, in general, the body must be secured from all irritating stimulation. (4) The mind of the aspirant is further to be freed from the petty worries of daily life. He should repair his robes and his begging bowl and clean his furniture and his room, before he begins his practice of concentration. (5) The place, lastly, in which the practice is to begin, should be carefully selected. Such a place should be a dwelling which is "neither too far nor too near, is easy of access, not crowded by day, with little sound or noise at night, scarcely exposed to wind, heat and crawling creatures."

(b) The Material Device of Kasina

The material upon which the monk is required to concentrate in the *Earth-device* is a quantity of earth of a particular quality. The object of concentration becomes unsuitable for the purpose if wrong colours arc mixed. Hence, the clay of the Ganges stream is recommended. The device should not be set up in the middle of the monastery where distractions are many. It should be within the confines of the monastery and in a covered place.

There are two kinds of device, movable and stationary. In the former case, a cloth or a piece of leather is tied to four sticks. On the cloth is spread finely ground earth from which all foreign matter has been eliminated. In the case of stationary device the sticks should be driven into the ground and creepers should be planted round the device. The size should be "that of tray or of pot-lid." The earth on its receptacle should be "smooth like the surface of a drum."

(c) Posture and Mental Adjustment

The monk, after he has performed his ablutions, should sit at a distance of about forty-five inches from the device. Too close a position would give a view of details of the fault ot the device, engrossing the attention. The position and the posture must both be comfortable so that they do not impede attention.

Even the manner of looking at the device is specifically prescribed. "By opening too wide, the eye gets tired and the circle becomes too clear on which account the sign does not manifest itself to him. When the eye opens too narrowly, the circle does not become clear, the mind slackens; thus, again, the sign is not manifested. Therefore like a man who sees the reflection of his face on the surface of a mirror, he should open the eye with an even gaze." The monk should begin by reminding himself that the device would prove efficacious as it has been to the various Buddha-personalities through the ages. He should also have faith in the ultimate success of his spiritual undertaking.

(iii) What Kasiṇa Aims at?

The set of concentration seems to consist of three phases. In the first phases. The monk tries to abolish the sense of separation from his particular device and the earth as an extended reality. "He (the monk) should let the device and the physical basis assume one and the same colour." Secondly, the monk directs his attention to the *concept* earth, helping the mind in its task by a recital of one of the synonyms of the term "earth". The third phase is called the *grasping of the sign*. So far as I am able to understand, it consists in the comprehension of the *full connotation* of the term "earth" together with a generalised image.

A note on this last point may define the nature of the experience that seems to be aimed at here. An image of an object when it appears in consciousness may undergo four types of change. (a). It fluctuates and gradually passes out of the field of attention, to reappear in dreams and day-dreams and also suddenly in moments of relaxation. (b). It may acquire a meaning and a verbal symbol which obscure the image-experience. In this way, it becomes a concept. (c). It stimulates associated images and builds up with them an entire configuration. (d). Lastly, it becomes a generalised image of the type that medieval realism spoke. The image "table" comes to posses a character of such wide generality that it can represent any particular kind of table. So far as I have been able to gather from the description, the fourth type of experience seems to be aimed at in the practice of *Kasina*.

It is thus enjoined in the case of *Paṭhavī-kasiṅa* that once the sign, has been grasped, the devotee should not sit at the place of the *Kasina-stimulus*. "He should enter his abode; there he should sit and develop." He must take all care not to make any delay in the continuance of the practice. "Then, if the tender concentration perishes for any reason of inappropriateness, the monk should go to the place where the *Kasiṅa* object is, "take the sign, come back, and sitting in comfort, develop it; he should repeatedly lay it to heart, consider it with applied and sustained thinking."

The distinction between this type of image of the *Kasiṇa object* and that which arises at the first moment when the monk fixates, is that "in the former the fault of the device appears; the latter is like the disc of a mirror taken out of a bag, or a well-burnished conch-vessel. It possesses neither colour, nor form". The absence of impurity seems to exclude after-image and idiotic image. The absence of colour and form seems to exclude the memory image. "To the winner of concentration", says the text, "it is just a mode of appearance, and is born of perception." This suggests the exclusion of the concept. Hence, I suggest that the *Kasiṅa* aims at developing a *generalised image which is psychologically midway between the conceptual processes, on the one hand, and the perceptual processes on the other.*

The purpose of developing a generalised image of this type seems to be three-fold:

(i) Since the senses are normally oriented to external objects, an image of this order would do less violence to human nature than fixation upon a conceptual object. It would be a better device than fixation upon memory images inasmuch as the latter are more fluctuating. Thus, a generalised image offers a better opportunity for steady application of attention. A concept trails away into new meanings. The memory image brings ever new associations in their wake. The generalised image remains relatively constant and is thus a better object of fixation.

(ii) Secondly, such generalised images seem to constitute the natural territory of mind in which the purely subjective and the object-contents meet. It is well-known that some of the processes of spiritual discipline aim at cultivating a kind of *spiritual cyclopean eye* which stands midway between introversion and extroversion. Fixation upon a generalised image may, in a sense, be the beginning of the *cyclopean outlook.*

(iii) A generalised image of this type, appearing both to the sensory function and the intellect, inhibits all particular mental functions *by virtue of its uniformity of constitution*. All is earth, air, fire or water. The other mental functions, associations, memories and attitudes are inhibited by the persisting uniformity of the *Kasina-image*. At the same time, the initial beliefs with which the practice begins, have a chance to proliferate on the relatively empty field of consciousness. It is thus that the *ecstasy-concentration* grows. The pattern of mind resembles that so often found among people on a holiday who gaze out at sea or look down upon the plane from the top of a hill. Both of these are said to expel the persistent thoughts and memories of daily life from the mind.

III—The Techinc of Attention in the Kāshmir Śaiva School

The most varied methods for securing concentration of attention for spiritual discipline are adopted by the Kashmir Śaiva school. These range from the adjustment of attention to specific sensory objects to fixation upon social situations, that offer fulfillment of instinctive drives to the intent contemplation of conceptual constructions. The aim of attentional discipline is to develop a non-relational (*Nirvikalpa*) mode of consciousness. This signifies a mode of experience that no longer fluctuates, lying midway between the opposite poles of subject-object consciousness and of internality and externality. It is said to be devoid of sensory contents and to implicate a sense of vastness, of the infinite expanse of reality. The feeling of self-hood and the consciousness of the body totally disappear.[14]

(i) ***Sensory Objects of Attention***

(a) One should fixate on hollow vessels such as jars, taking care not to pay any attention to the sides and the base. When concentration is complete and the mind rests on the object of fixation, the desired non-relational state arises.

(b) It is again, suggested that the eyes should be directed to treeless regions at the base of hills. All the mental states disappear and the predispositions (*Vritti*) that build up mental configurations, diminish in their potency.

(c) One should stand near wells or other deep depressions and look downwards. If one stands, says the commentator, on the top of a hill and looks downward, the same purpose will be served. When the plane of experience becomes non-relational the habitual mental states and operations subside.

(d) Fixate visual attention on any object and immediately withdraw it. The mental functions would come to a cessation; they would lapse into a non-relational state.

(e) Fixate attention on the tones produced from a stringed musical instrument. The pitch of these tones should be serially given from the higher to the lower scales. When the sensory experience ceases, the mind becomes "like the supreme space-expanse"; it becomes dissociated from all experiences past and present.[15]

(f) Keep up a continuous fixation on the placid sky. The mind becomes immobile and enters into the nature of the *Bhairava* representing an expanse of non-relational consciousness.

(g) It is recommended that the eyes should be fixated on the sun at day time, on the moon at night, and on the glow of the lamp inside the house. The mind under such condition slowly touches upon the pure consciousness.

(h) A finger or any other part of the body may be pierced with a needle. Attention should be fixated to such parts. The mind under such conditions smoothly proceeds to the *Bhairava* state.

These are some of the methods suggested in a text which is regarded as authoritative by competent scholars. These are probably many more of such methods. The aim of all them seems to be induce a non-relational plane of experience.

(ii) Fixation upon Imaginal Objects

(a) Think of the skin of your body as the base of all inert matter and external objects. Think of the interior of the cover of skin as empty. Your self-consciousness will disappear and a consciousness of supreme expanse will gradually grow upon the mind.

(b) Picture to yourself that the fire of final dissolution has caught the big toe of your right leg. Imagine that the whole body is burnt into nothingness. A placid self-illuminating and, therefore, conscious reality emerges out of such contemplation.

(c) The whole universe should be pictured as consumed by the fire of dissolution in the same way. A self-consciousness as the residual reality would finally emerge.

(d) Concentrate your mind on the idea, says the text, that the universe all around you is entirely empty. The field of knowledge becomes non-relational and the mind finally loses itself in the vast expanse of reality.[16]

(e) Think of a night of impenetrable darkness, says the text. Concentrate on the image of darkness with eyes closed. The Bhairava, as represented by the non-relational state will descend on your mind. Concentrate on the darkness around you with the eyes open. The same goal will be reached.

Many such situations are recommended for attentional fixation. The ends sought are three-fold: *the attainment of a state of pure consciousness devoid of any definite content, of self-consciousness or 'I'-consciouness, and of a non-relational plane of experience.*

(ii) Concentration upon Certain Momentary Phases of Experience: The Middle State (Madhyabhāva).

(a) A sense of reality is said to dawn upon the mind when two different ideas are entertained and when they are simultaneously and completely inhibited, attention being given to a contentless consciousness which constitutes the interval between the two ideas.

(b) The same principle is suggested in a simpler form. When a specific meaning-configuration fades away and consciousness through skillful practice, is maintained in an objectless condition, a vivid sense of reality gradually appears.

(c) When the mind ceases to think of gross objects, attention is to be directed to internal states. The mind reaches a non-relational plane and a sense of reality emerges.

(d) When the adjustment of a sense-organ for the perception of external objects ceases or when a sensory process is inhibited through its *rivalry* with others, consciousness lapses into an objectless state. Fixation upon such consciousness leads to the growth of a sense of reality.

(e) A desire or impulse about to take shape should at once be brought to an end. Mind relapses into a state of placidity. Fixation upon consciousness in its pure and objectless state is a step towards the comprehension of reality.

(f) A dual operation of attention is suggested in the following method: let the mind be directed to objects that stimulate the emotion-impulse systems, such as, sex, anger and greed. Such concentration leaves a residual awareness which is the essence of the conscious reality. Concentration upon this phase would naturally lead to the revelation of the nature of reality.[17].

Attention in these instances is directed to *transitional states of consciousness.* It is a difficult task of introvert self-observation, rendered more uncertain by the rarity of the states. Yet it is not impossible to secure the conditions necessary for such manipulation of attention. The psychology of such fixation will be considered later.

IV—Attention Directed to Certain Conceptual Constructions

(a) It is recommended that attention should be concentrated on the *inspiratory and the expiratory pauses neglecting altogether the processes of inspiration and expiration.* In the alternative, attention may be directed to the state when air has been completely breathed in. Under such conditions, says the text, there arises a sense of joy similar to the joy of sex.

(b) There are words in Sanskrit that end in an aspirate sound. It is recommended that attention should be fixated on the aspirate alone, leaving out the other vowels and consonants. When the mind loses all other contents excepting this, it comes into contact with the reality as pure consciousness.

(c) Conceive of your consciousness as an entity apart from your body. Think of this consciousness as belonging to other bodies as well. Direct your attention to the conception of a consciousness as common to all bodies. A few days of such attentional practice, says the text, cultivates the feeling that one's consciousness expands all over the universe.

(d) When the attention is directed to one object, all other things should be thought of as nothing. Thus, the higher degree of attention, the focus, is directed to the object, while the field of dispersed attention consists of a sense of nothingness. Such contemplation leads to quiescence of all mental activities.

(e) When the awareness of 'I' and 'Mine' ceases and attention is directed to the conception of nothingness, says the text, the conscious life comes to its own natural state of balance and quiescence.[18]

The object of attention, in all these instances, is a meaning that intellect seizes upon. The conceptual processes isolate and define a specified phase of conscious-life which normally appears as a short-lived moment in the continuum of experience. Such fixation is said to secure balance and quiescence of mind, expansion of consciousness and revelation of reality.

V—Psychological Theory of the Śaiva Technic

(1) What the Technic Aims at

The technic of attention described in the preceding section is said to usher in several types of psychological state.

(a) In the first place, attention to certain types of objects precipitates a non-rational plane of experience which is often said to herald the rise of the *Bhairava* state. The latter is described in the following manner: there arises an internal sense of joy blended with a complete awareness of the ago or the I-feeling (*A hantā);* there emerges a sense of freedom from all rational experience; the whole universe and the self are felt as a single completed reality. The manifoldness of experience lies latent in the mind as in the *Madhyamā* state, "in the manner of ovules inside the pod."

(b) The second type of experience which the technic aims at securing is pure consciouness, as a general expanse of mere awareness without any object. It also aims at projecting ("expanding" and "spreading" are translations of the term) the pure awareness grasped in self-observation to all things in the universe. The world thus becomes a vast expanse of consciousness.

(c) Thirdly, there arise in this technic, a supreme sense of reality which may attach itself to any of the planes of experience described above.

(d) Fourthly, the process of fixation of attention is correlated with a sense of joy. (This last phase has been explained in another paper previously published.)

(e) And lastly, the process of fixation and the consequent transformation of mental functions bring into relief a vivid sense of the self. The explanation to be aimed at in this section will consist in exhibiting how the process of attentional fixation may produce these changes in the field of consciousness.

2. *Sensory Attention and its Possible Consequences*

Attention directed to sensory phenomena is said to give rise to a non-relational field of experience. The process may be described in the following manner:

(a) The process of fixation in the context specified above, involves: (i) the inhibition of all tendencies to action; (ii) A strict limitation of attention to a specified phase of experience, e.g., attention to a sound and not to the instrument, to the base of the hill and not to the surroundings, to the small injury on a finger and not to any other part of the body (iii) the consequent inhibition of the function of judgment which usually accompanies the action attitude and the tendencies of integration operative in the field of perception.

(b) Such fixation induces what in structural Psychology, is called the *'Process'*-attitude as distinguished from the *'meaning'*-attitude.

(c) Experimental evidence shows that the continuum of experience divides itself, under such condition, into a number of phenomenal units. It is found, for instance, that there appear in aesthesiometric experiments "several perceptive forms between exact oneness and clear twoness. Under the *process*-attitude all of these intermediate forms are reported. Under the *stimulus*-attitude, however, whatever is not one, is reported as two. The experiments of Britz, again, showed how in the Tachistoscopic presentation of coloured geometrical figures, forms not presented were reported by the subjects. Dallenbach also found a similar phenomenon in his experiments on attention. The subjective forms comprise from 'spots', 'flicks' and 'blurs' to well-defined geometrical figures.[19]

(d) The continuity and unity of experience is thus broken up into phenomenal phases which are usually observed as parts of a single field in an immediate mode of awareness. The inhibition of the reaction attitude and of the processes of perception and association places the experience of the environment on the lower level of attention,—in the field of "apprehension" in Wundt's sense. Hence, the whole field of consciousness comprising the focus and the fringe becomes a field of non-relational experience.

(e) A non-relational field of experience is said to convey a sense of reality that no other form of knowledge possesses. Such

experience, according to Bradley, carries a "sense of living emotion" and comprises "everything of which in any sense I am aware"; it is a "knowing and being in one."[20] It is also the neutral base from which opposing types of beliefs and judgments may emerge, as Bradley's own dialectical presentation shows. It is possible, then, that a new scheme of beliefs and judgments will take shape in the context of the principles, attitudes and imagery of the Śaiva cult.

(f) Again, the non-relational experience considered in this context is very similar to the fore-conscious of Frendian Psychology. It is the point of confluence of the unconscious and conscious stresses and trends of the personality. As perceptions and ideals become articulate in beliefs and judgments the nuances of the unconscious tendencies interlace with the thought processes. There grows up in this manner, a new plane and pattern of personality in the wake of the technic of attention dissolving the ordered scheme of daily experience into the melting pot of non-relational immediacy.

3. The Theory of Attention to Image-objects

Attention directed to objects and situations represented in terms of images, gives rise to three types of transformation:—

(i) There is a growth of non-relational experience.

(ii) A self-illuminating conscious reality is immediately felt.

(iii) A witnessing consciousness, i.e., a self-conscious observer of mental functions, gradually emerges. It is necessary to explain how these transformations take place.

(a) The Imaginable situation to which attention is fixated in Śaiva technic is a visual expanse. The picture of void or of the dense darkness of the night, both build up a vision of uniform expanse. But such uniformity would break up into phenomenal units in the course of attentional exercises as considered above. A non-relational experience will emerge in the same manner as in the case of a sensory continuum.

(b) A fixation on the picture of dissolution of the body and of things of the universe, leaves the mind without any content.

A contentless consciousness, then, is grasped in immediate experience and becomes, for this reason, the sole reality. For, imagination has dissolved away everything else.

(c) The mechanism of the witnessing consciousness is somewhat different. The feeling of self-hood is a complex of organic and kinaesthetic sensations according to both James and Wundt. It may be physiologically correlated with a complex process of circulation of the nervous impulse between the various cortical and thalamic regions. Thus, the self-feeling may be represented as (i) a system of memories (cortical associations), (ii) a system of emotions, impulses and organic sensations (thalamic associations), (iii) a system of idea or plans connected with the action and emotional functions (thalamo-cortical associations), and (iv) an experience of durable unity or subjective point of reference (correlated with a nodal point in the circulation of the nervous impulse).

The image of dissolution of the world upon which attention is fixated gradually leads to the cessation of the memory pictures and of emotions. The inhibition of the action, attitude, and disappearance of specific objects of the environment dissolve the ego conceived as a process of realisation of a plan or idea. The self-feeling is thus experienced as a durable unity—as a point of reference that persists *vis a vis* the image of the void into which all else has been dissolved.

The psychological constitution of this point of reference or the witnessing consciousness is of considerable theoretic interest. Freud suggests that the separation of an observing function from the totality of mental life is most likely a normal process. The witnessing ego is the superego which represents the parental function, an impression of which every mind carries within itself. The separation of the super-ego is really a schism between the traditional authority and the desires and impulses of the individual.[21] This interpretation, however, would not readily be applicable in the present context. For, in the instance that we are considering, the impulses and the objects which they implicated have both, for the time being, lost their specificity in the general expanse which imagination is called upon to represent to the mind. The punitive function that the tradition and the parental authority imply, has no part to play when both impulses and their objective have come to nought.

We may approach the problem on the basis of the analysis of self-consciousness or the pure 'I' offered by James and Wundt. Though old, there is nothing of a more recent date to supersede the perspicacity of the view. According to James, the self is the "intermediary between ideas and overt acts and would be a collection of activities, physiologically in no essential way different from the activities themselves....The nuclear self would be adjustments collectively considered."[22] Hence, the constituents of the self-feeling, conceived as a psychological complex, are the organic and kinaesthetic sensations.

Wundt also thinks of the experience of self as a permanent mass of feelings immediately or remotely subject to will. He speaks of two kinds of awareness of the self: a wide and a narrow one. In the former case, every mental act comes to standing relation to the will. In the latter case, the self-feeling adheres more upon the "inner activity of apperception, over against which our own body and all representations connected with it, appear as external objects, different from our proper self". The consciousness "contracted down to the process of apperception" is called by Wundt, the 'Ego'.[23]

Wundt postulates a specific function of apperception, with a well-defined physiological basis. The consciousness that arises as a resultant of this function is, for him, the self-consciousness. The questionable validity of the conception of apperceptive function and the more questionable validity of localisation of that function, render the notion of the self in this narrow sense insecure. Hence, neither Freud's nor Wundt's views are of help to us in this context.

I suggest the following interpretation in the light of these theories: when the external world dissolves into a sense of uniform emptiness, attention directed to this expanse of void builds up either a non-relational field in the manner considered above, or it recoils towards other termini. The other dominant sensory object is the complex of organic and kinaesthetic sensations of which James and Wundt speak. These become better integrated and more vivid in the field of attention. For, the organic sensations do not usually yield to attentional analysis. There is no chance, therefore, of their building up *phenomenal phases* as in the cases of visual and auditory sensations.

All experience that man acquires enters into fusion with this group of dominant sensations and are part and parcel with the ego-feeling which is the correlate of the organic-kinaesthetic sensation-complex.

The experiences which are not assimilated into this complex are inhibited due to their small attention value. Hence, there remains only the ego-feeling as the residual experience.

4. *What Attention to Conceptual Constructions Achieves*

Attention directed to the phases of sensory experience and conceptual constructions are said to achieve four different kinds of result: (a) feeling of joy resembling that of sex, (b) realisation of pure-consciousness, (c) the whole universe as consciousness or expansion of consciousness, and (d) a sense of balance and quiescence. We shall try to understand how far these consequences may be expected to ensue from the specific type of attentional adjustment.

(a) A sense of joy of a specific order arises when attention is fixated to the inspiratory and the expiratory pauses. In the phenomenon of abdominal breathing and in the respiration of the intercostal type, there is also a movement, more or less extensive, of the reproductive organs. The sensations from these are obscured by those of deep respiration in the normal course of things. When, however, the pauses are fixated, the feeling of pleasure from the stimulation of the reproductive mechanism readily blends with the experience of relative relaxation. Hence, arises the joy that resembles the pleasure of sex. I follow in this interpretation very largely the idea conveyed to me by one whom I have every reason to believe, to be skilled in the breathing practices and to be reliable observer.

(b) The short lived aspirated sound at the close of a syllable, called in Sanskrit the *Visargaḥ,* when isolated from the rest of the syllable, is the last phase of expiration. When attention is fixated to it, there is seemingly an empty awareness. For, the dying phase of expiration does not provide consciousness with any vivid content. And the feeling of relative relaxation that accompanies the process of expiration blends with such awareness. This is probably the pure consciousness referred to in the practice.

(c) Fixation of attention upon consciousness as distinct from the body, is said to lead to the experience of the world as pure consciousness. The phase of consciousness grasped

within the span of the particular act of attention spreads all over the universe. The phenomenon can be explained in the following way: when attention is directed to self, or consciousness itself, one grasps an organic kinaesthetic sensation-complex, a *bewusstseinslage* or some experience similar to the *Pure-phi,* which is an experience of pure change or movement. The successive acts of attention serve to define the character of this experience as they do in the *Ausfrage* experiment. If one observes his experience in the light of what is called the *process-attitude,* the pure experience appears merely as a phase of a total mental in the background. When one assumes the *meaning-attitude,* the pure experience slides into the background and the meanings, objects and contents gain in vividness. If these two attitude oscillate, pure consciousness would appear to interlace with all the objects of daily experience. These would, then, appear to posses the pure consciousness that attentional practice has singled out. There would be an expansion, of the consciousness felt by the individual subject. Or, again, the technic of attention may cure some kind of a balance or a middle position between the two attitudes. In that case, too, the pure consciousness would seem to pervade the entire world of men and things.

(d) A sense of peace and balance is said to set in, when there is a fixation of attention on a specified object on the one hand, and 'thinking away of the rest of the world', on the other hand. The interpretation seems to be as follows. Each object and situation is a terminus for a group of emotions and reaction attitudes. A world of manifold objects and situation, then, would be likely to precipitate a conflict between these response patterns. When it becomes possible to think away the external world, incongruity of emotions, rivalry of the several motor attitudes, and the sense of incoherence of ideas, all cease. The process of fixation on a single object makes such inhibition easier and, at the same time, serves to direct the interests already dissociated from their objects, to a new terminus, namely, the object of fixation. A condition of peace and quiet would thus set into the extent to which the twofold act of attention and inhibition succeeds.

(iv) ***The Role of Attention in the Scheme of Spiritual Discipline: A Resume and Conclusion.***

The process of attention is utilised for many purposes in our daily life. We attend to things for their clear perception and retention, for precise comprehension and evocation of latent associations, for withdrawing our mind from unpleasant situations and for gaining an easy control over our mental life. The scheme of spiritual discipline, too, utilises the technic of attention for securing a number of ends.

(i) ***We have seen that a common technic of attention is to project all mental functions upon mythic scenes and mythical personalities. This type of culture is recommended alike in Christianity and in the various strands of Hindu tradition. It seems to serve three different purposes:***

(a) The myth-pictures, like dreams, possess a manifest as also a latent meaning. Just as a dream haunts the mind suffusing all thoughts and feelings with its implicit significance, so does the myth. The mythic objects thus displace the normal perceptions and ideas. The latent significance of myths steals into the fringe of consciousness and insinuates itself into the unorganised mass of purposes and meanings yet to take shape. The process of attentional fixation of mythic images and scenes thus transforms the conscious states impregnating them with a new strand of meanings concealed in the myths.

(b) The new perspective of mind serves to interlace the mythic images with the facts and events of daily life and thus to give rise to a new plane of experience. This order of mental life which refers neither to the facts of the external world nor to a conceptual scheme, henceforth undergoes a process that the Gestalt school calls 'structuration' as attention dwells on it continuously.

(c) The new order of experience thus established in the field of attention reacts and is reacted upon by the entire range of the personality-processes, manifest and latent, the processes of knowledge, desire, feelings, purposes and attitudes. Thus, a new kind of integration is achieved between the vital, experiential and the mythic planes, between the conscious and the unconscious thoughts and impulses.

(ii) Such integration, inasmuch as it resolves the endemic conflicts of mind, secures a certain degree of stability of the mental personality and a sense of independence of the forces of environment that operate upon man. The personality can alter its orientations to things and its inner dispositions at will. It can also carry its spiritual adjustments and objects across the vicissitudes to which the mental life is subject. For, the mythic pictures have become 'generalised' images in the course of attentional fixation. This is the kind of transformation that occurs in the case of the Buddhist *Kasiṅas*. Henceforth, they attain a peculiar status: (1) they do not change with the changing moods and thus give rise to a sense of their objectivity; and (2) yet, they remain the content of a particular mind. In this manner, the personality can dwell in a *milieu* of things, ideas and personalities that it itself creates.

(ii) The practice of attention by this method thus helps to secure a condition of introversion. For, the mind need not make any excursion outside of itself for any adjustment that implicates an emotion or an abiding purpose. This is what the *Yoga-sūtras* describe as the process of *Dhāranā* and this is what the Buddhist technic of attention aims at.

(iv) Such withdrawal of the personality from its setting in the world of men and things works a profound change in the psycho-physical organism. Its moods, and impulses, its ideas and outlook, in fact, its whole character gradually alters its pattern. Side by side, there occur profound physical changes. These send the signals of their progress and direction in the form of sensory and attitudinal experiences, of which there are many instances in the writings of the mystics, both Eastern and Western. The personality, psychically and physically, becomes renewed into a fresh configuration.

(v) Out of the perpetual process of renewal that leads novelty and romance to the seeming monotony of the mystic life, are born two characteristic modes of experience:

(a) There grows upon the mind a sense of unison with the ideas and the mystic personalities that attention selects out of the rich pattern of tradition and culture. The identity of the self

with the *Haṁsa,* the symbol of reality, considered in another paper, is an instance in point.[24] This may, probably, be similar to the phenomenon described by Freud as the process of identification of the ego with the super-ego.[25]

(b) The continued process of attention upon the mythic scenes naturally induces change in the object of fixation . The personalities, Rādhā and Krishṅa, Christ, Mary and the angels of whom the medieval saints speak, appear in the course of the practice of attention in varying roles and configurations. Such change reflexively alters the *Aufgabe* that lies implicit or explicit in the process of attentional preparation. A changing *Aufgabe* induces new attitudes and new *Bewusstseseinslagen*. These, however, are processes that are said to be free from sensory contents; they may be regarded as p'-ases of consciousness that have not taken up any sensory or conceptual form. It is for this reason that Kāshmir Śaivism prescribes fixation of attention upon the transitional phases of sensory and emotive experiences. Attentional process serves in this manner to bring into relief the phase of consciousness, that survives, even when all the meanings and images that senses and interest of action impose upon it, are subtracted.

Such a residual consciousness must in some sense be timeless. For, it eludes the change and transformation that go on in the world of perception and are reflected into the mental life. For, the pure consciousness rejects all material and sensory images and imports.

—N.N. Sen Gupta

References

1. Rhys Davids, Buddhist Psychology, p. 97. *Yoga-sūtra,* i. I See also the *Bhāshya. Gitā,* ii 66; note the concept of *Bhāvanā*
2. *The Path of Purity,* II, Ch. xi, pp. 402 and 431. (P.T.S. Trans. Series).
3. Comm. to *Chhāndogya,* VII. vi. 1.
4. Boehme, *The Supersensual Life* (Allenson), pp. 40-43.
5. *Haṁsa-Upanishat.*F. 36
6. *Kshurikā-Upanishat,* 3. *Maitrāyanī,* IV. 3-9. *Maṇdala-brahmana-Upanishat,* 1.

7. *Abhidhammāvatāra* (P.T.S.), Ch. viii, Verses 510-11.
8. *Ibid.*, p. 25. Rhys Davids, *Buddhist Psychology*, p. 89.
9. *Path of Purity*, II. pp. 170 ff.
10. *Abhidhammāvatāra*, XIV, 910, XXIV, 1394.
11. *Path of Purity*, II. pp. 430-31.
12. Washburn and Severance, *Am. Jl. Psych.* 1907, pp. 182-86.

    Sen Gupta, *Sir Ashutosh Silver Jubilee Vol. (Science)*, pp. 155-161.
13. *Śikshāsamuchchaya*, Ch. xiii.
14. *Vijnāna-Bhairava*, 26, 32, and 40.
15. *Ibid.*, 41, 59, 60, 77, 84, 93, 115 and 120.
16. *Ibid.*, 48, 52, 53, 87 and 88.
17. *Ibid.*, 61, 62, 80, 89, 101, 116, and 129. Also note the commentaries to the verses.
18. *Ibid.*, 68, 91, 107, 122, and 131.
19. Fernberger, 'An Experimental Study of the Stimulus Error'; Dallenbach, 'Subjective Perceptions', *Jl. of Exp. Psychology*, 1921, pp. 62-76, and pp. 143-163.

    Sen Gupta—"Joy" "Delight" and "Consolation" as Phrases of Mystical Experience (*Rev. Phil. and Religion*, 1940).
20. *Essays on Truth and Reality*, Ch. vi.
21. Freud, *The New Introductory Lectures*, pp. 83-86.
22. James, *Principles*, i. p. 302.
23. *Ibid.*, p. 303; Wundt's view quoted in the foot-note.
24. "The General Theory of Recital'. See *Journal of the U.P. Historical Society*, 1941. (*Ajapāmantra*).
25. Freud, *The New Introductory Lectures*. See the Chapter on the Anatomy of the Mental Personality.

7. Karma-Yoga Purification

Brothers,

When first I spoke in this Hall two years ago, I led your attention to the building of the Kosmos as a whole, to the steps through which that evolution took place, the methods, as it were, of the vast succession of phenomena. Last year I dealt with the evolution of the Self, the Self in man rather than the Self in the Kosmos, and tried to show you how from sheath after sheath the Self gained experience and obtained sovereignty over its lower vehicles—still with the man as with the universe, still with the individual as with the Kosmos, seeking ever reunion with the Self, seeking ever that whence it had come. But sometimes men have said to me when discussing these lofty topics: "What bearing have these on the life of men in the world, surrounded as we are with the necessities of life, surrounded as we are with the activities of the phenomenal world, continually drawn away from the thought of the One Self, continually forced by our Karma to take part in these multifarious activities? What bearing, then, has the higher teaching on the lives of men, and how many men in the world rise upward until the higher life becomes possible also for them?" It is that question that I am going to try to answer this year. I am going to try to show you how a man in the world, surrounded with family obligations, with social duties, with all the many activities of worldly life, may yet prepare himself for union and take the first steps on the path that leads him to the One. I am going to try to trace for you the steps of that path, so that, beginning in the life that any man may be leading, starting from the standpoint where most of you may be standing at the moment, you may recognise a goal to be reached, you may recognise a path to be trodden—the path which begins here in the life of the family, of the community, of the State, but which ends in that which is beyond all thinking and lands the traveller ultimately in the home which is his for evermore. Such is the object, then, of these four lectures, such the steps along which I trust you will accompany me; and in order that we may understand our subject, let us glance for a moment at the course of evolution, at its meaning, at its object, so that, from what must be but a bird's-eye view of the whole, we may be able, appreciating the whole, to understand the congruity of the steps which one by one we are to take. We realise that the One has become the many. Glancing backward into the primal darkness that shroudeth all, we can hear out of that darkness but a whisper—a whisper: "I will multiply." That multiplication is the building of the universe, and of the individuals who live within it. In that will to multiply of the "One which is without a second," we see the source of manifestation, we recognize the primal germs, as it were, of the Kosmos,. And as we realise that beginning of the universe, and as we see the complexity, the multiplicity, that results from the primal simplicity, from the primal unity, we realise also that in each of these phenomenal manifestations there must be imperfection, and that the very limitation which makes a phenomenon possible is also the inevitable mark that it is less than the One, and therefore by itself imperfect. So we understand why these should be variety, why there should be this vast multiplicity of separate and living things. And we begin to understand that the perfection of the manifested universe must needs lie in this very variety; that if there be more than the One then there must be welling infinite multiplicity, in order that the One, which is as a mighty sun sending forth beams of light in all directions, may send beams everywhere, and in the totality of the beams will be the reflection of the lighting of the world. The more numerous, the more wonderful, the more various the objects, the more nearly, though still imperfectly, will that universe image forth That whence it comes.

The first effort in the evolving life must be to make many, to make separated existences—apparently separate—so that looked at from without there shall seem many, although looked at in their essence we see that the Self of all is One. Realising that, we understand that in the process of multiple individualising, the one as individual comes into manifestation as a faint and limited reflection of the Self. And we begin to understand also what is to be the outcome of this universe, why it is that these many individuals should be evolved, why it is that this separateness should be a necessary part in the evolution of the whole. For we begin to see that the result of the universe is to be the evolution of the Logos of another universe, of the mighty Devas who are to be the guides of all the kosmic forces of that universe in the future, and of the divine Teachers whose duty it will be to train the infant humanity of another Kosmos. What is going on to-day in all these worlds of individual existences is a steady process of evolution, by which one universe gives to a future universe its Logos, its Devas, the earliest of its Manus, and all those great Ones that will be necessary for the building, for the training, for the governing, for the teaching of the universe which is yet unborn. Thus are the universes linked together, thus does Manvantara succeed Manvantara, thus are the fruits of one universe the seeds of the universe that succeeds it. In the midst of all this multiplicity there is being evolved a yet vaster unity which shall be the framework of the unborn Kosmos, which shall be the Power which in the future Kosmos shall guide and rule. And then the question arises—as I know it arises in many minds, for it has been put to me both in the East and in the West over and over again—why so much difficulty in the evolution, why so much apparent failure in the working, why should men go wrong so much before they go right, why should they run after the evil that degrades them instead of following the good that would ennoble them? Was it not possible for the Logos of our universe, for the Devas who are His Agents, for the great Manus who came to guide our infant humanity—was it not possible for Them to plan so that there might be no such apparent failure in the working out? Was it not possible for Them to guide, so that the road might have been a straight and direct one instead of so devious, so circuitous?

Here comes the point that makes the evolution of humanity so difficult, having in view the object which is to be gained. Easy in truth would it have been to have made a humanity that might have been perfect, easy to have so guided its dawning powers that those powers might have travelled towards what we call the good continually, and never have turned aside towards what we call evil. But what would have been the condition of such an easy accomplishment? It must have been that man would have been an automation, moved by a compelling force without him which imperiously laid upon him a law which he was compelled to fulfil, from which he could not escape. The mineral world is under such a law; the affinities that bind atom to atom obey such an imperious compulsion. But as we rise higher we find greater and greater freedom gradually making its appearance, until in man we see a spontaneous energy, a freedom of choice, which is really the drawing manifestation of the God, of the Self, which is beginning to show itself through man. And the object, the goal which was to be attained, was not to make automata who should blindly follow a path sketched out for their treading, but to make a reflection of the Logos Himself to make a mighty assemblage of wise and perfected men, who should choose the best because they know and understand it, who should reject the worst because by experience they have learnt its inadequacy and the sorrow to which it leads. So that in the universe of the future, as amongst all the great Ones who are guiding the universe of today, there should be unity gained by consensus of wills, which have become one again by knowledge and by choice, which move with a single purpose because they know the whole, which are identical with the law because they have learned that the law is good, who choose to be one with the Law, not by an outside compulsion, but by an inner acquiescence. Thus in that universe of the future there will be one Law, as there is in the present, carried out by means of Those who are the Law by the unity of Their purpose, the unity of Their knowledge, the unity of Their power—not a blind and unconscious Law, but an assemblage of living beings who are the Law, having become divine. There is no other road by which such goal might be reached, by which the free will of the many should reunite into the one great Nature and the one great Law, save a process in which experience should be garnered, in which evil should be known as well as good, failure as well as triumph. Thus men become Gods, and because of the experience that lies behind them, they will, they think, they feel, the same.

Now in working towards this goal the divine Teachers and Guides of our humanity planned many civilisations, all moulded towards the end that was in view. I have no time to go back to the great civilisation of the Fourth Race that preceded that birth of the mighty Āryan people. I may only say in passing that there was a great civilisation which was tried, which for a time under its divine Rules succeeded; then the divine Rulers withdrew. Their immediate guiding—as a mother withdrews her hand from her babe that is learning to walk, in order to see if, without her supporting arm, it is able to make its own steps, it is able to use its own limbs. So for the same purpose They withdrew into the darkness—the divine Guides and Rulers—to see if the child-humanity making these early steps would walk or would stumble on its way. And that infant humanity stumbled and fell, and the great civilisation—mighty as it was, perfect in its social order, glorious in the strength and the wisdom by which it was builded—broke into pieces under the selfness of man, broke into pieces under they yet unconquered lower instincts of humanity. Another attempt had to be made, and the great Āryan race was found—again with divine Rulers, again with divine Guides, with a Manu who gave it its law, founded its civilisation, sketched out its polity, with the Ṛṣhis who gathered round Him, who administered His laws and guided the infant civilisation; thus again humanity was given a pattern, again the race was shown a type towards which it should evolve. Then once more the great Teachers drew back for a while to let humanity again try its own strength, again experiment if it were strong enough to walk alone, self-reliant, guided by the Self from within, instead of by outer manifestations. And again, as we know, the experiment has largely been a failure. Again, as we know, glancing backward, we see this civilisation, originally divine, gradually degenerating under the still unconquerred lower nature of man, again going downward for a while under the still uncurbed passions of humanity. Looking back, as we know do, to the India of the past, we see its perfect polity, its marvellous spirituality, and we trace its degradation millennium after millennium as the guiding hand withdraws out of the visible sight of man, and once more humanity blunders and fails as it tries to walk. We see how in each case there has been the failure of the realisation of the divine ideal. We glance over the modern world and we see how the lower nature of man has triumphed over the divine ideal, which was set before him at the beginning of the Āryan race. We see how in that day there was the ideal of the Brāhmana, an ideal that might be summed up as that of her soul approaching liberation, which asks no longer for the goods of earth, which asks no longer for the enjoyments of the flesh, which asks no longer for any gifts of wealth, of power, of authority, of earthly pleasure, the type of the Brāhmana being that he was poor, but wise; whereas to-day we too often find the man who bears the brāhmana name not poor and wise but wealthy and ignorant. There in that caste you have one of the signs of the degeneration by which the ancient polity fell; and the same with each of the four castes.

Let us now see how it was proposed by the great Teachers that man by experience should learn to choose of his own free will the ideal which was placed before him, and from which he turned aside; how the great Teacher endeavoured to build up from the imperfect humanity towards the perfected ideal manifest in the beginning for the guidance of the race, and unrealised in evolution, by the weakness and the childishness of men.

In order that this might in the course of ages come, what is called Karma-Yoga was taught to the people—Yoga, or union, by action. That is the form of Yoga which is fitted for the men of the world, beset with life's activities; it is by these very activities, by the training afforded by them, that the first steps towards union must be taken. And so you find laid down for the training of men this Karma-Yoga.

Note the juxtaposition of the words "action" and "union". Action so performed that union may result, action so carried out that union may be the outcome. It is a thing to remember that it is our activities that divide us, it is our actions that separate us, it is all this changing and multifarious activity by which we are drawn and kept apart. It seems almost a paradox then to speak of union by action, union by that which was ever a means of division, union by that by which separation was brought about. But the wisdom of the divine Teachers was equal to the task of reconciling, of explaining, the apparent paradox. Let us follow the steps of the explanation and see what it is.

Man runs wild, runs wild in every direction under the influence of the three energies in Nature, the gunas. The dweller in the body finds himself under the domination of these gunas. They are at work, they are active, they make the manifested universe, and he identifies himself with these activities. He thinks he is acting when these are acting. He thinks he is busy when these are bringing about results. Living amongst them, blinded by them, under the illusions which they produce, he loses entirely all recognition of himself, and is taken here and there, blown hither and thither, carried away by the currents, and so the activity of the gunas is all that the man sees in life; clearly he is not fit under these conditions for the higher forms of Yoga. Clearly, until these illusions are at least partially conquered, the loftier steps on the path will be beyond his treading. He must begin then by understanding the gunas, by separating himself from these activities of the phenomenal universe. And the great scripture of Yoga, as it may be called, the scripture of this Karma-Yoga, is that which was reproclaimed by Shri Krshna on the field of Kurukshetra, when He taught this form of Yoga to Arjuna, to the prince, to the warrior, the man who was to live in the world, to fight in the world, to rule the State, and take part in all external activities; here is the eternal lesson for men who are living in the world, how gradually they may arise beyond the gunas and so reach union with the Supreme.

It will then first be in what we may call the training and regulation of the activities of the gunas that this Karma-Yoga will consist. There are, as you know, three gunas, Sattva, Rajas and Tamas, the three gunas out of which all around us is builded and combined together in various ways, mingled in various fashions. Here one is acting and the other is working in every direction. They have to be brought into equilibrium; they have to be reduced to subjection. The dweller in the body, the lord of the body, must become sovereign master and distinguish himself from the guṇas. That, then, will be the work that has to be done; their functions must be realised, their activities must be controlled and directed. You cannot at once rise above them, you cannot at once cross beyond them—any more than a child can do the work of a full-grown man. Can humanity in its unevolved and in its imperfect state accomplish perfection of Yoga? Nay, it is not even wise that man should try; for if the child be put to the work of the full-grown man, he will not only fail to accomplish it, but he will overstrain his powers in the attempt, and the result will be not only failure in the present, but also failure in the future. For the task too great for his powers will thwart and distort them. They must be trained to strength before they can accomplish, and the child must grow to manhood before manhood's work should be his. Take for a moment the function of Tamas-translated darkness, or sluggishness, or inertia, or negligence, and so on. What function can that play, if it is to be used for human evolution? What use has this particular guna in the growth of the man, in the liberating of the soul? The particular use of that guṇa, the use to which it will be put in Karma-Yoga, is to act as a force which is to be struggled against and overcome, so that strength may be evolved in the struggle, power of will may be developed by the effort, self-control and self-discipline may be accomplished by the attempt. It may be said to serve in the evolution of man as the club or dumb-bell serves the purpose of the athlete. He could not strengthen his muscles unless there was something against which he exercised them. He could not gain muscular vigour unless there were opposing weights by struggling to lift which the muscles should grow strong. The value is not in the weight itself, but in the use to which it is put, and if a man wants his physical muscles, the muscles of his arms, to grow very strong, the best way to strengthen them is to take a club or dumb-bell and daily exercise the muscles against that opposing force. In this way Tamas, negligence or darkness, plays its part in the evolution of the man; he has to overcome it, he develops his strength in the struggle; the muscle of the soul grow powerful as he overcome the negligence, the sloth, the indifference which is the tamasic quality in his nature.

So you will find for the overcoming of these the rites and ceremonies of religion are ordained, part of their function being to train man to overcome the sloth and the laziness and the indolence of his lower nature, and by placing before him certain duties to be done at a particular time—whether at that time he is inclined to do ţhem or not, whether at that time he is feeling active or feeling lazy—by imposing on him duties at a particular time he is trained to overcome the sloth and heedlessness and obstinacy of his lower nature, to compel it to walk along the path that the will has determined it should follow.

And so if we take Rajas: you will find the activities of man are guided in Karma-Yoga along certain definite path which I now propose to follow, so that you may see how this quality of activity, which is so much at work in the modern world, which is manifesting itself in every direction, which leads to hurry, bustle and constant effort to accomplish things in the lower life, material manifestations, material results, material phenomena—how this shall be gradually directed, trained and purified until it no longer has the power to hinder the real manifestation of the Self. The object of Karma-Yoga is to substitute duty for self-gratification; man acts to gratify his lower nature; he acts because he wants to get something; he acts for fruit; he acts for desire for reward. He works because he wants money in order that he may enjoy. He works because he wants power in order that the lower self may be gratified. All these activities, these rajasic qualities, are set going with the purpose of ministering to his lower nature. In order that these activities may be trained and regulated to serve the purpose of the Higher Self, he is to be taught to substitute duty for self-gratification, to carry on work at work because it is his duty, to turn the wheel of life because it is his function to turn it, that he may do as Shri Krṣhṇa said He does Himself. He does not act because there is anything for Him to gain either in this world or in any other; but He acts because without His action the world would cease; He acts because without His action the wheel would no longer revolve. And those who accomplish Yoga must act in the spirit of His acting, for the whole and not for the separated part, acting for the carrying out of the divine will in the Kosmos and not for the pleasure of the separated entity that imagines itself to be independent when it ought to be a co-worker under Him. This object is to be gained by gradually raising the sphere of these activities. Duty is to be substituted for self-gratification, and religious rites and ceremonies are ordained to train men gradually towards the true life that is their function. Every religious ceremony is but a way of training men into the true and higher life. A man meditates in the early morning and at the going down of the sun, but ultimately his life will be one long meditation. He meditates for an hour to prepare himself for meditating always. All creative activities are the result of meditation, and you will remember that it is by tapas that all worlds are created. In order, then, that man may reach that mighty and creative power of meditation, in order that he also may be able to exercise that divine power, he must be trained towards it by religious ceremonies, by intermittent thought, by Tapas taken up and laid down again. Set meditation is a step towards the accomplishment of constant meditation; it takes a part of daily life in order to permeate the whole, and men practise it daily in order that gradually it may absorb the life. The time comes when for the Yogi there is no fixed hour for meditation, for all his life is one long meditation. No matter what outer activities he may be going, he meditates; and he is ever at the feet of his Lord although both mind and body may be active in the world of man. And so with all other forms of action; first a man learns to perform action as a sacrifice to duty and a paying of his debt to the world in which he is—the paying back to all the different parts of Nature of that which they give to him. And then later, sacrifice becomes more than the paying of a debt; it becomes a joyful giving of everything the man has to give. The partial sacrifice is the debt that is paid, the perfect sacrifice is the gift of the whole. A man gives himself, with all his activities, with all his powers, no longer paying part of his possessions as a debt, but all of himself as a gift. And when that stage is reached, Yoga is accomplished and the lesson of Karma-Yoga has been learned.

Take as one step towards this those five daily sacrifices which are familiar, in name at least, to all of you, and realise what underlay the ordination of those sacrifices. Each one of the five is the payment of a debt, the recognition of what man as a separated individual owes as a debt to the whole around him. And if you consider them for the moment one by one, however hastily, you will see how thoroughly each is this payment of a debt. Take the first: the sacrifice to the Devas.

Why is that sacrifice ordained? It is because man has to learn that his body owes a debt to each and to the Intelligences that guide the processes of Nature by which earth brings forth her fruits, by which she produces nourishment for man; as man takes the nourishment for his body, his body owes back, in payment of the debt, the returning to Nature an equivalent for that which has been given it through the instrumentality of those kosmic Intelligences, those Devas, who guide the forces of the lower world. And so man was taught to pour his sacrifice into the fire. Why? The phrase that was given as an explanation was: "Agni is the mouth of the Gods," and people repeat the phrase and never try to understand its meaning, nor to go below the surface of the external name of the Deva to His function in the world. The real meaning, of course, that underlies the phrase is that all around on every side there are the conscious and subconscious works in Nature in grade after grade, a great kosmic Deva at the head, as it were, of each division of that vast army, so that below the Deva as a Ruler in fire, in air, in water, in earth, below that particular Deva come a vast number of lower Gods who carry on the different and separated activities of the natural forces in the world, the rain, the productive powers of the earth, the fertilising agencies of various sorts. And this first sacrifice is a feeding of these lower agencies, a giving to them of food by fire; and fire is called "the mouth of the Gods" because it disintegrates, because it changes and transmutes the solid and fluid things which are placed in it, turns them into vapour, disintegrates them into finer materials, and thus passes them on into etheric matter to become the sustenance of those lower grades to elemental lives that carry out the commands of the kosmic Devas. And in this way a man pays his debt to them, and then, in return, in the lower regions of the atmosphere the rain falls and the earth produces, and nourishment is given to man. And that was what Shri Krshna meant when he bade man "nourish the Gods and the Gods shall nourish you". For it is that lower cycle of nourishment, as it were which man has to learn. At first he accepted it as a religious teaching; then came the period in which he thought it superstition, knowing not the inner working and seeing only the outer appearances; and then comes deeper knowledge when Science, which tends first to materialism, by deeper study rises towards recognition of the spiritual realm. Scientific knowledge begins to say in scientific terms what the Riṣhis said in terms of the spirit, that man may rule and regulate the working of the lower powers of Nature by action that he himself performs, and in this way growing knowledge justifies the ancient teaching, justifies to the intellect what the spiritual man sees by direct intuition, by the spiritual sight.

Next, there is the sacrifice to the Ancestors; the recognition of what man owes to those who went before him in the world, the payment of the debt that he owes to those who worked in the world for us, and brought about improvements that we, should inherit them. That service is a debt of gratitude due to those immediately before us in human evolution, who took their part in it during their earthly lives and bequeathed to us the result of their labours. As we reap the benefit of their work, we pay back the debt of gratitude. And so this is one of the daily sacrifices, the recognition of this debt of gratitude to those who have gone before. And then of course comes the sacrifice of knowledge, that of study, in order that by the study of the sacred words men may be able to help and train those more ignorant than themselves, and may also evolve in themselves the knowledge necessary for the manifestation of the Self within them.

Fourthly, the sacrifice to men, the payment to some particular man of the duty owed to humanity, the feeding of some particular man as a recognition that men owe to each other all kindly deeds in the physical world, all the assistance that brother can give to brother. The sacrifice to men is the formal recognition of this duty, and in feeding those who are hungry, and in showing hospitality to those who are in need of it, while you feed one man as a concrete fact you feed all humanity ideally and in intention; when you give hospitality to one man who comes past your door, you open the door of your heart to humanity as one great entity, and in helping and sheltering one you give help and shelter to humanity as a whole.

And so also with the last of the five sacrifices, that to Animals; food is to be placed on the ground by the householder that any passing animal may take. In this you recognise your duty to the lower world, your duty of giving help, of giving food, of giving training to them. The sacrifice to animals is meant to impress on his mind that we are here as trainers, as directors, as helpers, of the lower creatures that stand beneath us on the ladder of evolution. Every time we sin against them by cruelty, by harshness, by brutality of any sort, we sin against Him who is dwelling within them and whose lower manifestations they also are. And in order that man might recognize the God within the brute, in order that he might understand that Shri Kṛṣṇa is in the lower animal, although more veiled than He is in man, man was bidden to sacrifice to the animals, not to the outer form but to the God within. The only way we can sacrifice to them is by kindness, by gentleness, by compassion, by training, by helping forward the animal evolution, and not by beating it back by the brutality and by the cruelty we see around us on every side.

Thus man was taught by these outer rites and ceremonies the inner spiritual truths, by which his lie was to be permeated. And when the five sacrifices were over, he was to go out into he world of men still to sacrifice by other forms of action, still to sacrifice by the performance of his daily duties. And his daily life that was begun by these five sacrifices passed out consecrated into the outer life of men. With gradual carelessness as to the five sacrifices has grown carelessness of duty in that outer life of man. Not because these sacrifices in themselves will be for ever necessary, for a time comes when a man rises above them. But remember this; he only rises above them when his whole life has become one long and living sacrifice. Until that is accomplished, these formal recognition of duty are necessary for the sake of the raising of the life. And unhappily in India today, these have largely dropped out of account, not because men have risen above them nor because all their lives are pure, spiritual and lofty, so that they have no need of the lower training and the continual reminder; but because they have become careless and materialistic, and have fallen so far below the ideal of their Manu. They refuse all dutiful recognition to the Powers above them, and therefore they fail in their duty to the men around them.

Let us consider next the outer daily life—the duty of the individual in the outer world. Wherever it is, he is born into some particular family; that marks his family duties. He is born into some community; that marks out his communal duties. He is born into a particular nation; that marks out his national duties. For each man the limitations of duty are set by the circumstances of his birth, which, under the good Law, under the karmic direction, give to each man the place of his working, the training ground on which he is to learn. Therefore is it said that each man should do his own duty, his own Dharma. Better to do your own, although imperfect, than to try to do the higher Dharma of another. For that into which you are born is that which you need; that into which you are born is your wisest training. Do your own duty, careless of results, and then you will learn the lesson of life, and you will begin to tread the path of Yoga. At first, of course, action will be done for its fruit; men will do it because they desire to gain its reward. And here we understand their early training, where men were taught to work for results in the world of Svarga. The child-man is trained by rewards; Svarga is held out to him as a thing to be gained by work; as he accomplishes his religious rites and duties he ensures their svargic recompense. And in this way he is induced to practise morality, just as you induce a child to learn its lessons by giving it some reward or some prize. But if action is to be used for Yoga and not for the gaining of reward, either here or in any other world, then it must be done only as duty. Consider for a moment the four great castes and see how each of these was meant to be used. The Brāhmaṇa was to teach in order that there might be a succession of wise teachers to guide the evolution of the race. He was not to teach for money, he was not to teach for power, he was not to teach for anything he got for himself; he was to teach in fulfilment of his Dharma, and he was to have knowledge that he might in turn hand it on to others. Thus in a well-regulated nation there would be always teachers to instruct, able to guide and advise unselfishly and without a selfish object; thus nothing would be gained by him for himself, but everything would be gained by him for the people. In this way his Dharma would be accomplished and the soul set free.

Then there came the Yoga which was the fitting of the active man of the world for governing and regulating, the training of the dominant class, the Kṣhattriya. There you had the man who was to rule. Why? Not that he might gratify himself by power, but in order that justice might be done, in order that the poor man might feel secure and the rich man might be unable to tyrannise, in order that fairness and impartial justice might prevail in the struggling world of men. For in the midst of this world of struggle, in the midst of this world of anger and strife, in the midst of this world where men are seeking to gratify the spirit of self instead of the common good, they have to be taught that justice must be done, that if the strong man abuses his strength the just ruler will restrain that unfair exercise of strength, that the weaker shall not be trampled upon, that the weaker shall not be oppressed. And the duty of the king was to do justice between man and man, so that all men might look to the throne as the fountain from which divine justice flowed. That is the ideal of the divine kingship, that is the ideal of the divine ruler. Rāma came to teach it, Shrī Kṛṣhṇa came to teach it; but men were so dull that they would not learn the lesson. The Kṣhattriya used his strength to gratify himself and oppress others, and took their wealth for his own and used their labour for his personal advantage. He lost the ideal of the divine ruler who incarnated justice in the warring world of men. But he was meant to make that ideal the object of his life, and his duty, therefore, was to administer the land, to administer it for the good of the nation and not for the gratification of himself. And so also when his duty was the duty of the soldier. The nation was to carry on its functions in peace. Poor men and harmless men were to live secure with their house-holds round them in happiness and prosperity. The merchant was to carry on the work of a merchant in peace. All the various avocations of life were to be carried on fearlessly, secure against aggression. And so the Kṣhattriya was taught that when he was to fight, he fought as the defender of the helpless and gave his life freely that they might enjoy their lives in peace. He was not to fight because he wanted gain. He was not to fight because he wanted a land. He was not to fight because he wanted power of dominion. He was to stand as an iron wall round the nation, so that every attack should break itself against his body, and within the circle made by him all men should live in peace, in security and in happiness. If he was to follow Yoga within the duty of the Kṣhattriya, he must look on himself as the agent of the divine Actor, and therefore it was that Shrī Krṣhṇa taught that He had done all and that Arjuna but repeated the action in the world of men. And when the divine Actor is recognised in every action of the man, then he can accomplish action as duty without desire, and it loses its binding power on the soul.

So again with the Vaishya, who was to accumulate wealth. He was to do it not for his own gratification but for the support of the nation. He was to be rich in order that every activity that needed wealth should find a store of wealth at hand and be carried out in every direction. So that everywhere there might be homes for the poor, everywhere resthouses for the traveller, everywhere hospitals both for men and beasts, everywhere temples for worship, and everywhere the wealth which was needed to support these activities of perfect national life. And so his Dharma was this accumulation for the common good and not for individual self-gratification. In this way he too might follow Yoga, and by Karma-Yoga prepare himself for the higher life.

So also with the Shūdra, who was to perform his Dharma in the commonwealth. His work lay in accomplishing the duty of forming the great hand of the nation, which brought into it was wanted and carried on the serving external activities. His Yoga, if it were to be accomplished, lay in gladly discharging his duties, doing them for the sake of doing them and not for the reward that by doing them he might gain.

First, men do action for self-gratification, there only progress in experience is grained; then they learn to do it as duty, and so they begin to practise Yoga in their daily life; lastly they do it as a joyful sacrifice for which they ask nothing back, but give every power they possess for the accomplishment of the work. And in this way union is accomplished.

We understand what is meant by purification when we notice these stages of self-gratification, of doing duty as duty, of giving everything as a free-will sacrifice. These are stages of the path of purification. But how shall such purification be made as shall lead to the higher steps, to the beginning of the discipleship for which all created activity is to be the preparation? Every part of man must be purified, body as well as mind. On the purification of the body I have no time to dwell, but I may remind you that according to the teaching of the *Bhagavad-Gītā* it is by way of moderation that this purification is accomplished and not by self-torturing ascertism, torturing the body and Him that dwells within it, as Shrī Krṣhṇa says. Yoga is accomplished by temperate self-control, by deliberate training of the lower nature, by quietly choosing the pure path in food, by care and moderation in all physical activities, thus gradually training and regulating and moderating until the whole body comes under the control of the will and of Self. Therefore the household life was ordained; for men were not fit for the hard road of celibacy, save here and there a few. Brahmacharya was not for all. By household life were men taught to control and moderate their sexual passions, not by crushing them out–which is for the mass of men impossible, and if attempted with unwise energy often results in a reaction that throws the unwise person into the worst profligacy of life—not by a single effort which tries to kill and to uproot in a moment, but by gradual training in moderation, and by practising the self-denial of the home, where the lower nature should be slowly trained to temperance and be accustomed to be controlled by the higher, trained out of its over-activity and made utterly subordinate to the One. There is where this Karma-Yoga comes in. The householder has gradually to learn self-control, moderation–*i.e.*, making the lower nature yield to the higher, training it day by day until it is absolutely subject to the will. In that way he purifies the body and becomes fitted for the higher paths of Yoga.

Then again he must purify the passions of the lower nature all through. Take as an illustration of it—I want to give you three illustrations of this, so that you may work it out in your lives—take the passion of anger and see how it may be worked upon in Karma-Yoga, in order that it may be transmuted in quality. Anger is an energy, an energy that goes out of man to fight his way. You see it in an undeveloped and untrained man as passion, showing itself in many brutal forms, beating down opposition, caring not what methods are used if he strikes out of his way all that which opposes the gratification of his will. And in that form it is an undisciplined and destructive energy of Nature which he who would do Karma-Yoga must most certainly subdue. How shall he subdue and train the passion of anger? He gets rid of the personal element to begin with. When a personal injury is done to him he trains himself to ease to resent it. There is the duty which lies before many of you. Some man does you a wrong; someone does an injustice against you. What shall you do? You may let the passion of anger carry you away and you may strike at him. He has cheated you: you try to injure him in return, and to take advantage of him. He has injured you: you try in turn to injure him. He has gone behind your back: you go behind his back and do him wrong in turn. And so the passion of anger rages and destruction is seen on every side in what should be the society of men. How shall this passion be purified? You may take the answer from any one of the great Teachers who taught Karm-Yoga, who taught how action in the world of men might be used for the purposes of the Self. You may remember that amongst the tenfold system of duty which Manu laid down, forgiveness of injuries is one of the duties. You may remember that when the Buḍḍha was teaching, He taught: "Hatred ceases not by hatred at any time, hatred ceases by love." You may remember that the Christian Teacher followed the same line of thought, and He said: ``Be not overcome of evil, but overcome evil with good." That is Karma-Yoga. Forgive the injury; give love for hatred; overcome evil with good. In that way you will eliminate the personal element; you will no longer feel angry because you are wronged; you will have purified away the personal element, and anger in you will no longer be of this lower kind. But still a form of anger may remain of a higher kind. You see a wrong done to the weak: you are angry with the wrong-doer; you see an animal ill-used: you are wrathful with the person who is cruel; you see a poor man oppressed: you are angry against the oppressor. Impersonal anger—far nobler than the other and a necessary stage in human evolution; far nobler and better to the angry with a wrong-doer than pass by in stolid indifference, because you have no sympathy with the suffering that is inflicted. That higher, impersonal anger is nobler than indifference, but it is not the hightest. It also in turn has to be changed and it has to be changed into the quality of doing justice to the strong and the weak alike; which compassionates the wrong-doer as well as the wronged; which sees that he injures himself even more than the person whom he hurts; which is sorry for him as well as for the person who suffers under him; which embraces all, wrong-doer and sufferer, in one embrace of love and of justice. The man who has thus purified the passion of anger stops the wrong because it is his duty to stop it, and is gentle to the wrong-doer because he also must be helped and trained; thus what was anger striking back against a personal wrong becomes justice which stops all wrong and makes the strong and the weak equally safe and equally protected. That is the purification which is done in the world of action, that the line of daily effort by which the lower nature is purified in order that union may be attained.

Take again love. You may have that in the lower, brutal form—the animal passion between the sexes of the every lowest and the poorest kind, which cares nothing for the character of the one for whom the attachment is felt, which cares nothing for the beauty of the mental and of the moral nature; it cares only for the physical beauty, the physical attraction, and the physical pleasure. There is passion in its lowest form. Self is sought and only self. That is purified by the man who follows Karma-Yoga into love which sacrifices for the one who is loved; he performs family duties, he takes care of wife and of child and does his very best for them at the sacrifice of his own inclinations, of his own leisure and his own gratification; he works in order that the family may be better supported, he works in order that the family wants may be supplied; in him love no longer seeks only its own pleasure, but seeks to help those who are beloved and to take on itself the evil that threatens them in order that they may be sheltered and spared and guarded; by following Karma-Yoga the man purifies his love from the selfish elements, and that which was an animal passion for the other sex becomes the love of the husband, of the father, of the elder brother, of the relative, who fulfils his duty, working for the sake of the love and in order that their lives may be fairer and happier. And there comes the last stage, when the love that is purified from self goes out to all. Not only in the narrow circle of the home does it work, but it sees in everyone whom it meets a person who is to be helped, sees a brother to be fed in every starving men, sees a sister to be protected in every woman who is left forlorn. Finding anyone who is lonely, a man thus purified becomes father and brother and helper to that one, not because he loves personally but because he loves ideally, and because he seeks to give for love's sake and not even for the gratification of being loved in return. The highest love, the love that grows out of Karma-Yoga, asks nothing back in return for what it gives; it seeks no gratitude; it asks for no recognition; it is willing to work unknown; nay, it is more glad to work unknown and unrecognised than to work in a way that brings recognition and that brings praise. And the ultimate purification of love is where that love becomes absolutely divine, where it gives because it is its nature to spread happiness, where it asks nothing for itself but seeks only that others should be glad.

And so again with greed, convetousness. Men seek to gain in order that they may enjoy; they desire to gain in order that they may have power; they strive to gain in order that they may be lifted up. They purify that first form of greed; and they begin to desire to gain that the family may be better off, that the family may be in a better position, that the family may be beyond suffering and want and starvation; thus they grow less selfish than before. Then they go further. They desire power in order that they may use it for good, that they may spread it to do good over a wider area than the family, that they may serve in a wider field than the home; and at last, as in the case of love, they learn to give without any return. They learn to desire knowledge and power, not that they may hold it; but that they may give it, not that they may enjoy it, but only in order that it may be spread. And in this way selfishness is burned up.

Have you ever wondered why He to whom is given the name of Mahāḍeva, why He dwells in a burning-ground? A strong place, men would have thought, in which the Mightiest One should dwell. Strange surroundings with which to environ Him who is purity itself. What is hidden under the symbolism of the burning-ground is human life; and in that burning-ground where Shiva dwells, all the lower things in human life are consumed as by fire. If he dwells not within it, then these earthly things remain to putrefy, to corrupt, to be a source of danger, to spread disease and corruption everywhere. But in the burning-ground in which He dwells, through which His fire passes from side to side, is burned up everything that is selfish, every thing that is personal everything which is of the lower nature; out of those regenerating flames the Yogi rises triumphant, with nothing of the personal element left within him; for the fire of the Lord has burned up all lower passions, and there is nothing there remaining to corrupt or to spread diseas. Therefore He is called the Destroyer, the Destroyer of the lower in order that regeneration may come; for out of His Fire the soul was originally born, and from that burning-ground the purified Self arises.

Thus do these first steps lead onward; lead onward towards true discipleship, lead onward towards the finding of the Guru, lead onward topwards the Inner Temple, the holiest of holies, where the Guru of humanity resides. These are the first steps that you must take, this is the route by which you must travel. Men you are, living in the world and bound by worldly ties, men living the social and political life; and yet at the back of your hearts you are desiring true Yoga and the knowledge which is of the permanent and not only of the transitory life. For in the hearts of everyone of you, if you go down to the very bottom of them, you will find a yearning to know something more, a desire to live more nobly than you live to-day. You may have the outer appearance of loving the things of the world and you do love them with your lower natures; but in the heart of every true Hinḍū, who is not absolutely renegade and apostate to his religion and his country, there is still an inner yearning for something more than the things of earth, still a faint longing, if only from the past traditions, that India shall be nobler than she is today and her people more worthy of her past. Here, then, is the route that you must begin to tread: no great nation unless individuals are great; no mighty people if individuals are sordid and poor and selfish in their lives. You must begin where you are today, in the life that you are leading; and following these lines that I have roughly sketched, you will take your first steps towards the Path.

Let me close by reminding you of what the end of that Path is, although I have still to take you further towards it in the lectures that lie before us in these morning hours. The end of the Path is union—the Karma-Yoga which we have been studying in Union by Action. There are other steps to take, but what is "union"? You remember how

Shrī Krṣhṇa gave the marks of the man who had passed beyond the guṇas, the marks of the man who had crossed beyond them and who was fit for the nectar of immortality, the man who was ready to know that which is Highest, to come into union with the Supreme. He perceives no agent save the guṇas, He knoweth That which lies beyond. He sees the guṇas acting; he desires them not when they are absent, he repels them not when they are present. He is balanced amidst friends and foes, balanced in praise and in shame, self-reliant, looking on all things with an equal eye, on the clod of earth, on the piece of gold, on friend and on enemy alike. He is the same to all, for he has crossed over the guṇas, and is no longer deluded by their play. That is the goal that we are seeking. These are the first steps towards the Path that crosses over. Until these are trodden no other steps are possible; but as these are gradually accomplished the beginning of the true Path is seen.

—*Annie Besant*

8. The Doctrine of Karma

The *Upaniṣads* exhibit an attitude of ambivalence in their exposition of the doctrine of *karma.* On the one hand the *upaniṣads* establish and uphold *karma* as a moral law of good and evil which forms as the basis of Indian ethics. At the same time they teach how *karmas* can be destroyed or arrested and rendered sterile or one can obtain release from their binding force.

In the *upaniṣads karma* as a law of rewards and retribution for good and evil acts replaces the *yajña karma* or sacrifices of the *Brāhmaṇas* for attainment of human desire for material prosperity and physical well being. This law explains the cosmic phenomenon of inequality and suffering as a consequence of *karmas.* This forms the basis of Indian ethical discipline.

All *karma,* whether good or evil, is also deemed to be bad in the ultimate sense: it is a bond and source of bondage leading to transmigration and rebirth and the consequential suffering inherent in existence. The *upaniṣads* expound the means to achieve *mokṣa* or release from the bondage of *karma.* In a sense this trend is anti-*karma,* being life-negating aiming to bring the life process to an end. The *upaniṣads* draw a distinction between good, (*śubha, sukrta, puṇya*) and evil (*aśubha, duṣkṛta, pāpa*) acts. *Bṛhad. up,* III.2.13 says: *puṇyo vai puṇyena karmaṇā bhavati pāpaḥ pāpeneti:* By good deeds indeed one becomes good, evil by evil deeds. Again *Bṛhad, up.* IV. 4, 5 tellingly distinguishes between good and evil:

Yathākāri yathācāri tathā bhavati; sādhukāri sādhur bhavati,
Pāpakāri pāpo bhavati; puṇyaḥ pāpena
Karmaṇā bhavati, pāpaḥ pāpena

According as one acts, according as one behaves, so does he become. The doer of good becomes good, the doer of evil becomes evil. One becomes virtuous by virtuous action, bad by bad action. *Praśna up.* III.7 says: *puṇyena puṇyam lokam nayati pāpena pāpam ubhābhyāmeva manuṣya lokam.* Virtuous acts lead to virtuous world, evil acts to the sinful world and both (such acts) lead to the world of men. *Kaṭha up.* II.11.7 explains *yonim anye prapadyante śaīratvāya dehinaḥ Sthāṇu manye anusamyanti yathākarma yathāśrutam.* Some souls are reborn as sentient creatures, others as stationary objects according to their deeds and according to their thoughts. The *Kauṣitaki up.* 1.2 links rebirths to a person's *karmas:*

> *sa iha kiṭo vā, patango vā, matsyo vā,*
> *śakunir vā, simho vā, varāho vā,*
> *paraśvān vā, śārdulo vā, puruṣo,*
> *anyo vā teṣu sthāneṣu pratyājāyate*
> *yathā karma yathā vidyām*'

"Either as a worm, or as an insect, or as a fish, or as a bird, or as a lion, or as a boar, or as a snake, or as a tiger, or as a person, or as some other in this or that condition, he is born again according to his deeds, according to his knowledge...." Likewise the *Maitrī up.* III.1 reiterates that the fruits of good and evil *karma* (*sitāsitaḥ karma phala*) lead to good and evil birth (*sad-asal yonim*). The *Śvet. Up. V.* clearly makes the doer of an act as the bearer of the consequences of that act: *phala karma kartā kṛtasya tasyai va sa copabhoktā.* Further the effect or consequence of a *karma* is a limited potential. *Bṛhad. up.* III.8.10 proclaims that the fruits of fire offerings (*yajñas*) and penances (***tapaḥ***) for many thousand years are all transitory or impermanent (***antavat***) *Chānd. Up.* VIII. 1.6 says: "Just as here on earth the world which is earned by work perishes, even so there in the other world, the world which is earned by righeous deeds perishes: *tadyatheha karmajito lokaḥ kṣiyate evamevāmutra puṇyajito lokaḥ kṣiyate.*

Thus in the *upaniṣadic* texts we see the formulation of the doctrine of *karma:*

(i) good acts produce good results, evil acts produce evil results;

(ii) good acts lead to happiness, bad acts lead to unhappiness and misery.

(iii) the results or fruits which any *karma* can produce are limited and hence the *karmas* are liable to exhaust themselves.

(iv) he who does an act reaps its consequences.

While the *upaniṣads* established a powerful moral law of *karma,* they also discounted the utility of good *karmas;* in fact the *karmas* are considered to be responsible for transmigration and rebirth. Hence they teach the means to escape the bondage of *karmas,* for the following reasons:

(i) All life suffers from certain infirmities: *Jarā* (old age) and *maraṇa* (death). Even a person, who has committed no evil whatsoever and in fact has done excellent deeds, is liable to suffer from old age and death. Old age and death are considered evil.

(ii) The good or merit earned by an individual is necessarily limited in its duration. All the doers (*kartās*) are ***bhoktās*** (experiencers): while they are exhausing the results of their past actions, they accumulate fresh *karmas* by their new actions as *kartās* and this chain continues. In other words, like the external world the potentiality of *karmas* is *anitya,* it is not abiding; it is essentially transient. So merit (*puṇya*) and demerit (*pāpa*) both produce sorrow. *Chānd. Up.* VIII.12.1 emphasises that there is no freedom from pleasure and pain for one who is embodied: *śarirasya sataḥ priyāpriyayorapahatiḥ.* All *karmas* are therefore *pāpman,* evil, *mala,* impurity.

So the *upaniṣads* shift their emphasis from doing good deeds, *puṇya karma* to annihilation of the deeds so that liberation or *mokṣa* from transmigration and rebirth can be attained.

Thus the *Kaṭha up.* I.ii.5 says that the ignorant government round and round (*pariyanti mūḍhā*) in this world. *Katha* I.ii.6 proclaims a person who thinks that there is only this world and no world hereafter, *ayam loko nāsti paraḥ,* due to ignorance is subject to repeated births and death. *Muṇḍ up.* III.1.10 states that a pure person, a person of excellent conduct (*Viśuddhasattva*) whose mind seeks fulfilment of its wishes (*manasā samvibhāti*) and craves (*kāmayati*) to obtain various objects of desire or enjoyment (*Kāmān*) fulfils them and attain them. *Muṇḍ up.* III.2.2 adds that a person who covets desirable objects (*Kāmān Kāmayate*) is born with those desires. *Praśna up.* 1.9 observes that those who perform *iṣṭāpūrta, Vedic* sacrifices (*iṣṭa*) and charitable works (*pūrta*) come back to the world (*punaḥ āvartante*) that is, are reborn.

Praśna up. III.3 teaches that rebirth is the product of mental desires: *manok tema āyāti asmin śarire:* life comes to this body through the actions of the mind (however noble) So *Praśna up.* V.3-5 and 7 proclaims that the recitation of the *mantras* of the *Rg Veda* leads to this world (and brings about birth as a human being), practice of austerity (*tapas*), self control, continence (*brahmacapa*), faith (*śraddhā*) can only bring him (worldly) greatness; the recitation of the *mantras* of the *yajurveda* leads to the intermediate world, the world of the moon, from which he is born again in this world; the recitation of the *mantras* of the *Sāmaveda* leads to the world of Brahmā (which again is a temporary abode).

The *upaniṣads* find an answer for this situation in cultvating detachment, *tyāga;* desirelessness (*akāmatāh*). So *Brhad up,* IV.4.7 says that a mortal becomes immortal only when all the desires have totally left him (*sarve pramucyante kāmāḥ*) *Chānd up.* VII.26.2 says that he who sees *ātman* everywhere does not see death, not illness nor any sorrow *na paśyo mṛtyum paśyati na rogam nota duhkham.* Again *Chānd.* VIII.4.1 reiterates that *ātman* is unaffected by old age, death, sorrow, merit or demerit: *na jarāna mrtyur na śoka na sukrtam na duṣkrtam sarve pāpmāno. Katha up.* II.3.14-15 says that when all the desires *kāmāḥ* (which are the source of *karmas*) clinging to one's heart are discarded, then a mortal attains the supreme (*Brahman*) and becomes immoral (*martyaḥ amṭtaḥ bhavati*). *Kaṭha up.* 11.3.18 reiterates that Naciketa attains *Brahman,* the Supreme Reality, after he becomes free from desire which leads to *Karma* (good and evil). *Iśa up.* I teaches renunciätion (*tyāga*) and giving up of covetousness (*grdhaḥ*). *Muṇd up.* III.2.1 is more explicit. It says that desirelessness (*akāmaḥ*) enables a person to transcend the human seed, that is, to overcome rebirth and transmigration. *Muṇd up.* III.2.2 emphasises that a person who has fulfilled all his desires (*paryāptakāmasya*) and III.2.5-6 who is free from attachment (*vitarāgaḥ*) attains liberation (*parimucyanti sarve)* at the time of death (*parāntakāle*).

It is natural the *upaniṣads* derive the logical, though extreme conclusion that, on attaining liberation a man is free from good and evil; his existing *karmas* are destroyed or become sterile and now *karmas* are abortive; therefore he is free to act anyway he likes. *Chānd* IV. 14-3 says "just as water does not cling to lotus leaf so also sin does not cling to him who knows *Brahman*". Again *Chānd up.* VII. 25-2, VIII. 4-3 and VIII. 5-4 states that he who attains the *ātman* becomes self sovereign (*svarāṭ bhavati*) and becomes free to act as he wishes in all the words, *sarveṣu lokeṣu kāmacāo bhavati*. According to *Chānd. Up.* VIII 1-5 and 7-1, the *ātman* is, *inter-alia*, free from evil, *eṣa ātmāpahatapāpmā*. *Kaṭha up.* II. 3.18 says that a person on attaining *Brahamn* becomes free from vice and virtue (*Brahmaprāptaḥ virajaḥ*) *Kena up.* IV.9 reiterates *yo vā etāmevam vedāpahatya pāpmānam* any one who knows this (*Brahmn*) dispels sin.

The *Śvetāśvatara upaniśad* strikes a radically different note. No doubt it fully accepts the law of *karma*, *Śvet up.* V. 7 & 12 avers that the doer of the deeds wanders about and obtains rebirth according to his deeds but it also postulates an omnipotent creator and the doctrine of grace. It believes in an Iśvara Lord, who is the great refuge of all *sarvasva śaraṇam brhat* (*Svet. Up.* III.17) and that a person attains immortality when blessed by him (the Lord) or at his pleasure (*Śvet. Up.*[1] I. 6). It teaches that a person becomes free from sorrow through the grace of the creator. *Vita śoko dhātuḥ prāsadan mahimānam Śvet. Up.* III. 20. Again it says that a man is helpless or powerless and becomes freed from sorrow by seeing the Lord. *Yadā paśyaty...iśam asya mahimānam iti vita śokaḥ*. *Śvet. Up.* IV. 7. So the seeker of liberation according to *Śvet. Up.* VI. 18 seeks his refuge.

Thus the *Śvetāśvatara upaniṣad* seeks to abrogate the law of *Karma* so far as the devotees of the Lord are concerned. *Śvet. Up.* I. 7 avers that the knowledge of *Brahaman* frees a person from birth, *yoniḥ muktaḥ*; *Śvet up* I. II (and also II. 15, IV. 16, V. 13 & 8, VI. 13) proclaim that knowledge of God leads to falling of the fetters and cessation of birth and death: *jñātvā devam sarva pāśāpahiniḥ kṣinaiḥ kleśair janma mrtyu prahanih*. So in *Śvet up.* VI. 6 God is descriebd *inter alia* as the producer of good and remover of evil *dharmāvaham pāpanudam*; in *Śvet. Up.* VI. II he is called ordainer of *karmas*: *karmādhyakṣa*.

Thus the *Śvetāśvatara upanisad* postulated a God whose grace to his devotees provided a way of escape from the law of *karma*.

The *upaniṣads* propagated contradictory trends of thought. They .ablished a doctrine of *karma*, of rewards and retribution, which is strongly ethical in character; inequality and suffering are explained as consequences of good and evil action. The doctrine of *Karma* was a philosophy of self-effort as the means of improving one's lot.

Simultaneously they maintain that rebirth and transmigration *per se* are bad in that (I) certain suffering in inherent in life such as craving or desires, old age and death, however meritorious a person's deeds might be (ii) the consequences of deeds already done have limited potentiality. Once actions have borne fruit, happiness and suffering caused by those *Karmas* come to an end but the process of fresh accumulation of *karmas* 'and their fruition continues. Thus it is an endless chain of birth and death, of happiness and suffering.

Escape from this cycle of existence, subject to suffering, lay not in doing *karma* but in *karma nirodha* suppression of *karmas.* One way to achieve this is by attaining the state of desirelessness, non-attachment, renuciation, which, in effect, would result in cessation of worldy activity. Another way was that enunciated in the *Śvetāśvatara upaniṣad,* the path of devotiion and divine grace and seeking reguge in Him.

It is paradoxical that the *upaniṣads* which postulated *karma* as a law of ethical discipline also seek escape from the operation of that law either in renunciation of worldy activity or in the grace of god. It is naïve to explain away the paradox by justifying the law of *Karma* in the context of the empirical reality and which loses its validity with reference to transcendental reality, or through an omnipotnet creator who can liquidate *Karmas.* In doing so the *upaniṣads* unwittingly blurred the distinction between good and evil, *duṣkṛta* and *sukṛta* pregnant for the growth of antinomianism in Indian philosophy and religion.

—*Y. Krishan*

9. Contributions of Kashmir to Civilisation

Kashmir in Indian mind has become a symbol of pristine beauty in the broadest sense of the term. Thus it embraces beauty associated with nature, race, heart and mind. In all these spheres Kashmir, since early times, has played an important role and has made remarkable strides in literature, religion, philosophy and culture of India. In the context of today, Kashmir has further become an embodiment of our most cherished democratic ideals, catholic and humanistic outlook and integrated culture. A résumé of Indian-Cultural history in all its ramifications will be impossible without reference to and insight into the genius of Kashmir.

We are, therefore, not surprised when Kashmir is found to have become famous as the abode of Sarasvatī, the Indian Muse. *Bālacandra, the Gujarati author of the epic called* Vasantavil*āsa,* echoes the very idea.

काश्मीरवासव्यसना सनाऽपि सरस्वती पुण्यवशादुपेत्य।
वसत्यवश्यं कविता विलासरूपेण चिद्रूपमुखाम्बुजेषु।।

For a man of letters Kashmir used to serve as final test of his merits. Śri Harsa recalls with great pride the reception of his work in Kashmir as a great intellectual achievement—

काश्मीरैर्महिते चतुर्दशतयीं विद्यां विद्‌द्रिर्महा
काव्ये चारूणि नैषधीयचरिते सर्गो निसर्गोज्जवल:।।[2]

Even in the valley itself we are reminded of Bilhaua's pithy description of his home-land, the land of Śāradā. He says it is only Kashmir[3] which has unique privilege of producing saffron filaments together with poetic ingenuity. And were we to add that Kashmir is equally the land of philosophical speculation and creative thinking as it is a country of saffron flowers and bunches of grapes, we need not be accused of resorting to hyperbole. The long history and voluminous literature of religio-philosophical thought of Kashmir only goes to exemplify the above contention. Jayaratha has not failed to take note of these twin peculiarities[4] of Kashmir, the seat of the Goddess of learning[5], with special reference to Kashmir Śaiva monism. Even the plan and design of the city of Srinagar has been patterned on that of the Śricakra, according to a tradition current even to day.[6]

The moment we think of Kashmir's philosophical and cultural heritage, we are immediately reminded of Kashmir Śaivism, the greatest humanistic attainment of Kashmir. This Kashmir Śaivism is generally believed to be monistic in temper and idealistic in ideology. We have, however, to be very clear that the word Kashmir Śaivism has extremely wide connotation and includes within tis range all the branches of Śaiva speculation-monistic, monistic-cum-dualistic and dualistic associated with Kashmir. This Śaivism is elastic enough as to include Śākta schools of thought within its ambit. If Abhinavagupta's *Tantrāloka* is any guide, the Trika of Kashmir Śaivism stands for the total *tāntrci* lore of Kashmir. It has to be specifically stated that in his *magnum opus* i.e., *Tantrāloka* (the light of Tantras), Abhinavagupta dwells on both the diverse currents of thought namely Tantraprakriyā and Kulaprakriyā.[10] While Tantra Prakriyā is traced straight to Tryambaka, the first ancestor referred to by Somānanda, the Kula Prakriyā is traced to Tryambaka through his[9] daughter and is therefore designated as "Ardha-Tryambaka." To be brief, the Kula system is identified with Kula Prakriyā, while the three independent monistic systems namely Trika, Krama and Pratyabhijñā are subsumed under the Tantraprakriyā or the Traiyambaka School.

In this scheme Abhinavagupta does not include the Spanda branch, possibly because of its lack of *tāntric* character and deep affiliation to this Śākta mode of thinking. This fact has been noted by Kṣemarāja, though in a different context.[10] With all their differences, however, they constitute what is precisely meant by Kashmir Śaivism. So far these four represent the monistic trend of thought. The schools founded by Amardaka and Śrinātha and continued by their spiritual descendants, relate to the dualistic and dualistic-cum-monistic currents of thought respectively and are also covered by the term Kashmir Śaivism. Out of these two, the Kashmir School of Śaiva Siddhānta, headed by Sadyojyoti, is a logical development of the dualistic line emanating from Amardaka. It may need be stressed in passing that all these systems, though have different secular history, they seem to be one in their *tāntric* origination.

From the foregoing lines it is apparent that the popular classification of the monistic Śaiva thought into Āgama Śāstra, Spanda Śāstra, and Pratyabhijñā Śāstra does not stand the strict logical scrutiny. It is an overlapping through handy attempt to classify the Śaiva Monism in a non-orthodox manner. At the most, we may resu.t to one classification from the point of view of the lauds of their origin. Thus broadly we have two types of schools:

(i) those which originated in Kashmir, and

(ii) others which were associated with other parts originally through the ancestral line of preceptors but were nurtured and developed afresh in Kashmir.

Under the previous head we have Krama, Spanda and Trika system which are brought into existence by Śivānanda (800 A.D.), Kallaṭa (825 A.D.) and Vasugupta (800 A.D.), respectively. The roots of the Krama system even go much earlier and may be consistently traced to one Gandhamādana (675 A.D.), who is said to be the preceptor of one *Vātūlanātha-Sūtrāṇi*. This work, alleged to be a work on the Śāhasa School, is now conclusively proved to be a text on a sub-school of the Krama system. It is interesting to note that the system has two phases-earlier and later—which develop into two full—grown schools and may be designated as Northern and Southern Schools respectively. The Northern, that belongs to Kashmir, is Śaiva-oriented with obvious Śākta leanings and has claimed contributions from Siddhanātha (900-950 A.D.), Bhaṭṭa Utpala, Bhūtirāja (900-950 A.D.), Cakrabhānu (1050-1100 A.D.), Ramyadeva (1100-1150 A.D.), Śrivatsa (13th Century) Śitikaṇṭha (15th Century) etc. in addition to the recognised stalwarts like Abhinavagupta and Jayaratha etc. The Southern School, which also traces its origin to Kashmir, in fact belongs to Cola in Deccan and is primarily Śakti-oriented. This tradition is nurtured by Śivānanda II (12th Century), Mahāprakāśa (12th Century) and Maheśvarānanda (13th Cent.), the illustrious author of the *Mahārtha-mañjari*, Thus the Southern School of the Krama has made very substantial coantribution to the Tripurā School. This we know on the authority of Śivānanda and Maheśvarānanda themselves.

Kallaṭa, the first exponent of the Spanda system, is a famous Siddha during the reign of Avantivarman (855-883 A.D.) as recorded by Kalhaṇa. His *Spanda Kārikā*[1] is commented upon by himself Utpala Vaiṣṇava (10th Cent.), Rāmakaṇṭha (10th Cent.) and Kṣemaraja (10th-11th Century). Vasugupta's famous *Śivasūtras* furnish a philosophical foot-hold to the *tāntric* lore and accord a mystic bias to the Trika line of thought. He is commented upon by Kallaṭa (9th Century), Bhāskara (10 Century), Kṣemarāja, Varadarāja (11th Century) and others.

Under the second head may be placed Kula and Pratyabhijñā. Of the two the Kula system, as propagated by Abhinavagupta, by and large appears to be of foreign origin. Abhinavagupta owes his initiation in the system to one Śambhunātha who hailed from Jālandhara and has received deepest veneration at the hands of the former. The alien origin of the Kula system is further corroborated by Jayaratha's observation that the Vāmakeśvari branch of the system was promulgated in Kashmir by Iśvaraśiva (9th Century), the celebrated author of the *Rasamahodadhi* and Śaṅkara Rāsi (9th Century).[12] Jayaratha seems to have inherited this tradition straight through Viśvāvarta (9th Century)[13] who happens to be a precursor of Śambhunātha. Other Kashmirians of eminence are Dipikānātha (10th Cent.) and Kalyāṇavarman (11th Century). Somānanda, Abhinava's great-grand teacher in Pratyabhijñā also wrote a commentary on the *Parātriṁśikā,*[14] avowedly a Kula tantra. It, therefore, appears certain that its alien character could not be sustained longer so much so that this system is represented to have originated in Kashmir[15] by the Southern School of the Kula system. However, this Kula culminates in Pratyabhijñā i.e. Anupāya according to Abhinavagupta's own verdict in the *Tantrāloka*.

On the threshold of the Pratyabhijñā system, though we notice that ancestral lineages of the two stalwarts of the system, Somānanda and Abhinavaguta, were brought to Kashmir from outside, yet the enormous gap that entailed between their settling down and taking philosophical exposition hardly justifies us to treat them as immigrants. Thus Somānanda (9th Century) is credited with breaking an entirely new ground towards human emancipation and furnishing a logical and rational basis in his *Śivadṛṣti* for the scattered *tāntric* ideals.[16] He is rightly hailed as the 'originator of the reasoning' (तर्कस्य कर्ता). He is followed by a galaxy of great authors e.g. Utpala, Lakṣmanagupta, Kṣemarāja, Yogarāja, Jayaratha and others. Utpala enlarges the scope and consolidates the rational side of the system in his learned commentary on *Śivadṛṣti* and his independent treatises like *Iṣvara Pratya-bhijña-Kārikā* and *Siddhitrayī,* though logical continuation of his master's work. Through Lakṣmanagupta, the author of *Śrīśāstra,*[17] he is succeeded by Abhinavagupta (950-1020 A.D.) the greatest of all Kashmirian thinkers and one of the greatest among the Indians. Abhinavagupta is credited with the authorship of more than forty-two works.[18] Of which the *Tantraloka, Vīmarsinī* and *Bòhatī* on *Utpala's Kārikās* and *Vivṛtti* respectively, *Vivaraṇa* on *Parā Triṁsīkā, Dhvanyāloka-locana* and *Abhinavabhāratī* are the works of extreme value and have been serving as reference books in their respective fields for centuries. He, with his unparalled genuis, synoptic vision, tremendous study and creative insight, enriched and illuminated the Śaiva philosophy, *tāntric* culture and aesthetic thought all the same time. In him Somānanda's aim of establishing the system on sound footing against the onslaughts of Buddhists, Grammarians, Śākta Monists, and Śaiva Dualists, a hint of which is echoed in the preamble of the *Śiva-sūtravārtika* of Varadarāja[19] is realised for good.

Coming to the thought-content of these systems, their agreement of fundamental principles impresses a keen student. Their mutual differences centre round varying orientations and emphasis, which cannot be taken up here. Their originality lies in the novel approach to the problems of philosophy and human emancipation which may be summed up as below:

(i) Reality is consciousness, not only pure, but perfect also. Perfection and totality result in self-spontaneous manifestation of the Absolute as psycho-metaphysical subjectivity on the one hand and objective data on the other.

(ii) Reality, though kinetic, is continuous and suffers no gap. This is brought about by *tāntric* transformation of the Sāṁkhya thesis of Sadṛśapariṇāmavāda into Ābhāsavāda, that of Sāmya (perfect harmony of three *guṇas* in Prakṛti) into Sāmarasya of the subjective and the objective. In addition, the *yogic* concepts of Parināmi-nityatā and Kūṭasthanityatā referring to different states are compressed and fused into one as Maheśvara, the dynamic Absolute or autonomous consciousness (*svatantrā saṁvit*).

(ii) The autonomy of consciousness, by its very implication, reconciles contradiction (*parasparaparihāra*) and synthesises dichotomy of subjective and objective of the dualists into pure, perfect and intuitive experience. Thus the ultimate unity is not an abstract unity but a concrete unity.[20] In the words of Dr. Pandey "It is not only the unity of opposites, as Hegel maintains his Absolute to be, but also the unity of distincts as Croce maintains".[21] Hence the Reality is essentially unity in multiplicity.

(iv) The autonomy i.e. self-spontaneity or consciousness also renders the entire causal explanation as futile and dogmatic. In Hegel the instances of reality are "deduced" from Absolute, here they are 'manifested' or 'expressed'. The cosmic law of causation is, therefore, transformed into Absolutic functionalism.

(v) This perfect consciousness is not something remote but essentially identical with self-consciousness and is 'ever present point of reference in every experience, actual or possible'.

(vi) Such a view of reality revolutionises the very mode and method of our time-old thinking and the following conclusions, of necessity, follow:

(a) Axiologically, emancipation of human soul is the highest value. Here *Mokṣa* consists in inculcation of synthesis of worldy enjoyments and transcendental experience of self (भोगमोक्षसामरस्यात्मामोक्षः). The world is liberation in changed perspective. This is a minimum pre-supposition of any definition of absolute perfection.

(b) This leads to a marked difference from other systems of Indian thought. Notwithstanding their mutual divergences, most schools are unanimous that *Mukti* follows in the wake of our distinguishing the self from the not-self. Broadly speaking *Mukti* is negation or sublation of not-self. On the countrary, here the self-realisation consists in synthesis of these two opposites and rules out the negation of either.

(c) Self-realisation is, therefore, 're-cognition'. Whatever has been passing through as 'this' hitherto, is now recognised

as 'I', because of intrinsic oneness of their character as freedom and consciousness (*Kartṛtva* and *Jñātṛtva*).

(d) Hence, knowledge is not 'knowing afresh' but 'knowing the known', that is, it is a removal of veil of ignorance which is defined as imperfect consciousness (अपूर्णम्मन्यता).

(e) Such a view of reality, apart from its epistemic implications, contains cultural margins of no mean consequence. It has a very optimistic appeal and culminates into deep commitment to life putting a seal of approval on all that life contains or stands for. This may be termed as a life-affirming attitude of the *tāntric* culture that makes it a truely humanistic movement where all spiritual pathways form part of one integrated scheme[23] and cease to be isolated events and where entire mankind is welcomed to the threshold of true wisdom without reference to caste, creed, sex and social status.[24] Thus Tagore's tribute that Trika "has penetrated to that living depth of thought where diverse currents of human wisdom unite in a luminous synthesis"[25] is amply borne out.

Side by side the growth of monistic schools, another branch line of Śaivism preaching dualistic ideology was very active.[26] This dualistic school also originated from Tantras and sought its anchorage in Ten Dvaita Tantras. Later on, but long before Abhinavagupta, the fusion of these Ten Dualistic Tantras and Eighteen dualistic-cum-non-dualistic Tantras[27] was responsible for the rise of a school now known as Śaiva Siddhānta.[28] This school is quite identical in its approach with its counterpart in South. In Kashmir, it produced great philosophers like Sadyojyoti, Bòhaspati and Śaṅkaranandana. From Somānanda down to Varadarāja there are glaring evidences that there existed direct confrontation between the monistic and dualistic schools. This accounts for Abhinavagupta's disdain fo the dualism. Sadyojyoti's (9th Century) *Nareśvara Parīkṣā* is an important work of this school. This was commnted upon by Rāmakaṇṭtha II (1100-1130 A.D.). This work is available in print. This masterpiece highly speaks of the philosophical acumen of the author as well as the commentator. The *Bhogakārikā, Mokṣakārikā* etc. are among his six other works. Bòhaspati is supposed to be as great an authority as Sadyojyoti himself and is the author of the *Śivatanu Śāstra*. Śaṅkaranandana is referred to by Abhinava as the author of the *Prajñālaṁkāra*.[29] Vidyāpati, Devabala are also the dualistic Śaiva authors preceding Abhinavagupta. In poet-Abhinavagupta period we meet King Bhojadeva (1018-60 A.D.), the author of the *Tattva-Prakāśikā;* Rāmakaṇtha I (1035-1050 A.D.), the author of the *Nādakārikā* and *Vṛtti* on *Mṛgendra Tantra;* Śrīkaṇṭha (1050-1075 A.d.), the author of *Ratnatraya;* Nārāyaṇa Kautha (1075-1100 A.D.), the author of a commentary on *Mògendra Tantra;* Rāmakantha II and Aghoraśiva (1130-58 A.d.). The last one is credited with writing commentaries on all the major works of dualistic Śaivism. This is a very impressive list and explains why the monistic Śaivism viewed it as a formidable opponent. In fact, the Śaiva dualists made deep inroads into the monistic philosophy and tried to interpret the monistic *āgamas* in the dualistic light. Kṣemarāja in his commentary on the *Svacchanda Tantra* makes a pointed reference to it.[30] Similarly Aghora Śivācārya charges Monists to have commented upon the *Tattva-Prakasikā* of Bhoja without any insight into the discipline and he, in order to undo the wrong, had to undertake a commentary on the same.[31]

Still another line of Śaivites, declaring their adherence to the Eighteen Dvaitādvaita Tantras, arrests our attention. This system is known as Lakulīśa Pāśupata. Abhinavagupta seems to have a soft corner for the system and preferes it to Śiddānta, avowedly the dualistic system[32] But it is difficult to say whether it was a Kashmirian system.

Outside the pale of Śaivism, yet within the *tāntric* fold, we have sufficient reason, according to Dr. Schrader, to believe that a considerable part of Pāñcarātra Āgamic literature was produced in Kashmir[33]. Utpala Vaiṣava, the early 10th century author of the *Spanda Pradāpikā,* mentions the following Śaṁhitās by name, *Jayāhkya, Hamsaparameśvara, Vaihāyasa, Śrikālaparaā* and *Śrī Sāttvata*.[34] In addition, he gives eight quotations from Pāñcarātra scriptures without naming them. Pt. V. Krishnamacharya, the editor of Adyar edition of the *Lakṣmītantra,* is of the view that those extracts are most probably taken from *Ekāyanaveda*.[35] It is to be noted that of all these Saṁhitās *Pauṣkara, Sāttvata* and *Jaya* have "on the whole been considered the most authoritative part of the Pāñcarātra scripture."[36] *Ahirbudhnya Saṁhitā* was definitely composed in Kashmir in early eight century as is indicated by the episode of Muktāpīda (699-735 A.D.) contained in the 48th Chapter. Again *Lakṣmītantra* is quoted by Yogarāja.[37] (11th Century), Abhinavagupta's pupil, and by Mahesvarānanda (13th Century),[38] a South Indian author on Kashmir Śaivim. Even the authors in the dualistic line, notably Rāmakaṇṭha II among them groups the adherents of the Pāñcarātra system into two classes, viz. Saṁkarṣaṇa Pāñcarātra[39] and Saṁhitā Pāñcarātra.[40] Kṣemarāja, another student of Abhinavagupta, assigns the Pāñcarātra concept of the ultimate reality to the realm of *Avyakta.*[41] The most significant thing in this connection is a work known as *Kāśmīrāgama-prāmānga* by Yāmunācārya (11th Century) which is not lost but of which we are told in his *Āgamaprāmanya.*[42] A man of Yāmuna's eminence would never write a work on Kashmir scriptures unless he found something of intrinsic worth in them. Vedāntadeśika echoes this very contention.[43] It is an irony of history that after these few celebrated names, the centre of Pāñcarātra activity shifted to South and the tradition died out in the land of its origin.

Another allied system of thought which seems to have evoked considerable interest in Kashmir is that of Bhartṛhari. Though Kashmir has received more from him than it has given to Bhartṛhari, the contribution of Kashmir cannot be left unaccounted for. Philosophy of language has remained an integral part of basic structure of every *tantric* system. Language in its most subtle and universal form is implied in the concept of *Vimarśa* which serves as the very core of Reality. It is the concept of *Parā* (the ultimate) stage of Supreme Speech, evolved in course of criticism of the grammarian's concept of *Paśyantī,* the *Śabdabrahman* that had led post-Somananda grammarians to conceive *Parā* as distinct from and transcendental to *Paśyanth.* Kaiyata's *Pradīpa,* a commentary on Patañjali's *Mahābhāṣya,* apart from its grammatical importance, is full of philosophical observations. In tradition, he is held to be Mammata's brother (11th Century). Similarly Helārāja, to whom we owe most of our understanding of Bhartṛhari, belongs to Kashmir and on his own testimony is the son of Bhūtirāja (भूतिराजतनयहेलाराजकृते). Abhinavagupta was its student in dualistic branch (भूतिराजतनय: स्वपितृप्रसाद;)[44] On internal evidence he appears to be the brother of Bhaṭṭendurāja, Abhiuava's teacher in literature (900-950 A.D.).

Let us now divert to the other side of the picture. Coming close to the scene of the orthodox Indian philosophy, no account is deemed to be complete without a study of *Prasthānatrayī* constituting the basic texts of Indian philosophy. Of these the *Bhagavadgītā* has enjoyed a unique place in the annals of Indian thought and culture through the ages. In this sphere too, Kashmir claims its share of originality. First of all attention was drawn to the existence of Kashmir recension of *Gītā by Dr. Schrader*[45] as back as 1930. Since then considerable amount of work has been produced on the problem.[46] Kashmir recension of *Gītā* contains 745 verses as against 700 verses of the popular recension adopted by Śaṅkara etc. The text seems to have been commented upon by a host of Kashmirian scholars headed by Vasugupta who wrote the *Vāsavītikā*. He was followed by Ānandavardhana, Bhāskara, Abhinavagupta, Lāsaka and others. Of these, only two commentaries have come down to us; one by Abhinavagupta under the *title Gītārthasaṁgraha* and the other by Rāmakaṇṭha under the title *Sarvatobhadra,* Abhinavagupta, true to his synthetic ideology, lays equal emphasis on each of the tripple approaches-*Jñāna, Karma* and *Bhakti* as conducive to spiritual enlightenment. To Abhinavagupta the fight between Kauravas and Pāṇdavas is symbolic of a war that is constantly raging between the lower and upper impulses of our personality.[47] Rāmakaṇṭha, the younger brother of Muktākaṇa, a contemporary of Avantivarman (855-888 A.D.), advocated *Jñānakarma-samuccaya* as a way to spiritual realisation in his *Sarvatobhadra.* According to Chintamani[48] Rāmakaṇṭha adopts *Bhedābhda* fashion in his commentary. On the affinity of this identity-in-difference attitude, Chintamani has raised a doubt as to whether Bhāskara, the known Bhedābhedavādin and a commentator on *Gītā*, is identical with his namesake in Kashmir to whom also is attributed the authorship of a commentary on *Gītā*. This is indeed a very important problem of Indology as well as Indian thought that calls for further investigation by the scholars. It is premature to say on the problem, because the *Jñānakarma-samuccaya* may also be explained in the light of synthetic thesis of the Monistic Śavisim which is ideologically different from identity-in-difference.

Kashmir, from early times, has been a meeting ground of a variety of faiths and divergent thought currents. Kashmir's attachment to Buddhism dates back to the time of Aśoka (273-232 B.C.). Nāgasena (150 B.C.), the author of *Milind-Panho,* is said to be a Kashmiri.[49] Kaniṣka (78-102 A.D.) convened the 2nd Buddhist Council in Kashmir and brought Aśvaghoṣa to act as its Vice-President.[50] Kumāralabdha, one of the famous four luminaries of Buddhism, is believed to be a Kashmiri.[51] Jan Yun-Hua in his learned paper[52] draws our attention to the activities of Kashimrian monks in medieval China and evaluates their contribution to Buddhism in the Far East. This tradition begins about the early fourth century and continues upto 11th century. Kashmirians' contribution, at large, includes translations into Chinese of Buddhist canons and ritualistic texts. They also translated *tāntric* Texts. Among the early authors, he mentions Prajñākūṭa (307-317 A.D.) Saṅgha-bhūti, Puṇyatara (404 A.D.), Dharma Mitra (356-442 A.D.) and a host of others. Similarly the Gilgit Manuscripts, published by the Research Department of the Kashmir Government containing a large number of Buddhist manuscripts found in 1931 in Gilgit, now under Pakistani occupation, were written around 5th century according to Nalinaksa Dutta and belong to a section of Mahayāna Sanskrit Canon.[53] As the tradition has it, Nāgārjuna, a devout Mahāyānist, came to power after receiving Kashmir (Kaniṣka-Puram) as a gift from Kaniṣka and propagated his faith. This may possibly explain the prevalence of Mahāyānic literature in these manuscripts which form a solid creative block of Buddhist genius in Kashmir.

The Kashmir School of Buddhist logic, according to Stcherbatsky,[54] begins with Dharmottara whose main aim is to unearth the "deep philosophic contents of the system of Diṅṇāga and Dharmakīrti, regarding it as a critical system of logic and epistemology".[54] He was invited by the King Jayāpīḍga (778-813 A.D.) as reported by Kalhaṇna,[55] to Kashmir which he chose as a centre of his academic pursuits. He wrote detailed commentaries on *Pramāṇaviniścaya* and *Nyāyabindu*, the first being called his Great comment and the second his Small comment. This may be treated as a possible source of inspiration to Abhinavagupta who also wrote the small and great commentaries. Dharmottara's importance as a first rate logician and philosopher can be gauged from the fact that Abhinavagupta's celebrated *Vimarśinī* and *Bṛhatī Vimaśinī* have been attempted primarily as a critique of Dharmakīti as interpreted by Dharmottara. He has written some other works also which are preserved in Tibetan translation alone. From Abhinavagupta[56] we learn that Ānandayardhana[57] wrote a commentary called *Pramāṇaviniścayatīkāvivṛti*. This work is now lost to us. Another sub-commentary on the same was written by Kashmirian Jñānaśri. Its Tibetan translation is preserved in this Tanjore collection. This tradition was continued by Śaṅkarananda (middle of 11th Cent.). He undertook to write an exhaustive commentary on *Pramāṇavārtika*, but could not complete it. He also wrote other works. All of them are available now in Tibetan translation only. In addition, a passing reference may be made to Ravigupta (725 A.D.), the author of the *Pramāṇavārtikatīkāvṛtti.*[58] Among others Arcaṭa, the author of the *Hetubindutīkā;* Dānaśila (988-1038 A.D.) who migrated from Kashmir to Jaggadal monastery of Bengal[59] and wrote *Pustakapāthopāya;* Jinamitra (close of 10th Century), the author of the *Nyāyabindu-piṇḍārtha,*[60] and Ratnavajra (10th Century), the author of the *Yuktiprayoga* deserve special mention.

As is evident from the foregoing account Śaivism and Buddhism have been extensively cultivated in Kashmir, while other systems grew and developed sporadically. Among these our attention is arrested by Jayanta Bhaṭṭa, an outstanding scholar of the Nyāa system. He is the author of famous *Nyāyamañjurī* and a contemporary of King Śaṅkaravarman (883-902 A.D.). This Jayanta was a great-grandson of Śivasvāmin, minister of King Muktāpīḍa and author of *Kapphiṇābhyudaya* epic. Jayanta Bhaṭṭa has sarcastically attacked the Buddhists for the gap between their profession and performance. For instance:

नास्त्यात्मा फलभोगमात्रमथ च स्वर्गाय चैत्यार्चनम्।
संस्काराः क्षणिका युगस्थितिभृतश्चैते विहाराः कृताः।।
संर्व शून्यमिदृं वसूनि गुरवे देहीति चादिश्यते।
सौद्धनां चरितं किमन्यदियती दम्भस्य भूमिः परा ।।

Jayanta's other work on Nyāya Philosophy is the *Nyāyakalikā.* He is also said to have written a drama called *Āgamaḍambara* on the six orthodox systems of Indian philosophy. Jayanta's *Nyāyakalikā* is a commentary on the *Nyāyasāra* of Bhāsarvajña. There is no unanimity with regard to the latter's time, but he must have flourished before the end of ninth century as Jayanta has commented upon him. In this short tract on logic, Bhāsarvajña departs from the tradition inasmuch as he rejects the claim of *Upamāna* as an independent means of knowledge. His concept of *Mokṣa* as characterised by eternal happiness and final elimination of pain[63] also does not fall in tune with the traditional viewpoint. This clearly betrays the influence of Kashmir Śaivism on him.

We now come to another phase of Kashmir's cultural heritage. In the context of Indian philosophy, three approaches are generally noticed for self-realiaation-cognitive, moral and emotional (*Jñāna, Karma* and *Bhaktimārgas*). The cognitive and the moral both pin up their faith in human agency. In the former demands are put on a *priori* intuition as the only way, whereas in the latter on ideal action. This is the domain of philosophy and ethics. But in emotional approach human agency and cognitive movements are totally resigned to the divine will. This is the realm of devotion i.e. *Bhakti*. The cognitive approach lays more stress on the transcendent side of reality while the emotive leans towards the immanent side—both following from the very definition of reality. In fact, the *Jñāna* blooms forth into *Bhakti* (समावेश पल्लवा एव).[64] It is the expression of the *Ānanda* aspect according to Gopinath Kaviraj,[65] where unity is fundamental and duality is deliberate in order to realsie the self-hood.

Like Vaiṣṇava Bhakti cult in other parts of India, Śaiva cult of Bhakti in Kashmir has flooded the valley since the time of Utpala's *Storāvalī*. It is followed by Kalhaṇa's *Ardhanārīśvara Stotra*. During this period the *Kramastotra* attributed to Siddanātha[66] is worthy of mention. Abhinava has composed a number of devotional songs. *Stavacintāmaṇi* of Nārāyaṇakaṇṭha, *Bhāvopakhāra* of Cakrapāṇi are other hymns of repute. Kṣemarāja and Jayaratha have also composed qutie a few *stotras*. This cult of total dedication and absolute self-surrender to the Divine reaches its culminating point in Lalla De (1335 A.D.). According to Nilla Cram Cook in her book *The way of the swan,*[67] a close parallel is descernible between the poet philosophers of Erfan in Central Asia and Śaiva writers of Kashmir. The two movements of Śaiva philosophers and Erfan met in Kashmir in the fourteenth century when Lalla De met Shah-I Hamdan,[68] resulting in fusion of the two streams of thought e.g., Śaivism and Erfanism (i.e. Sufism). Thus Lalla De was acclaimed by all sections of society as the prophet of the new movement[69] preaching social equality of mankind and essential unity of all creeds. This process of fusion, engineered by the Bhakti movement, got a fillip in the hands of King Zain-ul-abidin who embraced tolerance and catholicity as his inner faith. Says Cook "Had the example of Kashmir been followed (by Akbar) a secular India might have come into being then and there".[70] This cult was continued by Sheikh Nooruddin (1438 A.D.),[71] a Hindu saint converted to Islam, who all through his life stood by the basic unity and fraternity of humanity. Jaggadhara's (1450 A.D.) *Stuti Kusumāñjali* is a work of the same time which is fresh with its devotional fervour. After him this movement starts fading out and by the time we reach Sahibakaula's *Devīnāma Vilāsa* (1666 A.D.), we hear only decadent notes of Sanskrit poetry presented in the garb of devotional poem. This tradition, however, blossomed outside the skirts of Kashmir, in the "confluence of two oceans" of Darashikoh but that too could not survive the religious fantacism of his brother.

Kashmir's contribution to the realm of thought and culture is manifold. From abstract metaphysics let us now switch over to the field of applied philosophy. For example, in the precincts of fine arts Abhinvagupta's contribution is matchless. As poetics is not presently our concern, we refrain from referring to his theory of aesthetic experience which he evolved after a careful examination of a galaxy of illustrious thinkers preceding him. But the observations on music in the 3rd Ānhika of the *Tantrāloka* and *gānādhyāyas* of *Abhinavabhāratī* and those of his teacher Utpala as preserved by him in his *Abhinavabhāratī,* and of Ratnakaṇtha and Rāmakaṇṭha as contained in the *Ratnatraya* and *Nādakārikā respectively*[72] are comparable only to those of Bhartṛhari and merit our careful consideration. Śarṅgadeva (1132-1169 A.D.), the celebrated author of an encyclopaedic work on classicial music called *Sañgītaratnākara,* haild from a Kashmirian family. His grand-father, Bhāskara, migrated from Kashmir and settled down at Deogiri. Hence the credit on this account is to be shared between Kashmir and South equally. Similarly a small tract on the science of architecture named *Prāsādamaṇḍana* by Sūtradhāra Maṇḍana has been brought out by the Research Department of Kashmir Government.[73] It contains an outline sketch of architectural and sculptural aspects of temple and palace. Professor Rasiklal C. Parika tells[74] us on the basis of *Vastupālapraśasti* that Sarada temple in Kashmir had influenced the Jain architecture in Gujarat and small temples of Saravatī were built along with the bigger temples of Tirthañkaras. These were called Kāśmīrāvatāra (काश्मीरावतार-श्रीसरस्वतीमूर्तिदेवकुलिय) and were designed on the architectural pattern of Śāradā temple in Kashmir.

Coming to the secular sciences we find the celebrated combination of Vāmana and Jayāditya as co-authors of *Kāśikā-Vòtti* on *Aśtādhāyī.* This Vāmana is said to be identical with the famous poetician who was also a minister of King Jayāpīḍa (779-813 A.D.). Similarly the typically cultural treatises in the form of *Nīlamata Purāṇa* and *Viṣṇu Dharmottara*, an Upapurāṇa, are in all probability texts of Kashmirian origin and afford to us a deep insight into the culture, life, religion of the people and topography of the valley. Buhler refers to two recensions of the *Nīlamata Purāṇa* in his report.[75] In the same tradition we find

Kïemendra's *Lokaprakāśa* which seems to have received finishing touches by several authors as late as 17th century. This work is indispensable for an understanding of the social, political and commerical conditions of the then Kashmir.

The subject is to challenging and vast that, before concluding, attention of the scholars needs be drawn to the observations made by Pushp in his brilliant analysis entitled *Requisites of Kashmirology.*[76] As suggested by him, with each passing world of the present paper, the author has been increasingly convinced of the urgency of a concerted, planned and determined effort to fathom the intellectual beauty and rhythm that is Kashmir. While closing, we are remained of a feeling reference made by Kalhaṇa, the illustrious author of the Royal Chronicle, which even today rings tune in our memory:

विद्यावश्मानि तुङानि कुङ्कुमसहिंत पथः।
द्राक्षेति यत्र यत्र सामान्यमस्ति त्रिदिवदुर्लभम्।।

—*Navjivan Rastogi*

References

1. Quoted by Rasiklal C. Parikh in 'Classical Sanskrti', *Proceedings of AIOC,* 21st Session, Srinagar, p. 118.

2. *Naiṣadha* 16, 121.

3. सहोदराः कुंकुमकेसराणां भवन्ति नूनं कविताविलासाः।
   न शारदादेशमपास्य दृष्टस्तेषां यद्न्यत्र मया प्ररोहः।। *Vik.* 121.

   This we find repeated in the concluding *Praśasti of Karṇa-sundarī-nāṭkā*

4. श्री सोमानन्दपादप्रभृतिगुरूवराद्दिष्टसत्रीतिमार्गो
   लब्ध्वा यत्रैव सम्यवपदिमनि घटनानीश्वराद्वैतवादः
   कश्मीरेम्यः प्रसृत्य प्रकटपरिमलो रञ्जयन् सर्वदेशान्
   देशेऽन्यस्मित्रदृष्टो धुासृणविसरन्सर्ववन्द्यत्वमाप।।

   T.A.V., XII, p. 429, verse 7

5. युत्का बोधाप्रधााना स्थिनिजमहसा शारदापीठदेवी
   विद्यापीठे प्रथीयः प्रथितनिखिलवाग्यत्र काश्मीरनाम्नि।।

   Ibid, Verse 4

6. In the Asiatic Society of Bengal, there is a manuscript of the text named *Vidyārṇava* by a student of some Pragalbhācārya, which also records this tradition. By implication 'Srinagar' is an abbreviation of the original "Śrividyanagara".

7. Although Somānanda, at the very outset of his third Āhnika, castigates the Śakta Monists, yet he calls them a kith and kin of his own (स्वयुथ्यानद्वयवादिन: प्रतीदानीप्रारम्भ: । *Śivadṛsti,* p. 94). This Śāktism is later assimilated into the Tripura School, which iss an off-shoot of the Kula system, as well as in the Southern School of the Krama system. This point will be enlarged upon in the sequel.

8. अतश्र वक्ष्यमाणशास्त्रस्य कुलतन्त्रप्रक्रियात्मकेन द्वैविघ्यं *T.A.V.* I, p. 24. For details see Author's doctoral thesis entitled *Philosophy of Krama Monism of Kashmir: An Analytical Study,* Part I, Chapter 3 (submitted to Lucknow University in 1967).

9. *T.A.V., I. P. 27.*

10. अनन्तापरटीकाकृन्मघ्ये रिथतिमगृष्यता।
वृितं स्पन्दशास्त्रं नो गुरूणा नो, मयास्य तु ।। A*sp. N.* p. 77, concluding verse no. 2.

11. The authorship of *Spanda Kārikā* is a controversial point. In the traditional circle the group headed by Utpala, the author of the *Pradipikā* commentary on *Sp. K.,* ascribes authorship of the *Kārikās* to Kallaṭa, whereas the one headed by Kṣemarāja to Vasugupta. In this tussle we have two recensions of *Sp. K.* It forms a very interesting episode of the contemporary philosophical scene, which for want of relevance and space has to be skipped over here. For further discussions see author's thesis on Krama system, Part I, Chap. 4.

12. वस्तुतो हि अस्य दर्शनस्य एतदेव आचार्यद्वयं कश्मीरेषु अवतारकम्। *Vāmakeśvarimataviva-raṇam* by Jayaratha, p. 48. (K.S.S.).

13. ततश्र श्रीविश्वावर्तमुखैनैवं लक्ष्यते यत्, तदेव इदमस्मत्पर्यन्तं शिष्यप्रशिष्यक्रमेण सर्वषामापि प्राप्तम्। *Ibid.*

14. *Parātrimśikāavivaraṇa,* Abhinavagupta, p. 16, (K.S.S.),

15. संप्रदास्य काश्मीरदेशोद्भूतत्वात्। *Rjuvimarśinī* on *Nityāṣoḍaśikārṇavatantru,* Śivānanda, Varanasi, p. 114.

16. इति प्रकटितो मया सुघट एष मार्गो नवा।
महागुरूभिरूच्यते स्म शिवदृष्टिशास्त्रे यथा।
Iśvara Pratyabhijña Kārikā 4.1.16.

17. Identical with the Śāradātilakatantra on the authority of Rāghava Bhatia, author of the commentary called *Padārṭhādarśa,*

18. Vide *Abinavagupta: An Historical & Philosophical Study,* K.C. Pandey, 2nd edition, pp. 27-76; vide also *Works of Abhinavagupta,* V. Raghavan, 'Jori, Vol. XIV, IV, 1933, pp. 318-28.

19. नागाबोघ्यादिभि: सिद्धैर्नास्तिकानां पुरमरै:।
आक्रान्ते जीवलोकऽस्मित्रात्मश्वरनिरासक: ।। *S.S. V. ā, K.S. 1.1.*

20. तस्मात्प्रत्यभिज्ञानबलात्-एकोप्यसौ पदार्थात्मा स्वभावभेदान् विरूद्धान् यावत् अंगीकुरूते तावत् ते विरोधादेव क्रमरूपतया निर्भासामाना: तमेकं क्रियाश्रयं संपादियन्ति। *Bhāskari,* Pt. II, edited by Iyer and Pandey, p. 9.

21. *Comparative Aesthetics*, Vol. I, Indian, K.C. Pandey, second edition, p. 101.
22. [Annals, B.O.R.I.]
23. तद्भूमिकाः सर्वदर्शनस्थितयः। *Pratyabhijñā Hṛdaya*, Kṣemarāja, Sūtra S.
24. केचिदाचक्षते द्विजराजन्यपशंसापरमेतद्वाक्यं न तु स्त्र्यादिष्वपवर्गप्राप्तितात्पर्येण। ते डि भगवतः सर्वानुग्राहिकां शक्तिं मितविषयतया खण्डयन्तः ... मात्सर्यावहित्थलज्जाजिह्मीकृतावङ्मुखदृष्टयः ... हास्रसिविषयभावमात्मनि आरोपयन्ति। *Gitārthasaṁgraha* on B.G. 9. 35, Abhinavagupta, ed. by Lakshman Raina, p. 108.
25. *A Description Analysis of Kashmir Series of Text and Studies* p. 2.
26. Prof. P.T. Raju has confused these two different and anomalous lines of thought as analogous in his *Idealistic Thought of India*, London, pp. 136-145.
27. Vide *Abhinavagupta*, Pandey, pp. 167-169.
28. अष्टाविंशतिसंख्योऽसौ सिद्धान्त इति संज्ञितः।

    Mṛgendratantra, Introduction, K.S.S., p. 2.
29. विस्तरेण च प्रज्ञालङ्कारे द्शितम् आचार्यशङ्करनन्दनेन। *Bhāskari*, Pt. I, p. 225.
30. Vide *Bhāskari*, Pt. III, Pandey, Introduction, p. xviii.
31. Vide *Bhāskari, Pt. III, p. xviii.*
32. *Vide* Abhinavagupta, Pandey, p. 169.
33. Introduction to *Pāñcarātra* and the *Ahirbudhnya Saṁhitā*, F. Otto Sohrader, Adyar, 1916, pp. 96-97.
34. *Spanda Pradipika*, edited by Islampurkar, 1898, pp. 9, 11, 20, 3-34 and 54.
35. *Lakṣmī Tantra*, Introduction, p. 5.
36. Vide Introduction to *Pāñcarātra*, p. 21.
37. *Paramārthasāra-vivaraṇa*, K.S.S., p. 164.
38. *Mahārtha-mañjari Parimala*, T.S.S., pp. 67, 182.
39. अंतःकरणचैतासिकाः सङ्कर्षणपांचरात्रिकाः। *Nareśvaraparikṣā*, K.S.S., p. 87.
40. परिणतिवेदान्तविदः संहितापाञ्चरात्राः। *Ibid.* p. 91.
41. *Pratyabhijñahṛdaya*, K.S.S.., p. 55.
42. Vide *Lakṣmi Tantra*, Introduction, p. 55.
43. यथा चैकायनशाखायाम् अपौरूषेयत्वं, तथा काश्मीरागमप्रामाण्य एवं प्रपांचितमिति नेह प्रस्तूयते।

    Pañcarātra-rakṣā, Vedāntadeśika-granthamālā, p. 95; *Nyāya-Pariśuddhi* (same series), p. 168.
44. Vide author's thesis on the *Karma system*, Pt. I, pp. 207-213.
45. Vide *Śrimadbhagavadgītā with Śarvatobhadra*, edit by T.R. Chintamani, Introduction, pp. xiv, xxi.

46. Vide R. Belvalkar's two papers in *New Indian Antiquary*, July, 1939, pp. 211-251 and *Annals BORI*, Vol. XIX, pp. 335-348.
47. *Gītāthasaṁgraha*, on 1.1., p. 3.
48. *Śrimadbhagavadgītā with Sarvatobhadra*, Introduction, p. xii.
49. *Doctrine of Recognition*, R.K. Kaw, V.V.R.I. p. 5; vide also, *History of Philosophy: Eastern & Western*, ed. Radhakrishnan, Pt. I, p. 38.
50. Vide *Doctrine of Recognition*, p. 5.
51. *Ibid.*
52. *Contribution of Kashmir to the Expansion of Buddhism in Far-East*, AIOC, Srinagar, 1961, Summaries of Papers, pp. 221-22.
53. *A Descriptive Analysis*, pp. 45-46.
54. *Buddhist Logic*, Vol. I., Dover Edition, p. 41.
55. *Buddhist Logic*, Vol. I, p. 41.
56. *Rājataraṅgiṇī*, IV. 498.
57. *Dh. Locana* (Kāvyamālā) p. 233.
58. *Buddhist Logic*, p. 42.
59. Vide *Cultural Heritage of Kashmir*, S.C. Banerji, Calcutta, p. 123.
60. *Ibid.*
61. *Ibid.*
62. *Nyāyamañjarī*, 7th Āhnika, quoted by Banerji, *Cultural Heritage of Kashmir*, p. 120.
63. Quoted from *Nyāya Sāra*, p. 41, *Ibid.*
64. *Bhāskari*, Pt. II, p. 258.
65. "काश्मीरीयशैवदर्शन" भारतीय संस्कृति और साधाना, भाग 1, पटना, प, 7-10.
66. Vide author's thesis on the *Karma system*, Pt. I, Ch. 6.
67. Vide *Kashmir Biannual*, Vol. I, No. I, pp. 89-91.
68. *Doctrine*, p. 365.
69. *Doctrine*, p. 365.
70. Vide *Kashmir Biannual*, p. 90.
71. *Doctrine*, p. 366.
72. Vide *Comparative Aesthetics 3*, Pt. I, pp. 540, 557-566.
73. K.S.S. No. LXVII.
74. *Proceedings of AOIC, 21st Session*, pp. 112-18.
75. Detailed Report of a tour in search of Sanskrit MSS, p. 38.
76. *Kashmir Biannual*, pp. 3-7.
77. *Rājataraṅgini*, I. 42.

10. The Masters

There is a stage in human evolution which immediately precedes the goal of human effort, and when this stage is passed through, man, as man, has nothing more to accomplish. He has become perfect; his human career is over. The great religions bestow on this Perfect Man different names, but, whatever the name, the same idea is beneath it; He is Mithra, Osiris, Krshṇa, Buddha, Christ—but he ever symbolises the Man made perfect. He does not belong to a single religion, a single nation, a single human family; he is not stifled in the wrappings of a single creed; everywhere he is the most noble, the most perfect ideal. Every religion proclaims him; all creeds have in him their justifications; he is the ideal towards which every belief strives, and each religion fulfills effectively its mission according to the clearness with which it illumines, and the precision with which it teachers the road whereby he may be reached. The name of Christ, used for the Perfect Man throughout Christendom, is the name of a *state,* more than the name of a *man:* "Christ in you, the hope of glory," is the Christian teacher's thought. Men, in the long course of evolution, reach the Christ state, for all accomplish in time the centuried pilgrimage, and he with whom the name is specially connected in Western lands is one of the "Sons of God" who have reached the final goal of humanity. The word has ever carried the connotation of a state; it is "the anointed". Each must reach the state: "Look within thee; thou art Buddha." "Till the Christ be formed in you."

As he who would become a musical artist should listen to the masterpieces of music, as he should steep himself in the melodies of the master-artists, so should we, the children born of humanity, lift up our eyes and our hearts, in ever-renewed contemplation, to the mountains, on which dwell the Perfect Men of our race. What we are, they were; what they are, we shall be. All the sons of men can be what a son of Man has accomplished, and we see in them the pledge of our own triumph; the development of like divinity in us is but a question of evolution.

COMMANDS: OUTER AND INNER

I have sometimes divided interior evolution into sub-moral, moral, and super-moral; sub-moral, wherein the distinctions between right and wrong are not seen, and man follows his desires, without question, without scruple; moral, wherein right and wrong are seen, become ever more defined and inclusive, and obedience to law is striven after; super-moral, wherein external law is transcended, because the divine nature rules its vehicles. In the moral condition, law is recognised as a legitimate barrier, a salutary restraint; "Do this"; "Avoid that"; the man struggles to obey, and there is a constant combat between the higher and lower natures. In the super-moral state the divine life in man finds its natural expression without external directional he loves, not because he ought to love, but because he is love. He acts, to quote the noble words of a Christian Initiate, "not after the law of a central commandant, but by the power of an endless life". Morality is transcended when all the powers of the man turn to the Good as the magnetised needle turns to the north; when divinity in man seeks ever the best for all. There is no more combat, for the victory is won; the Christ has reached his perfect stature only when he has become the Christ triumphant, Master of life and death.

THE FIRST INITIATION

This stage of the Christ-life, the Buddha-life, is entered by the first of the great Initiations, in which the Initiate is "the little child", sometimes the "babe", sometimes the "little child, three years old". The man must "regain the child-state he hath lost"; he must "become a little child" in order to "enter the kingdom". Passing through that portal, he is born into the Christ-life, and, treading the "way of the Cross", he passes onwards through the successive gate-ways on the Path; at the end, he is definitely liberated from the life of limitations, of boundage, he dies to time to live in enternity, and he becomes conscious of himself as life rather than as form.

There is no doubt that in early Christianity this stage of evolution was definitely recognised as before every individual Christian. The anxiety expressed by St. Paul that Christ might be born in his converts bears sufficient testimony to this fact, leaving aside other passages that might be quoted; even if this verse stood alone it would suffice to show that in the Christian ideal the Christ-stage was regarded as an inner condition, the final period of evolution for every believer. And it is well that Christians should recognise this, and not regard the life of the disciple, ending in the Perfect Man, as an exotic, planted in Western soil, but native only in far Eastern lands. This ideal is part of all true and spiritual Christianity, and the birth of the Christ in each Christian soul is the object of Christian teaching. The every object of religion is to bring about this birth, and if it could be that this mystic teaching could slip out of Christianity, that faith could no longer raise to divinity those who practise it.

The first of the great Initiations is the birth of the Christ, of the Buddha, in the human consciousness, the transcending of the I-consciousness, the falling away of limitations. As is well known to all students, there are four degree of development covered by the Christ-stage, between the thoroughly good man and the triumphant Master. Each of these degrees is entered by an Initiation, and during these degrees of evolution consciousness is to expand, to grow, to reach the limits possible within the restrictions imposed by the human body. In the first of these, the change experienced is the awakening of consciousness in the spiritual world, in the world where consciousness identifies itself with the life, and ceases to identify itself with the forms in which the life may at the moment be imprisoned. The characteristic of this awakening is a feeling of sudden expansion, and of widening out beyond the habitual limits of the life, the recognition of a Self, divine and puissant which is life, not form; joy, not sorrow; the feeling of a marvelous peace, passing all of which the world can dream. With the falling away of limitations comes an increased intensity of life, as though life flowed in from every side rejoicing over the barriers removed, so vivid a feeling of reality that all life in a form seems as death, and earthly light as darkness. It is an expansion so marvelous in its nature, that consciousness feels as though it had never known itself before, for all it had regarded as consciousness is as unconsciousness in the presence of this upwelling life. Self-consciousness, which commenced to germinate in child-humanity, which has developed, grown, expanded ever within the limitations of form, thinking itself separate, feeling ever "I", speaking ever of "me" and "mine"—this

Self-consciousness suddenly feels all selves as Self, all forms as common property. He sees that limitations were necessary for the building of a centre of Selfhood in which self-identity might persist, and at the same time he feels that the form is only an instrument he uses while he himself, the living consciousness, is one in all that lives. He knows the full meaning of the oft-spoken phrase the "unity of humanity", and feels what it is to live in all that lives and moves, and this consciousness is accompanied with an immense joy, that joy of life which even in its faint reflections upon earth is one of the keenest ecstasies known to man. The unity is not only seen by the intellect, but it is felt as satisfying the yearning for union which all know who have loved; it is a unity felt from within, not seen from without; it is not a conception but a life.

In many pages of old, but ever on the same lines, has the birth of the Christ in man been figured. And yet how all words shaped for the world of forms fail to image forth the world of life!

But the child must grow into the perfect man, and there is much to do, much weariness to face, many sufferings to endure, many combats to wage, many obstacles to overcome, ere the Christ born in the feebleness of infancy may reach the stature of the Perfect Man. There is the life of labour among his brother-men; there is the facing of ridicule and suspicion; there is the delivery of a despised message; there is the agony of desertion, and the passion of the cross, and the darkness of the tomb. All these lie before him in the path on which he has entered.

By continual practice, the disciple must learn to assimilate the consciousness of others, and to centre his own consciousness in life, not in form, so that he may pass beyond the "heresy of separateness", which makes him regard others as different from himself. He has to expand his consciousness by daily practice, until its normal state is that which he temporarily experienced at his first Initiation. To this end he will endeavour in his everyday life to identify his consciousness with the consciousness of those with whom he comes into contact day by day; he will strive to feel as they feel, to think as they think, to rejoice as they rejoice, to suffer as they suffer. Gradually he must develop a perfect sympathy, a sympathy which can vibrate in harmony with every string of the human lyre. Gradually he must learn to answer, as if it were his own, to every sensation of another, however high he may be or however low. Gradually, by constant practice, he must identify himself with others in all the varied circumstances of their different lives. He must learn the lesson of joy and the lesson of tears, and this is only possible when he has transcended the separated self, when he no longer asks ought for himself, but understands that he must henceforth live in life alone.

His first sharp struggle is to put aside all that up to this point has been for him life, consciousness, reality, and walk forth alone, naked, no longer identifying himself with any form. He has to learn the law of life, by which alone the inner divinity can manifest, the law which is the antithesis of his past. The law of form is taking; the law of life is giving. Life grows by pouring itself out through form, fed by the inexhaustible source of life at the heart of the universe; the more the life pours itself out the greater the inflow from within. It seems at first to the young Christ as though all his life were leaving him, as though his hands were left empty after outpouring their gifts on a thankless world; only when the lower nature has been definitely sacrificed is the eternal life experienced, and that which seemed the death of being is found to be a birth into a fuller life.

THE SECOND INITIATION

Thus consciousness develops, until the first stage of the path is trodden, and the disciple sees before him the second portal of Initiation, symbolised in the Christian Scriptures as the Baptism of the Christ. At this, as he descends into the waters of the world's sorrows, the river that every Saviour of men must be baptised, in, a new flood of divine life is poured out upon him; his consciousness realises itself as the Son, in whom the life of the Father finds fit expression, He feels the life of the Monad, his Father in Heaven, flowing into his consciousness, and realises that he is one, not with men only, but also with his heavenly Father, and that he lives on earth only to be the expression of the Father's will, his manifested organism. Henceforth is his ministry to men the most patent fact of his life. He is the Son, to whom men should listen, because from him the hidden life flows forth, and he has become a channel through which that hidden life can reach the outer world. He is the priest of the Mystery God, who has entered within the veil, and comes forth with the glory shining from his face, which is the reflection of the light in the sanctuary.

It is there that he begins that work of love symbolised in the outer ministry by his willingness to heal and to relieve; round him press the souls seeking light and life, attracted by his inner force and by the divine life manifested in the accredited Son of the Father. Hungry souls come to him, and he gives them bread; souls suffering from the disease of sin come, and he heals them by his living word; souls blinded by ignorance come, and he illumines them by wisdom. It is one of the signs of a Christ in his ministry, that the abandoned and the poor, the desperate and the degraded, come to him without the sense of separation. They feel a welcoming sympathy and not a repelling; for kindness radiates from his person, and the love that understands flows out around him. Truly they know not that he is an evolving Christ, but they feel a power that raises, a life which vitalises, and in his atmosphere they inbreathe new strength, new hope.

THE THIRD INITIATION

The third Portal is before him, which admist him to another stage of his progress, and he has a brief moment of peace, of glory, of illumination, symbolised in Christian writings by the Transfiguration. It is a pause in his life, a brief cessation of his active service, a journey to the Mountain whereon broods the peace of heaven, and there—side by side with some who have recognised his evolving divinity—that divinity shines forth for a moment in its transcendent beauty. During this lull in the combat, he sees his future; a series of pictures unrolls before his eyes; he beholds the sufferings which lie before him, the solitude of Gethsemane, the agony of Calvary. Thenceforth his face is set steadfastly towards Jerusalem, towards the darkness he is to enter for the love of mankind. He understands that ere he can reach the perfect realisation of unity he must experience the quintessence of solitude. Hitherto, while conscious of the growing life, it has seemed to him to come to him from without; now he is to realise that its centre is within him; in solitude of heart he must experience the true unity of the Father and the Son, an interior and not an outer unity, and then the loss even of the Father's Face; and for this all external contact with men, and even with God, must be cut off, that within his own Spirit he may find the One.

THE DARK NIGHT OF THE SOUL

As the dark hour approaches, he is more and more appalled by the failure of the human sympathies on which he has been wont to rely during the past years of life and service, and when, in the critical moment of his need, he looks around for comfort and sees his friends wrapt in indifferent slumber, it seems to him that all human ties are broken, that all human love is a mockery, all human faith a betrayal; he is flung back upon himself to learn that only the tie with his Father in heaven remains, that all embodied aid is useless. It has been said that in this hour of solitude the soul is filled with bitterness, and that rarely a soul passes over this gulf of voidness without a cry of anguish; it is then that bursts forth the agonised reproach: "Couldst thou not wath with me one hour?"—but no human hand may clasp another in that Gethsemane of desolation.

When this darkness of human desertion is overpast, then, despite the shrinking of the human nature from the cup, comes the deeper darkness of the hour when a gulf seems to open between the Father and the Son, between the life embodied and the life infinite. The Father, who was yet realised in Gethsemane when all human friends were slumbering, is veiled in the passion of the Cross. It is the bitterest of all the ordeals of the Initiate, when even the consciousness of the life of Sonship is lost, and the hour of the hoped-for triumph becomes that of the deepest ignominy. He sees his enemies exultant around him; he sees himself abandoned by his friend and his lovers; he feels the divine support crumble away beneath his feet; and he drinks to the last drop the cup of solitude, of isolation, no contact with man or god bridging the void in which hangs his helpless soul. Then from the heart that feels itself deserted even by the Father rings out the cry: "My God! my God! why hast *Thou* forsaken me?" Why this last proof, this last ordeal, this most cruel of all illusions? Illusion, for the dying Christ is nearest of all to the divine Heart.

Because the Son must know himself to be one with the Father he seeks, must find god not only within him but as his innermost Self; only when he knows that the Eternal is himself and he the Eternal, is he beyond the possibility of the sense of separation. Then and then only, can he perfectly help his race, and become a conscious part of the uplifting energy.

THE GLORY OF PERFECTION

The Christ triumphant, the Christ of the Resurrection and Ascension, has felt the bitterness of death, has known all human suffering, and has risen above it by the power of his own divinity. What now can trouble his peace, or check his outstretched hand of help? During his evolution he learned to receive into himself the currents of human troubles and to send them forth again as currents of peace and joy. Within the circle of his then activity, this was his work, to transmute forces of discord into forces of harmony. Now he must do it for the world for the humanity out of which he has flowered. The Christs and their disciples, each in the measure of his evolution, thus protect and help the world, and far bitterer would be the struggle, far more desperate the combats of humanity, were it not for the presence of these in its midst, whose hands bear up "the heavy karma of the world".

Even those who are at the earliest stage of the Path become lifting forces in evolution, as in truth are all who unselfishly work for others, though these more deliberately and continuously. But the Christ triumphant does completely what others do at varying stages of imperfection, and therefore is he called a "Saviour", and this characteristic in him is perfect. He saves, not by substituting himself for us, but by sharing with us his life. He is wise, and all men are the wiser for his wisdom, for his life flows into all men's veins and pulses, in all men's hearts. He is not tied to a form, not separate from any. He is the Ideal Man, the Perfect Man; each human being is a cell in his body, and each cell is nourished by his life.

Surely it had not been worth while to suffer on the Cross and to tread the Path that leads thereto, simply to win a little earlier his own liberation, to be at rest a little sooner. The cost would have been too heavy for such a gain, the strife to bitter for such a prize. Nay, but in his triumph humanity is exalted, and the path trodden by all feet is rendered a little shorter. The evolution of the whole race is accelerated; the pilgrimage of each is made less long. This was the thought that inspired him in the violence of the combat, that sustained his strength, that softened the pangs of loss. Not one being, however feeble, however degraded, however ignorant, however sinful, who is not a little nearer to the light when a son of the Highest has finished his course. How the speed of evolution will be quickened as more and more of these Sons rise triumphant, and enter into conscious life eternal! How swiftly will turn the wheel which lifts man into divinity as more and more men become consciously divine!

THE INSPIRING IDEAL

Herrein lies the stimulus for each of us who, in our noblest moments, has felt the attraction of the life poured out for love of men. Let us think of the sufferings of the world that knows not why it suffers;

of the misery, the despair of men who know not why they live, and why they die; who, day after day, year after year, see sufferings fall upon themselves and others and understand not their reason; who fight with desperate courage, or who furiously revolt against conditions they cannot comprehend or justify. Let us think of the agony born of blindness, of the darkness in which they grope, without hope, without aspiration, without knowledge of the true life, and of the beauty beyond the veil. Let us think of the millions of our brothers in the darkness, and then of the uplifting energies born of our sufferings, our struggles, and our sacrifices. We can raise them a step towards the light, alleviate their paints, diminish their ignorance, abridge their journey towards the knowledge which is light and life. Who of us is there that knows even a little that will not give himself for these who know naught?

We know by the Law immutable, by Truth unswerving, by the endless Life and God, that all divinity is within us, and that though it be now but little evolved, all is there of infinite capacity, available for the uplifting of the world. Surely then there is not one, able to feel the pulsing of the Divine Life, who is not attracted by the hope to help and bless. And if this Life be felt, however feebly, for however brief a time, it is because in the hearth there is the first thrill of that which will unfold as the Christ-life, because the time approaches for the birth of the Christ-babe, because in such a one humanity is seeking to flower.

THE MASTERS AS FACTS AND IDEALS

"The Masters, as Facts and Ideals."—I have taken the double title, for there are some who know Them not as facts, to whom yet the ideal is valuable, precious, and inspiring. Not every member of the Theosophical Society believes in the existence of (Mahātmās). There are many within the limits of the Society who have no knowledge and no belief upon the subject; and it is the rule of our Society that no declaration of faith shall be asked from anyone who enters, save in the Brotherhood of man, without the distinctions that on the surface are set up. So that within the limits of the Society you may have alike believer and non-believer in the present existence or the past existence of these great Teachers. But I, who believe in them, and know them to exist, speak here not in the name of the Society which has no creed, but in my own and in the name of orders who share this belief or this knowledge will myself and refers not I am going to place what I believe to be rational evidence worthy of consideration—evidence that you can think over at leisure and make up your minds upon as you will;

and I speak also for the sake of the ideal, for the ideals of the race are precious, and cannot lightly be either outraged or denied. For great is this ideal of the Mahātmā, despite the idle laughter that has been used—for the name is merely the Samskrit for Great Spirit. There is not one great religion that has raised and elevated the minds of men, there is not one mighty faith that has led millions to a knowledge of the spiritual life and the possibilities of human growth, there is not one that has not founded that belief on a Divine Man, there is not one that does not look back, as its Founder, to one of these mighty Souls who have brought knowledge of spiritual truth to the world. Look back to the past as you will, take what faith you choose. Every one of them is founded on this same ideal, and looks backward for its Teacher to a Man who is divine in his life. Around this ideal gather all the hopes of men, around this ideal gather the future destinies of humanity. For unless man be a spiritual Being, unless he has within himself the possibility of spiritual unfoldment, unless there be some evidence available that men have become perfect, that it is not only a dream of the future, but a reality which the race has already realised, unless it be true that for you and for me there are open the same mighty possibilities that have been proved possible in the past by those who have achieved me in longings of men after perception have in them no certainty of realisation, humanity remains but the thing of a day, instead of being heir to a boundless immortality. That man may become divine, that is an idea which has inspired the greatest of our race, which has cheered the miserable in their agony, and has glorified the future with hope. That is why I defend the ideal. For who is the Mahātmā? He is the man who has become perfect, he is the man who has reached union with the Divine, he is the man who by slow degrees has developed the possibilities of the spiritual nature, and stands triumphant where we are struggling today. Every religion has borne witness to him. Every religion of the world looks back to a Divine Teacher. You may have the name of Zoroaster in Persia, of the Kṛṣhṇa in India, of the Buddha in latter days, of the Christ in Palestine, every one of them is the Divine Man, who has brought the certainty of human perfection to those who have come within the range of His influence.

A THEORY

What shall be the line of our evidence? I first suggest a probable theory on the lines of natural evolution. Then I propose to turn to the evidence for the existence of these perfected Divine Men in the past;

to come on from that to the evidence for their existence in the present; then—because without this last part the lecture would remain unpractical for us—then to show how it is possible for men to become perfect, a slight sketch at least of the methods by which the Divine Man becomes.

First, then, for the theory that the existence of Masters in itself probable and in accordance with the analogy of nature as we see it around us, as we know it in the past. Few today, probably, will dispute the fact of evolution. Few will deny that our race progresses, and that cycle after cycle you will find nations advancing and reaching higher and higher pinnacles of knowledge, higher and higher pinnacles in growth and in development. Theoretically there is nothing impossible or absurd in the theory that taking into consideration the vast periods of time which have elapsed since man first trod this earth, taking into consideration the enormous differences between primitive and highly developed, and the vast spaces of time for evolution that lie behind us in the past, it is not, at least, irrational or absurd that evolution may have been carried to a point in the case of some individuals much above the evolution of the civilised man of today.

Nor is that all. It is not only that we have enormous ranges of time behind us, but that there are traces of mighty civilisation which show that the race had climbed high in knowledge, high in philosophy, high in science and in religion, thousands upon thousands of years ago, nay! I might say centuries of thousands of years. For looking backwards you see traces of might civilisations which imply the presence of men of a most advanced type, and it is scarcely rational to suppose that the so much talked-of-evolution has been nothing more than a mere ebb and flow, leaving nothing as result, nothing more than successive periods of high civilisation and then of utter barbarism, and civilisation again re-begun with no links to preserve continuity of knowledge. It is not at least impossible, and in a moment we shall see signs that it is probable, that out of that mighty past some will have grown upwards, advancing higher and higher and perfecting the human race in individuals, as slowly all will in turn become perfect. Not impossible, not even improbable, remembering that progress is the law of nature, and the vast spaces of time during which humanity has lived.

HISTORICAL EVIDENCE

But from that mere possibility, which I take because it is well to clear out of the way at the outset the idea that the theory is in itself impossible and absurd, let us take historical evidence and see whether history does not, from time to time, show some gigantic human figures which stand out above and beyond the men of their time and the ordinary height of humanity; whether there is not evidence which cannot be denied that such Men are not merely the products of popular imagination, that they are not merely men of the past, exaggerated by popular tradition and seen magnified, as it were, through the haze of centuries. I speak of those Great Ones to whom I alluded who have been the Founders of the great religions of the world.

It is not only that there is unbroken tradition, and that the religions remain which these Men builded, but there is more than tradition, there is more than a religion which has grown; there is a literature, marked, definite, distinct, whose antiquity no scholar denies, although some may claim for it a vaster antiquity than others may be ready to concede. Take the later dates that would be given by the Orientalists who have studied the literature of China, of Persia, of India, to say nothing of later times. Certain books are regarded as sacred, books for which the religion has claimed what may fairly be termed an immemorial antiquity. You have amongst the Chinese their ancient sacred books; you have amongst the Pārsis, the followers of Zoroaster, their books. You have from India the Veḍas, the Upanishads, to say nothing of the later works, and I might, without possibility of challenge, give long lists of mighty works which are held as Scriptures by the believers in these faiths.

Who wrote those works, and whence the knowledge? That they exist is obvious. That they must have authors can scarcely be denied. And yet those works from a far-off antiquity show a depth of spiritual knowledge, a depth of philosophic thought, a depth of insight into human nature, and a depth of moral teaching so magnificent, that the greatest minds of our own day, both in morals and in philosophy, must admit that the modern world can show nothing which even approaches them in sublimity.

It is not a question of tradition, but of books; not a question of theory, but of fact; for if the books are so great, the morality so pure, the philosophy so sublime, and the knowledge so vast, their authors must have had the knowledge which therein you find incorporated. And the testimony of millions upon millions of human beings answers to the reality of the spiritual truth, and nations are guided by the teachings that thus have come down. Nor is that all. These teachings are similar wherever you find them. The same teaching of the unity of the Divine Life out of which the universe has grown; the same teaching of the identity of the Spirit in man with the Spirit from which the universe has come; the same teaching that man by certain methods may develop the spiritual Life in himself and come into positive knowledge of divinity, and not only hope and faith.

So that you have, coming down from far-off times, at least this fact which cannot be denied: that some men lived in the far-off past whose thought was great enough, whose morality was pure enough, whose philosophy was sublime enough, to outlast the wrecks of civilisation and the destructive force of time. Today Orientalists are translating for the teaching of the modern world that which mighty men of old once taught, and find the grandest thoughts to which the human race has given birth in these Scriptures that have come down from the most ancient times.

That some then have lived far greater than ourselves, that some have lived whose knowledge goes far beyond the knowledge that we possess, that we still learn in philosophy and in spiritual matters from these Teachers who spoke millenniums ago; that is a fact that cannot be denied. That there have been Divine Men in the past that we speak of as Mahātmās, that they have left the testimony to their existence in this mighty and sublime literature, that is the first line of argument—the establishment of the existence in the past, the proof that such Men have lived and have taught, and that by their teaching they have guided and helped millions of the human race. That their teaching has been identical in its main outlines, that their teaching is identical in its moral force, that the spiritual truths enunciated an unchanged have come down through the centuries: so far, at least, can we speak with certainty, the ground so far is solid beneath our feet.

The statements in this literature appeal to human experience. They not only say that certain things are, but they say these things can be known. They not only declare the reality of the soul, but they say that that reality can be proved; so that the teaching stands in this position, that it announces certain alleged facts which remain verifiable for all time, thereby affording a continually accumulating proof of the reality of the knowledge of those who first gave the statements to the world.

FIRST-HAND EXPERIENCE

Pass from that to the next point in the argument—that these statements have been verified by experience and are being verified today. Take, for instance, such a land as India. There you have an unbroken tradition, a tradition which comes down to the present time, a tradition that there always have been Teachers who may be found, Teachers who possess the knowledge which is hinted at in the books of which I speak, who can add the practical teaching to the theoretical statement, and enable people to verify by experiment that which is said to be true in the literature to which I have alluded. Ask any Indian of today what is his belief on this question, and he will tell you, if he has not been westernised, and you can gain his confidence, that always in his land there has remained the belief that these Men have existed in the past and have not passed out of existence in the present; that they have more and more withdrawn from the ordinary haunts of men, that they have become more and more difficult to discover as materiality has made its way and spirituality has diminished; but that still they can occasionally be found, that still the first steps of the Path are open.

And not only is there that belief, but you will find scattered throughout India many, many men who, while they have not reached the point of Mahātmāship, have taken certain steps above the physical plane, and have developed in themselves powers and capacities which the ordinary Westerner would look on as absolutely impossible of attainment. I do not now speak of the Mahātmās, but of the hundreds of so-called yogis scattered through the jungles and the mountains of India, some of whom habitually exercise remarkable powers—powers which here would seem incredible, but of which there is ever-accumulating testimony coming from the mouths of travellers who collect and who record the facts with which they themselves have come in contact. For the earlier stages of the development of the inner man are not so difficult of attainment, and in a country like India, where there is not the difficulty of scepticism to overcome, because there the belief has existed for thousands of years, you will find many a man who exercises the lower psychical powers, and a few who have gone far beyond that stage and exercise either the higher psychic faculties or the really spiritual powers of man.

And you can find some who have personal experience, some who have individual knowledge of Teachers, of Masters, who train their pupils in the higher path of what is called the Rāja, or the Kingly, Yoga, that is, the Yoga which primarily trains the mind rather than the body, which works by concentration of the mind, by meditation and by the evolution of the higher mental faculties, on which there is so much discussion here, and who by a definite system of training are able to consciously use powers of the mind which enable the possessor to pass beyond physical limitations, and passing out of the body to receive instruction which he is able then to bring back to the lower consciousness and impress on the physical brain, proving by his knowledge the reality of his teaching, and proving the existence of his Master by his knowledge which from him he has obtained.

That then would be the next line of evidence available. Not available, you may fairly retort, to the majority. But then you are surely bound to remember, as reasonable men and women, that if you desire knowledge you must seek it where the knowledge is to be found, and that it is as absurd for a number of men, who have never investigated, who have never even tried to investigate, who have never travelled, to write on that of which they have no knowledge, as it would be for some simple Indian, who has never had the slightest experience of Western experiments, say in the Royal Institution, to sit down and declare that those are absolutely impossible and ludicrous, because he himself has not travelled here and has not had the opportunity of seeing them performed. You must deal with evidence on rational lines, and if you cannot yourselves come into contact with certain facts, with certain phases of human life, you must either remain ignorant—and then you should be silent—or you should take the testimony of those who have carefully investigated, and have laid the result of their investigations before you.

HOW CAN WE FIND THE MASTERS?

And that leads me to my next line of argument. Suppose such Men existed in the past, suppose we admit, as every religion admits for its own Founder—though it may deny as to the Founders of other religions—suppose we admit that in the past Divine Men have lived, suppose that, believing in the immortality of the Spirit, we admit that they must still exist somewhere if they ever existed at all; then the next question will be: Do these Men of the past exist in the present? Can they be reached? Can they be known? And are there others who have reached a similar point, whose existence may be supported by evidence which at least is worthy of consideration? Do they still exist?

Here I am going into a line of thought which I should adopt if I were trying to prove to you the existence of any person living in a country which you had not visited, living under conditions which you had not yourself experienced. That it can be absolutely demonstrated in every case I admit to be impossible. I cannot demonstrate to you, for instance, the existence of Count Tolstoi. If you do not travel to Russia, if he does not happen to come here, and you do not happen to meet him, I cannot show you as an absolute matter of demonstration that he exists. But I could bring evidence that would convince any reasonable man; I could show evidence which would be admitted in any Court of Law; I could show you that there is no reason for denying his existence merely because you have not personally met him, and therefore obtained what you would call ocular proof of his existence.

H.P. BLAVATSKY

Now what is the proof for the existence of Divine, of Perfect Men living at the present time, reachable under certain conditions? What evidence can I submit to you for that? There are many of you probably who will object to my first witness; but not for the objection am I going to hold back her name—I speak of H.P. Blavatsky. I know the attacks that from every side have been made upon her. In face of those, having read, and read them carefully, I say that there remains enough evidence coming through her, untouched by those attacks, sufficient to put before you for your consideration, and sufficient to win the assent of rational men. Take if you will, for a moment—though I should deny it—take if you will some of the worst of those charges—that she had no contact with the Mahātmās at all, that she invented them, that they did not exist outside her imagination, and that everything she said was falsehood, everything that she said and did was intended to mislead. Still you have to deal with the facts of her life, and with the facts of her books.

"THE SECRET DOCTRINE"

You have to deal with the book known as *The Secret Doctrine*, and if you want to understand that you must read it before you waive it aside, and study it before you laugh at it. Madame Blavatsky has been accused of plagiarism, that she borrowed here, there and everywhere from other books. But what you have to consider is this: that she never claimed that she discovered the knowledge she gave to the world; that her contention is that this knowledge comes down from a far-off past, is found in every Scripture, in every philosophy; and the very purpose of that book is to quote from every direction, from the Scriptures of every religion, from the writings of every people, in order to show the identity of the teaching and to prove the antiquity of the doctrine.

What is new in the book is not facts that therein you find. What is new in the book is not what has been found by Orientalists, and may be pointed to in one or another sacred book of the world. What is new is the knowledge which enabled her to select from the whole of these the facts which build up a single, mighty conception of the evolution of the universe, the evolution of man, the coherent synthesis of the whole cosmogony. And that is her title to be the greatest teacher of our time, because she had real knowledge, not mere book-learning, knowledge which enabled her to collect from scattered books the truths which, fitted together, made one mighty whole; because she held the clue which she was able to follow with unerring accuracy through the maze, and show that all the scattered materials contained within them the possibility of the single building. And her work is the more wonderful because she did it not being a scholar; because she did it not having had the education which would have enabled her to some extent to piece this knowledge together; because she did what no Orientalists have done with all their learning; what not all the Orientalists together have done with all the help of their knowledge of Eastern tongues and their study of Eastern literature. There is not one of them who out of that tangled mass brought out that mighty synthesis; not one of them who out of that chaos was able to build up a cosmos. But this Russian woman who was no scholar, and pretended to be none, somewhere or other she gained a knowledge that enabled her to do what none of your scholars can do, somewhere or other she had a teaching which enabled her to reduce this chaos to order, and to bring out a mighty scheme of evolution which makes us understand the universe and man. She said it was not hers, she never claimed to have originated it; she was always speaking of her own want of knowledge and referring to those who taught her.

But the fact you have to meet is this—the knowledge is there, and stands there for criticism. Not one other person has done it, although the same materials that she used are open to the whole of the world. And my answer is: Give us then some others who can do as she did. Let us have some more of this plagiarism which is able to gather from so many sources everything that is necessary for a mighty philosophy. Let your scholars do it, and help us to understand, as she helps us to understand, the religions of the world. Let them show us the identity, let them show us the reality, and then we may begin perhaps to revise our opinion of her; but until that is done her claim remains unshaken, even though you should prove that she may have erred in much, and even although stones may be thrown at her by those who can never rival her in unselfishness, in self-sacrifice and in knowledge.

The reason that you cannot shake us in our belief in this is because she helped us to knowledge, because we gained from her teaching that which none other gave, because she opened up to us ways of gaining further knowledge along the same lines, and from the same Teachers who had taught her. That is why we remain such fools as people think us, in clinging to her and clinging to her memory, for we owe her a debt of gratitude that we never shall be able to pay, and never shall stone be cast upon her grave which I will not try to lift off it, for the sake of the knowledge to which she led me, and the priceless benefits that she gave me in the teaching which she began.

Now the evidence that I ask you to take from her is not the evidence of phenomena. I put that on one side. It is not the evidence of scholarship. She had none, she never portended to it. It is not the question as to whether or not her life from her childhood was perfect. It is that she had certain definite knowledge acquired somehow, which cannot be accounted for by ordinary education, which she obtained in a comparatively short space of time, which astonished her own family and friends when first she produced it, and which she said she got from certain Teachers—the important fact being that she possessed it, however it may have come into her possession.

That is the evidence that I want to lay stress upon, because that is the point which cannot be shaken, and it removes her testimony for the moment from the whole question of fraud of any sort; it remains above it and beyond it. There remains the fact of this knowledge embodied in *The Secret Doctrine,* which stands there as a witness to her, and which I venture to say cannot be overthrown; and the more you degrade her, the less you make of her, the more you prove the existence of and exalt the Great Ones who worked through her, and gave her what she produced.

"THE VOICE OF THE SILENCE"

Now, there is another point about another book of hers which is to me of special interest, a book that you may know, *The Voice of the Silence:* that book happened to be written while I was with her at

Fontainebleau. It is a small book, and in what I am going to say I speak only of the book itself: I am not speaking of the notes; those were done afterwards. The book itself is what may be called a prose poem in three divisions. She wrote it at Fontainebleau, and the greater part was done when I was with her, and I sat in the room while she was writing it. I know that she did not write it referring to any books, but she wrote it down steadily, hour after hour, exactly as though she were writing either from memory or from reading it where no book was. She produced, in the evening, that manuscript that I saw her write as I sat with her, and asked myself and others to correct it for English, for she said that she had written it so quickly that it was sure to be bad. We did not alter in that more than a few words, and it remains as a specimen of marvellously beautiful literary work, putting everything else aside.

The book is as I said, a prose poem, full of spiritual inspiration, full of food for the heart; stimulating the loftiest virtue and containing the noblest ideals. It is not a hotch-potch drawn from various sources, but a coherent, ethical whole. It moves us, not by a statement of facts gathered from books, but by an appeal to the divinest instincts of our nature: it is its own best testimony to the source whence it came.

PERSONAL KNOWLEDGE

Pass now from Madame Blavatsky herself to those she taught. Mr. A.P. Sinnett is one of them. Many others are living, here and elsewhere, whom she taught at first, and who have passed from her training into and under the training of her Teachers. And here you have an accumulating testimony of men and women who, of their own authority, by first-hand evidence, out of their own experience, testify to the reality of the existence of these Teachers, and to their own personal knowledge of them, and of the teaching which they have personally received from them.

Mr. Sinnett has alluded to evidence extending in his own case over fifteen years. Many others have done the same, like Countess Wachtmeister, like Colonel Olcott, like others who have given their own individual testimony. Are you going to say that all these people are frauds? With what right do you so condemn them? Are you going to say that they are all fools? But they are men and women living the ordinary life, men and women who amongst those who know them stand as persons of education, of intelligence, showing the ordinary powers of discrimination and of knowledge that others possess. Are you going to say that we are all mad? That is rather a rash assertion to make against constantly growing numbers of apparently reasonable men and women. What other sort of evidence can you demand for the existence of anyone save the evidence of those who know him, of persons of integrity and of honour who are living amongst yourselves? We bear to these our personal testimony, not founded on documents, not founded on writings, not founded simply on letters, and so on, on which there is always possibility of deception arising, but on individual communion with individual Teachers, and teaching received which otherwise we could not have gained. That is the kind of evidence you have to deal with; and no case of proving fraud against one or two or three people will upset the accumulating testimony of reasonable men and women, who are coming into connection with those Teaches, and who bear testimony to what they themselves know. That is the kind of evidence that you have to meet, that the kind of testimony that you have to overthrow. And however much you may be amused at smart and clever writing, which takes advantage of the deception practised by one in order to discredit the whole, you can no more discredit this mass of testimony by proving one man to be fraudulent, than you can challenge, say, the reality of real coin because a forger may circulate some false coin in a community, and people may pass the coin for the moment, and may be deceived into believing that it is real.

But you may say: We want first-hand evidence for ourselves. You can have it; but you must take the way. You can have the evidence amounting to demonstration for yourselves if you choose to take the trouble, if you choose to give the time. Not an unreasonable demand.

If you want to verify for yourselves the experiments of some great chemist, can you do it by simply going into a laboratory and mixing together the things that you find there? If you want to verify some of the latest experiments in chemical science, do you suppose that you can do it for yourselves, without giving years of trouble and of study to master the science in which you want to carry out a critical experiment? And what would you think of the value of the criticism of some person absolutely ignorant of chemistry, if he said the experiment could not be performed, merely because he was not able to do it without training and without knowledge?

THE WAY TO ADEPTSHIP

Therefore I said that I would tell you how the Mahātmā becomes. For only those who are willing to aim at that goal can obtain the absolute demonstration of the existence of those who have achieved. That is the price that has to be paid. And without this only probability? Yes, reasonable probability; testimony of others which you would accept on any other matter, on which, in a law-court, you would pass vast sums of money, large estates, or anything else; that you can have by simply looking into the available evidence of which I have been sketching merely the outline. But personal demonstration? For that you must begin yourselves to develop in the way in which their development has been made; and in order that anyone who desires may begin to follow that line and follow it to its natural ending, there have been published to the world the preliminary steps upon the Path, the steps that are taken by those who attain the knowledge, the steps that anyone may begin to take, and by which he in his turn may acquire a certainty similar to that which some of us possess. Two little books, especially, have been published, which trace the beginnings of the Path, one called *Light on the Path,* the other, the one to which I alluded, before *The Voice of the Silence;* and in addition to those there are many hints scattered through Theosophical literature.

How then should ordinary man and women begin? If they desire to get evidence for themselves as to the possibility of this development, which in the end will make the Perfect Man—the man become Divine—the first, the early steps, are those which every religion has taught—carefulness and unselfishness in life, discharge of duty in whatever place in life man or woman may happen to be. To use the phrase which is used in this book[1]: "Follow the wheel of life; follow the wheel of duty to race and kin"; that is a preliminary. For those who would gain knowledge of the Soul must begin in this way, which has ever been taught by the leaving off of evil ways, and by the following of good; by purity in life, by service to men, by the unselfish effort, continually repeated, to be useful in whatever place one may be in by the law of nature. The endeavour to discharge to the fullest every obligation, the endeavour to live a life which shall leave the world better than it was found, the endeavour to live nobly, unselfishly, and purely—these are conditions laid down for those who would find the Path.

REINCARNATION

Here let me say that unless reincarnation be true, then most certainly this development is not possible. In no one human life could that long Path be trodden; in no new-born Soul could be developed these divine possibilities; unless it be true that the Soul of man comes back life after life to earth, bringing with it to every new life the experience of the lives behind, building up higher and higher character life after life, then indeed the Mahātmā would be an impossibility, and the perfection of man would be but the dream of the poet. Reincarnation is taken for granted in the whole of this teaching, as a fundamental fact in nature, on which the perfection of the individual must depend.

TO LIVE NOBLY

First then, a man through many lives must set himself to live well, to live usefully, to live nobly, so that he may be born time after time with higher and higher qualities, with nobler and nobler faculties. Next, there is a stage in this human evolution, marked and definite, where the Soul, having long been struggling upwards, raises itself a little beyond the ordinary evolution of man. There are men and women who are exceptionally unselfish, who show exceptional capacities, exceptional intuitions, exceptional love for spiritual things, exceptional devotion to the service to mankind; when those exceptional qualities begin to manifest themselves, then comes the time when one of the great Teachers takes that person in hand individually, in order to guide the further evolution and to train the evolving Soul. The earlier efforts must be made in concert with the great spiritual forces which spread through all the world. But when those have been utilised, when men and women have done their best, as it were, along this line of general spiritual growth, then comes the stage when the Teacher comes forward to guide the further evolution, and certain definite demands are made, if this further evolution is to proceed.

These are laid down in the books to which I alluded. Summed up in a phrase, or rather in two phrases, they might be called "the realisation of non-separateness", which I will explain in a moment, and "rigid self-discipline". Non-separateness on the one side, self discipline upon the other. Now "non-separateness" is a technical world, which means this: that you realise that you are one fundamentally with all that lives and breathes, that you do not separate yourself from any living thing, that you separate yourself neither from the sinner nor from the saint, neither from the highest nor from the lowest of mankind. Nay, not even from the lower forms of living things, and things called non-living, which you recognise as being one in essence, and one with your innermost Self. How shall it be shown? It is shown by the elaborate attempt and training to begin to identify yourself with the sufferings, with the feelings, and with the wants of man. You are told: "Let thy soul lend its ear to every cry of pain like as the lotus bares its heart to drink the morning sun. Let not the fierce sun dry one tear of pain, before thyself has wiped it from the sufferer's eye."

But that is not all. "Let each burning human tear drop on thy heart and there remain; nor ever brush it off, until the pain that caused it is removed."[2] There is the first note. Go out to the sufferer and relieve his pain; but relieving his pain, let it wring your own heart, and let it remain there as a constant suffering until the cause of that pain has been removed. That is the first stage of non-separateness. Identify yourself with the sorrows and the joys of the world; let the sorrow of every one be your sorrow, the pain of every one your pain, the joy of every one your joy. Your heart must answer to every thrill in other hearts, as the string gives back the note of music to which it has been attuned. You must feel the pain, you must feel the agony; you must feel the sin and the shame as your sin and your shame, and make it part of your own consciousness, and bear it, and never try to escape therefrom. You must train yourself in a sensitiveness which will answer to every suffering of mankind, and you must carry that out in deed as well as in feeling; for you are told again that "Inaction in a deed of mercy becomes an action in a deadly sin."

But you must not only realise the pain of the world and make it yours; you must be as hard to yourself as you are tender to those around. You have no time to spend on your own troubles, if the trouble of the world is to become yours. You have no strength to waste on 'aments over your own grief, if you are to be identified with the sorrows of mankind. And so it is said that you must be as hard as the stone of the mango-fruit to your own pains and sorrows, while soft as its pulp to the pains and sorrows of other men.

And thus life after life you must be trained, life after life becoming more and more identified with all, and breaking down everything that separates man from man. That is why brotherhood is your only condition; because the recognition of that is the first step towards this realisation of non-separateness, which is necessary if the disciple is to progress. And the definite training of the disciple is a training which makes him sensitive to the sorrows of all, in order that, feeling, he may be ready to help, and which trains him in this self-identification with the whole, in order that he may at last become one of the Saviorus of the world. For as this training proceeds life after life, there gradually develops in this human being an evergrowing sympathy, an ever-deepening compassion, a charity which nothing can stain, and a tolerance which nothing can shake. No injury can give offence, for the sorrow is for the one who does the injury, and not for the blow which is struck at oneself. No anger can arise against any wrong, for you understand why the wrong is done, and you sorrow for the doer and have no time to waste in anger. You will not condone wrong, you will not say that wrong is right, you will not pretend that good is evil, for that would be the greatest cruelty and would make the progress of the race impossible. But while rcognising the evil, there will be no anger against the evil-doer, for he is one with your Soul, and you recognize no separation between yourself and him.

To what end? Because, as this growth proceeds, memory and knowledge will grow; because, as this growth proceeds, the developing life of the Spirit within the disciple will show itself out more and more in the walks of men, and gradually he will become marked out as a worker for man, a helper for man, a toiler for man, working for him to enlighten his ignorance, to bring him knowledge, and to show him the reality that underies all the illusions in the world. And he must be hard to himself because he is to stand between man and evil, because he is to stand between his weaker brothers and the dark powers that otherwise might crush them.

The illustrations given here of what the disciple must be are that he is to be like a star which gives light to all, but takes from none; that he is to be like the snow which takes on itself the frost and the biting winds, in order that the seeds below may sleep uninjured by the cold, and have the possibility of growth when the season for growth shall come. There is the training to which submission is demanded by these Divine Teachers; there what they claim from men who desire to be disciples. Not accomplishment at first, but endeavour; not perfection at first, but effort; not certainly the showing out of the ideal, but the striving after it amid whatever failure and amid whatever error. And I ask you if those of us who realise this as ideal, and who know that this is the demand which our Teachers make upon us, is it likely that we should act for the injury of society, or be anything save the servants of men in obedience to those whose law we strive to obey?

And then, as I said, life after life these qualities develop, until there comes at last a time when the weaknesses of men have fallen away, when the frailties of human nature have gradually been overcome, when a compassion that nothing can shake, a purity that nothing can soil, a knowledge mighty in this scope, and a spirituality that makes itself felt—when these are the qualities that mark the disciple who is nearing the threshold of liberation; until the day dawns when the treading of this Path is finished, the time comes when the disciple's course is over, and the last possibility of the Perfect Man opens before his eyes. Then for a while the earth, as it were, drops into the background; he stands—the liberated Soul as he is called, the Soul that has now his freedom, the Soul that has conquered human limitations—he stands on the threshold of Nirvāana, of that a perfect consciousness and bliss which go beyond possibility of human thought, which go beyond possibility of our limited consciousness. And as he stands there it has been said that there is silence; silence in Nature, one of whose children is rising beyond her, silence which nothing for a time may break, when the liberated Soul has accomplished his freedom. Silence—and it is broken by a voice; it is a voice that unites into one mighty cry the whole of the misery of the world which has been left behind. A cry from the world in its darkness, in its misery, in its spiritual starvation, in its moral degradatiopn. And in that silence surrounding the liberated Soul, the cry that comes across is the cry of misery from the human race to the Soul that has gone beyond his brothers, to the Soul that is free while they are left in chains.

THE SENSE OF UNITY

How shall he go further? Life after life he has learned to identify himself with man; life after life he has learned to answer to every cry of pain. Can he go onward freed,. and leave others in chains? Can he go onward into bliss, and leave the world in sorrow? He whom we call the Mahātmā is the liberated Soul who has the right to go onward, but for Love's sake turns back, who brings his knowledge to the helping of ignorance, brings his purity to the cleansing of foulness, brings his light to the chasing away of darkness, and takes up again the burden of the flesh till all the race of men shall be free with him, and he shall go onward not alone, but as father of a mighty family, bringing humanity with him to share the common goal and the common bliss in Nirvāna.

That is the Mahātmā. Life after life of effort crowned with supreme renunciation; perfection gained by struggle and by toil, and then brought back to help others till they stand where he is standing. Every Soul that stretches out its hands, his hand is ready to help. Of every brother that asks for guidance, his heart answers to the cry; and they stand there waiting until we are willing to be taught, and give them the opportunity which they have renounced Nirvāna to secure.

A SUBLIME IDEAL

Is that an ideal for scoffing, for laughter, for idle ridicule? If it be only a dream, it is the noblest dream that humanity has ever dreamed; the fullest of self-sacrifice, and the most inspiring of ideals. To some a fact—a fact more real than life. But to those to whom it is no fact it might be an ideal; an ideal of self-sacrifice, of knowledge, and of love. That such Men are, some of us know. But even if you believe not in them, there is nothing in the ideal that is not noble, and by thinking of which you may not grow higher and higher towards the light.

The Christian has the same ideal in his Christ; the Buddhist the same ideal in his Buddha. Every faith has the same ideal in the Man whom it regards as Divine. And we stand as witness to all religions that their faifth is real and not false; their Teachers a reality, and not a dream; for the Teacher is the realisation of the promise in the disciple, and realisation of the ideal that we adore. And so to some of us these Divine Teachers, whom we know to live, are a daily inspiration. We can only come in contact with them as we strive to purify ourselves. We can only learn more as we practice what already they have taught. And it I have spoken at first of a theory, then of the historical past, then of the witness that we bear you in the present, and lastly of the steps that all may make if they will, it is because I want to lift the ideal out of all the ridicule that has been heaped upon it, away from all the mud that has been cast upon it, out of the jar and the strife which has been made to surround it.

Blame us as you will, but leave that noble ideal of human perfection untouched. Laugh at us as you will, but do not laugh at the Perfect Man, the man made God, in whom, after all, most of you believe. Do not, you who are Christians, be false to your own religion, and leave your Christ only as a matter of faith and not of living reality, as many of you know that he is today. And remember that whatever the name, the ideal is the same, whatever the title, the thought that underlies it is identical.

And as you think, you develop; as is your ideal, so gradually your lives will become. For there is this transforming power in thought, that if your ideals are paltry your lives will be paltry; if your ideals are material your lives will be material. Take then this ideal and think of it, and your lives will become penetrated by its purity; you will become the nobler men and the nobler women, because it forms a subject of your thought, and the thought transforms you into its own likeness. It is true that men become like that they worship; it is true that men become like that on which they think. And this ideal of the Perfect Man has in it the hope for the future of the race. Therefore I plead for it to you today, and I point you to the Path by which from an ideal it may become a living reality, turning from a hope into a living Teacher, and from a lofty ideal for aspiration into the Friend and the Master to whom you may give your life.

—Annie Besant

References

1. *The Voice of the Silence.*

2. *The Voice of the Silence.* The other quotations are from the same book.

11. Hinduism

THE SPIRIT OF HINDUISM

If we look at the various and sometimes conflicting creeds which it contains, we may wonder whether Hinduism is not just a name which covers a multitude of different faiths, but when we turn our attention to the spiritual life, devotion, and endeavour which lie behind to creeds, we realise the unity, the indefinable self-identity, which, however, is by no means static or absolute. Throughout the history of Hindu civilisation there has been a certain inspiring ideal, a certain motive power, a certain way of looking at life, which cannot be identified with any stage or cross-section of the process. The whole movement and life of the institution, its entire history, is necessary in order to disclose to us this idea, and it cannot therefore be expressed in a simple formula. It requires centuries for ideas to utter themselves, and at any stage the institution has always an element that is yet to be expressed. No idea is fully expressed at any one point of its historical unfolding.

What is this Idea of Hinduism, this continuous element that runs through all its stages from the earlier to the latest, from the lowest to the highest, this fundamental spirit which is more fully and richly expressed in the highest though it is present in the very lowest? Life is present in every stage of a plant's growth and it is always the same life, though it is more fully expressed in the developed tree than in the first push of the tender blade. In the Hindu religion there must be a common element that makes every stage and every movement an expression of the religion. The different phases and stages have proper content and meaning only in so far as this common element exists. With the perception of the unity which runs through error and failure up the long ascent towards the ideal, the whole achievement of Hinduism falls into coherent perspective. It is this essential spirit that any account of Hinduism would seek to express, the spirit that its institutions imperfectly set forth, the spirit that we need to develop more adequately and richly before a better age and civilisation can be achieved.

HISTORICAL OUTLINE

The spirit is not a dead abstraction but a living force. Because it is active and dynamic the Hindu civilisation has endured so long and proved so capable of adaptation to the growing complexity of life. The great river of Hindu life, usually serene but not without its rapids, reaches back so far that only a long view can do justice to its nature. From prehistoric times influences have been at work moulding the faith. As a result of the excavations in Harappā and Mohenjo-dāro we have evidence of the presence in India of a highly developed culture that 'must have had a long antecedent history on the soil of India, taking us back to an age that can only be dimly surmised'.[1] I age and achievement the Indus valley civilisation is comparable to that of Egypt or Sumeria. The noteworthy feature of this civilisation is its continuity, not as a political power but as a cultural influence. The religion of the Indus people is hardly distinguishable, according to Sir John Marshall, from 'that aspect of Hinduism which is bound up with animism and the cults of Śiva and the Mother Goddess'.[2] These latter do not seem to be indigenous to the Vedic religion.

Though the Śakti cult was later accepted by the Vedic people, their original opposition to it is not altogether suppressed. To the sacrifice of Daksha, all the Vedic deities are said to have been invited except Siva, who soon gained authority as the successor of the Vedic Rudra. Even so late as the *Bhāgavata Purāna* the opposition to Śiva-worship is present. 'Those who worship Śiva and those who follow them are the opponents of holy scriptures and may be ranked with *pāshandins*. Let the feeble-minded who, with matted locks, ashes, and bones have lost their purity, be initiated into the worship of Śiva in which wine and brewage are regarded as god.'[3]

It is a matter for conjecture whether the Indus people had any relation to the Dravidians. Nor can we say whether the Dravidians were natives of the soil or came from outside. Besides the Āryans and the Dravidians there was also a flat-nosed, black-skinned people who were commonly known as *dāsas*. The religion, in the first literary records that have come down to us, is that of the Āryans, though it was much influenced by the Indus people, the Dravidians, and the aborigines. The simple hymns of the *Ṛig-Veda* reveal to us an age when Pan was still alive, when the trees in the forest cold speak and the waters of the river could sing and man could listen and understand. The spells and the charms to be found in part of the tenth book of the *Ṛig-Veda* and in most of the *Atharva-Veda* suggest a type of religious practice based on fear and associated with the spirits of the dark. A religions synthesis of the different views and practices on the basis of monistic idealism is set forth in the early *Upanishads*. Soon after, a composite culture, springing from a union of Greek with Persian and Bactrian influences, dominated north-western India. Successive descents of Muslim conquerors from about A.D. 1000 affected Hindu life and thought. The Pārsī fugitives who were expelled from Persia by Muslim invaders found a welcome shelter in India. St. Thomas brought the Christian faith from Syria to south India and for over a thousand years this remained the only Christian centre of influence. In the sixteenth century St. Fracis Xavier introduced Latin Christianity. The Modern Christian missionary movement started over a century ago. The cultural invasion of the West has been vigorous, thanks to its political superiority and industrial efficiency.

Jainism, Buddhism, and Sikhism are creations of the Indian mind and may be interpreted as reform movements from within the fold of Hinduism put forth to meet the special demands of the various stages of the Hindu faith, Zoroastrianism, Islām, and Christianity have been so long in the country that they have become native to the soil and are deeply influenced by the atmosphere of Hinduism.

India was a thorough 'melting-pot' long before the term was invented for America. In spite of attacks, Hellenic, Muslim, and European among others, Hindu culture has maintained its tradition unbroken to the present day. The spiritual life of the Hindus at the present time has not precisely the same proportion or orientation as that of either the Indus people or the Vedic Āryans or even the great teachers, Śankara and Rāmānuja. Its changes in emphasis reflect individual temperaments, social conditions, and the changing intellectual environment, but the same persistent idea reappears in different forms. Hinduism grows in the proper sense of the word, not by accretion, but like an organism, undergoing from time to time transformation as a whole. It has carried within it much of its early possessions. It has cast aside a good deal and often it has found treasures which it has made its own. The history of Hinduism is chequered by tragic failures and wonderful victories, by opportunities missed and taken. New truth has been denied and persecuted occasionally. The unity of its body, realised at the cost of centuries of effort and labour, now and then came near being shattered by self-seeking and ignorance. Yet the religion itself is not destroyed. It is alive and vigorous and has withstood attacks from within and without. It seems to be possessed of unlimited powers of renewal. Its historical vitality, the abounding energy which it reveals, would alone be evidence of its spiritual genius.

UNIVERSITY

In its great days Hinduism was inspired to carry its idea across the frontiers of India and impose it on the civilised world. Its memory has become a part of the Asiatic consciousness, tinging its outlook on life. Today it is a vital element in world thought and offers the necessary corrective to the predominantly rationalistic pragmatism of the West. It has therefore universal value.

The vision of India, like that of Greece, is Indian only in the sense that it was formulated by minds belonging to the Indian soil. The value of that vision does to reside in any tribal or provincial characteristics, but in those elements of universality which appeal to the whole world. What can be recognised as peculiarly Indian is not the universal truth which is present in it, but the elements of weakness and prejudice, when even some of the greatest of Indians have in common with their weaker brethren.

RELIGION AS EXPERIENCE

Hinduism represents a development from the beliefs and practices of the Indus valley civilisation to the complex of changing aspirations and habits, speculations and forms which are in vogue today. There are, however, certain governing conceptions, controlling ideas, deep dynamic links which bind together the different stages and movement. The unity of Hinduism is not one of an unchanging creed or a fixed deposit of doctrine, but is the unity of a continuously changing life. In this essay we can only deal with the general drift of the current of Hindu religion as a whole, not with the many confusing cross-current and sects.

Religion for the Hindu is experience or attitude of mind. It is not an idea but a power, not an intellectual proposition but a life conviction.

Religion is consciousness of ultimate reality, not a theory about God. The religious genius is not a pedant or a pandit, not a sophist or a dialectician, but a prophet, sage, or a *rishi* who embodies in himself the spiritual vision. When the soul goes inward into itself it draws near its own divine root and becomes pervaded by the radiance of another nature. The aim of all religion is the practical realisation of the highest truth. It is intuition of reality (*brahmanubhava*), insight into truth (*brahmadarsana*).

In emphasizing the experiential as distinct from the dogmatic or cradle character of religion, Hinduism seems to be more adequate than other religions to the history of religion as well as to the contemporary religious situation. Buddhism in its original form did not avow any theistic belief. Confucius, like Buddha, discourage his disciples from occupying their minds with speculations about the Divine Being or the Unseen World. There are systems of Hindu thought, like the Sānkhya and the Pūrva Mimāmsā, which, in some of their characteristic phases, cultivate a spirit and attitude to which it would be difficult to deny the name of religion, even though they may not accept any belief in God or gods superior to oneself. They adopt other methods for achieving salvation from sin and sorrow and do not look to God as the source of their saving. We cannot deny to Spinoza the religious spirit simply because he did not admit any reciprocal communion between the divine and the human spirits. We have instances of religious favour and seriousness without a corresponding belief in any being describable as God. Again, it is possible for us to believe in God and yet by without any religious sense. We may regard the proofs for the existence of God as irrefutable and yet may not possess the feelings and attitude associated with religion. Religion is not so much a matter of theoretical knowledge as of life and practice. When Kant attacked the traditional proofs of God's existence, and asserted at the same time his faith in God as a postulate of moral consciousness, he brought out the essentially non-theoretical character of life in God. It follows that the reality of God is not based on abstract arguments or scholastic proofs, but is derived from the specifically religious experience which alone gives peculiar significance to the world 'God'. Man becomes aware of God through experience. Rational arguments establish religious faith only when they are interpreted in the light of that religious experience. The arguments do not reveal God to us but are helpful in removing obstacles to the acceptance by our minds of a revelation mediated by our capacity for the apprehension of the Divine which is a normal feature of our humanity.[4] Those who have developed this centre through which all the threads of the universe are drawn are the religious geniuses. The high vision of those who have penetrated into the depths of being, their sense of the Divine in all their exaltation of feeling and enrichment of personality, have been the source of all the noblest work in the world. From Moses to Isaiah, from Jesus and Paul on to Augustine, Luther, and Wesley, from Socrates and Plato to Plotinus and Philo, from Zoroaster to Buddha, from Confucius to Mahomet, the men who initiated new currents of life, the creative personalities, are those who have known God by acquaintance and not by hearsay.

THE VEDAS

What is final is the religious experience itself, though its expressions change if they are to be relevant to the growing content of knowledge. The experience is what if felt by the individual in his deepest being. What is seen by him (*drishti*) or heard (*śruti*) and this valid for all time. The Veda is seen or heard, not made by its human authors. It is spiritual discovery, not creation. The way to wisdom is not through intellectual activity. From the beginning, India believed in the superiority of intuition or the method of direct perception of the super-sensible to intellectual reasoning. The Vedic *rishis* were the first who ever burst into that silent sea of ultimate being and their utterances about what they saw and heard there are found registered in the *Vedas*. Naturally they attribute the authorship of the *Vedas* to superior spirit.

Modern psychology admits that the higher achievements of men depend in the last analysis on processes that are beyond and deeper than the limits of the normal consciousness. Secrets speaks of the 'demon' which acts as the censor on and speaks through him. Plato regards inspiration as an act of a goddess. Ideas are showered on Philo from above, though he is oblivious of everything around him. George Eliot tells us that she wrote her best work in a kind of frenzy almost without knowing what she was writing. According to Emerson, all poetry is first written in the heavens. It is conceived by a self deeper than appears in normal life. The prophet, when he begins his message 'Thus faith the Lord', is giving utterance to his consciousness that the message is not his own, that it comes from a wider and deeper level of life and from a source outside his limited self. Since we cannot compel these exceptional moments to occur, all inspiration has something of revelation in it. Instead of considering creative work to be due to processes which take place unwittingly, as some psychologists imagine, the Hindu thinkers affirm that the creative deeds, the inspiration of the poets, the vision of the artist, and the genius of the man of science are in reality the utterance of the Eternal through man. In those rare moments man is in tough with a wider world and is swayed by an oversoul that is above his own. The seers feel that their experiences are unmediated direct disclosures from the wholly other and regard them as supernatural, as not discovered by man's own activity (*akartrika, apaurusheya*). They feel that they come to them from God,[5] though even God is said to be not their author but their formulator. In the last analysis the *Vedas* are without any personal author.[6] Since they are not due to personal activity they are not subject to unlimited revision and restatement but possess in a sense the character of finality (*nityatva*).

While scientific knowledge soon becomes obsolete, intuitive wisdom has a permanent value. Inspired poetry and religious scriptures have a certain timelessness or universality which intellectual works do not share. While Aristotle's biology is no longer true, the drama of Euripides is still beautiful. While Viśeshika atomism is obsolete, Kālidāsa's *Śakuntalā* is unsurpassed in its own line.

There is a community and continuity of life between man in his deepest self an God. In ethical creativity and religious experience man draws on this source, or rather the source of power is expressing itself through him. In Tennyson's fine figure the sluices are opened and the great ocean of power flows in. It is the spirit in man that is responding to the spirit in the universe, the deep calling unto the deep.

The *Vedas* are more a record than an interpretation of religious experience. While their authority is final, that of the expression and the interpretations of the religious experience is by no means final. The latter are said to be *smriti* or the remembered testimonies of great souls. These interpretations are bound to change if they are to be relevant to the growing content of knowledge. Facts alone stand firm, judgements waver and change. Facts can be expressed in the dialect of the age. The relation between the vision and its expression, the fact and its interpretation, is very close. It is more like the body and the skin than the body and its clothes. When the vision is to be reinterpreted, what is needed is not a mere verbal changes. When the vision is to be reinterpreted, that is needed is not a mere verbal change but a readaptation to new habits of mind. We have evidence to show that the *Vedas* meant slightly different things to successive generations of believers. On the fundamental, metaphysical, and religious issues the different commentators, Sankara, Rāma-nuja, and Madhva, offer different interpretations. To ascribe finality to a spiritual movement is to bring it to a standstill. To stand still is to fall back. There is not and there cannot be any finality in interpretation.

AUTHORITY, LOGIC, AND LIFE

Insight into reality, which is the goal of the religious quest, is earned by intellectual and moral discipline. Three stages are generally distinguished, a tradition which we have to learn (*śravana*), an intellectual training through which we have to pass (*manana*), and an ethical discipline we have to undergo (*nididhyāsana*). [7]

To begin with, we are all learners. We take our views on the authority of a tradition which we have done nothing to create but which we have only to accept in the first instance. In every department, art or morality, science or social life, we are taught the first principles and are not encouraged to exercise our private judgement. Religion is not an exception to this rule. Religious scriptures are said to have a right to our acceptance.

The second step is logical reflection or *manana*. To understand the sacred tradition we should use our intelligence. 'Verily, when the sages or *rishis* were passing away, men inquired of the gods, "who shall be our *rishi*?" They gave them the science of reasoning for constructing the sense of the hymns.'[8] Criticism helps the discovery of truth and, if it destroys, anything, it is only illusions that are bred by piety that are destroyed by it. *Śruti* and *Smriti,* experience and interpretation, scripture and logic, are the two wings given to the human soul to reach the truth. While the Hindu view permits us to criticise the tradition, we should do so only from within. It can be remoulded and improved only by those who accept it and use it in their lives. Our great reformers, our eminently original thinkers like Śankara and Rāma-nuja, are rebels against tradition; but their convictions, as they themselves admit, are also revivals of tradition. While the Hindus are hostile to those who revile their tradition and repudiate it altogether, and condemn them as *avaidika* or *na-stika*, they are hospitable to all those who accept the tradition, however critical they may be of it.

The authoritativeness of the *Veda* does not preclude critical examination of matters dealt with in it. The Hindus believe that the truths of revelation are justifiable to reason. Our convictions are valuable only when they are the results of our personal efforts to understand. The accepted tradition becomes reasoned truth. If the truths ascertained by inquiry conflict with the statements found in the scriptures, the latter must be explained in a way agreeable to truth. No scriptures can compel us to believe falsehoods. 'A thousand scriptures verily cannot convert a jar into a cloth.' We have much in the *Vedas* which is a product not of man's highest wisdom but of his wayward fancy. If we remember that revelation precedes is record, we will realise that the *Veda* may not be an accurate embodiment of the former. It has in it a good deal of inference and interpretation mixed up with intuition and experience. Insistence on Vedic authority is not an encouragement of credulity or an enslaving subjection to scriptural texts. It does not justify the conditions under which degrading religious despotisms grew up later.

The Vedic testimony, the logical truth, must become for us the present fact. We must recapture something of that energy of soul of which the *Vedas* are the creation by letting the thoughts and emotions of that still living past vibrate in our spirits. By *nididhyāsana* or contemplative mediation, ethical discipline, the truth is built into the substance of our life. What we accept on authority and test by logic is now proved by its power to sustain a definite and unique type of life of supreme value. Thought completes itself in life and we thrill again with the creative experience of the first days of the founders of the religion.

GOD

If religion is experience, what is it that we experience? What is the nature of reality? In our knowledge of God, contact with the ultimate reality through religious experience plays the same part which contact with nature through sense perception plays in our knowledge of nature. In both we have a sense of the other, the trans-subjective, which controls our apprehension. It is so utterly given to us and not made by us. We build the concept of reality from the data of religious experience, even as we build the order of nature from the immediate data of sense.

In the long and diversified history of man's quest for reality represented by Hinduism, the object which haunts the human soul as a presence at once all-embracing and infinite is envisaged in many different ways. The Hindus are said to adopt polytheism, monotheism, and pantheism as well as belief in demons, heroes, and ancestors. It is easy to find texts in support of each of these views. The cults of Śiva and Śakti may have come down from the Indus people. Worship of trees, animals and rivers, and other cults associated with fertility ritual, may have had to same origin, while the dark powers of the underworld, who are dreaded and propitiated, may be due to aboriginal sources. The Vedic Āryans contributed the higher gods comparable to the Olympians of the Greeks, like the Sky and the Earth, the Sun and the Fire. The Hindu religion deals with these different line of thought and fuses them into a whole by means of its philosophical synthesis. A religion is judged by what it tends towards. Those who note the facts and miss the truth are unfair to the Hindu attempt.

The reality we experience cannot be fully expressed in terms of logic and language. It defies all description. The seer is as certain of the objective reality he apprehends as he is of the inadequacy of thought to express it. A God comprehended is no God, but an artificial construction of our minds. Individuality, whether human or divine, can only be accepted as given fact and not described. It is not wholly transparent to logic. It is inexhaustible by analysis.[9] Its inexhaustibility is the proof of objectivity. However far we may carry our logical analysis, the given object in all its uniqueness is there, constituting a limit to our analysis. Our thinking is controlled by something beyond itself which is perception in physical science and the intuition of God in the science of religion. The eternal being of God cannot be described by categories. An attitude of reticence is adopted regarding the question of the nature of the Supreme. Those who know it tell it not; those who tell it know it not. The *Kena Upanishad says*: 'The eye does not go thither, nor speech nor mind. We do not know, we do not understand how one can teach it. It is different from the known, it is also above the unknown.[10] Śankara quotes a Vedic passage where the teacher tells the pupil the secret of the self by keeping silent about it. 'Verily, I tell you, but you understand not, the self is silence.'[11] The deeper experience is a 'wordless' doctrine. The sages declare that 'wonderful is the man that can speak of him, and wonderful is also the man that can understand him.'[12] Buddha maintained silence about the nature of ultimate reality, 'Silent are The Tathāgatas. O, Blessed one.'[13] The *Mādhyamikas* declare that the truth is free from such description as 'it is', 'it is not', 'both', and 'neither'. Nāgārjuna says that Buddha did not give any definition of the ultimate reality. 'Nowhere and to nobody has ever anything been preached by the Buddha.'[14] A verse attributed to Śankara reads: 'It is wonderful that there under the banyan tree the pupil is old while the teacher is young. The explanation of the teacher is silence but the doubts of the pupil are dispersed.' This attitude is truer and nobler that of the theologians, who construct elaborate mansions and show us round with the air of God's own estate agents.

When, however, attempts are made to give expression to the ineffable reality, negative descriptions are employed. The real is the wholly other, the utterly transcendent, the mysterious being which awakens in us a sense of awe and wonder, dread and desire. It not only fascinates us but produces a sense of abasement in us. Whatever is true of empirical being is denied of the Real. 'The Ātma can only be described by "no, no". It is incomprehensible for it cannot be comprehended.'[15] It is not in space or time; it is free from causal necessity. It is above all conceptions and conceptional differentiations. But on this account it is not to be confused with non-being. [16] It is being in a more satisfying sense than empirical being. The inadequacy of intellectual analysis is the outcome of the incomparable wealth of intrinsic reality in the supreme being. The eternal being is utterly beyond all personal limitation, is beyond all forms though the sustainer of all forms. All religious systems in which mankind has sought to confine the reality of God are inadequate. They make of God an 'idol'.

While the negative characteristics indicate the transcendent character of the real, there is a sense in which the real is also immanent. The very fact that we are able to apprehend the real means that there is something in us capable of apprehending it. The deepest part of our nature responds to the call of the reality. In spiritual life the law holds that only like can know like. We can only know what is akin to ourselves, Above and beyond our rational being lies hidden the ultimate and highest part of our nature. What the mystics call the 'basis; or 'ground' of the soul is not satisfied by the transitory or the temporal, by the sensuous or the intellectual,[17] Naturally, the power by which we acquire the knowledge of God is not logical thought, but spirit, for spirit can only be spiritually discerned. While the real is utterly transcendent to the empirical individual, it is immanent in the ultimate part of our nature. God's revelation and man's contemplation are two aspects of one and the same experience. The beyond is the Within. Brahman is Ātman. He is the *antaryāmin,* the inner controller. He is not only the incommunicable mystery standing for ever in his own perfect light, bliss, and peace, but also is here in us, upholding, sustaining us: 'Whoever worships God as other than the self, thinking he is one and I am another, knows not.'[18] Religion arises out of the experience of the human spirit which feels its kinship and continuity with the Divine other. A purely immanent deity cannot be an object of worship and adoration; a purely transcendent one does not allow of any worship or adoration.

Hindu thinkers are not content with postulating a being unrelated to humanity, who is merely the Beyond, so far as the empirical world is concerned. From the beginnings of Hindu history, attempts are made to bring God closer to the needs of man. Though it is impossible to describe the ultimate reality, it is quite possible to indicate by means of symbols aspects of it, though the symbolic description is not a substitute for the experience of God. We are helpless in this matter and therefore are obliged to substitute symbols for substances, pictures for realities. We adopt a symbolic account when we regard the ultimate reality as the highest person, as the supreme personality, as the Father of us all, ready to respond to the needs of humanity. The *Ṛig-Veda* has it: 'all this is the person, that which is past and that which is future.'[19] It is the matrix of the entire being. The Vaishnava thinkers and the Śaiva Siddhātins make of the Supreme, the fulfilment of our nature. He is knowledge that will enlighten the ignorant, strength for the weak, mercy for the guilty, patience for the sufferer, comfort for the comfortless. Strictly speaking, however, the Supreme is not this or that personal form but is the being that is responsible for all that was, is, and shall be. His temple is every world, every star that spins in the firmament. No element can contain him for he is all elements. Your life and mine are enveloped by him. Worship is the acknowledgment of the magnificence of this supreme reality.

We have accounts of the ultimate Reality as both Absolute and God, Brahman, and Isvara. Only those who accept the view of the Supreme as personality admit that the unsearchableness of God cannot be measured by our feeble conceptions. They confess that there is an overplus of reality beyond the personal concept. To the worshipper, the personal God is the highest. No one can worship what is known as imperfect. Even the idol of the idolater stands for perfection, though he may toss it aside the moment he detects its imperfection.

It is wrong to assume that the Supreme is either the Absolute or God. It is both the Absolute and God. The impersonal and the personal conceptions are not to be regarded as rival claimants the exclusive truth. They are the different ways in which the single comprehensive pattern reveals itself to the spirit of man. One and the same Being is conceived now as the object of philosophical inquiry or *jnāna,* now as an object of devotion or *upāsana*. The conception of ultimate reality and that of a personal God are reconciled in religious experience, though the reconciliation cannot be easily effected in the region of thought. We cannot help thinking of the Supreme under the analogy of self-consciousness and yet the Supreme is the absolutely simple, unchanging, free, spiritual reality in which the soul finds its home, its rest, and its completion.

HOSPITALITY OF THE HINDU MIND

A religion that is based on the central truth of a comprehensive universal spirit cannot support an inflexible dogmatism. It adopts an attitude of toleration not as a matter of policy or expediency but as a principle of spiritual life. Toleration is a duty, not a mere concession. In pursuance of this duty Hinduism has accepted within its fold almost all varieties of belief and doctrine and treated them as authentic expressions of the spiritual endeavour, however antithetic they may appear to be. Hinduism warns us that each of us should be modest enough to realise that we may perhaps be mistaken in our views and what others hold with equal sincerity is not a matter for ridicule. If we believe that we have the whole mind of God we are tempted to assume that any one who disagrees with us is wrong and ought to be silenced. The Hindu shared Arstotle's conviction that a view held strongly by many is not usually a pure delusion. If any view has ennobled and purified human life over a wide range of space, time, and circumstance, and is still doing the same for those who assimilate its concept, it must embody a real apprehension of the Supreme Being. For Hinduism, though God is formless, he yet informs and sustains countless forms. He is not small and partial, or remote and ineffable. He is not merely the God of Israel or of Christendom but the crown and fulfilment of you and me, of all men and all women, of life and death, or joy and sorrow. No outward form can wholly contain the inward reality, though every form brings out an aspect of it.

In all religions, from the lowest to the highest, man is in contact with an invisible environment and attempts to express his view of the

Divine by means of images. The animist of the *Atharva-Veda,* who believes that nature is full of spirits, is religious to the extent that he is convinced of the Divine presence and interpenetration in the world and nature. The polytheist is right to the extent that the Divine is to be treated on the analogy of human consciousness rather than any other empirical thing. The gods of the *Vedas* resemble the Supreme no more than shadows resemble the sun, but even as the shadows indicate where the sun is, the Vedic deities point to the direction in which the Supreme reality lies. All forms are directing their steps towards the one God, though along different paths. The real is one, though it is expressed in different names, which are determined by climate, history and temperament. If each one follows his own path with sincerity and devotion he will surely reach God. Even inadequate views help their adherents to adapt themselves more successfully to their environment, to order their experiences more satisfactorily, and to act on their environment more creatively. In the great crises of life, our differences look petty and unworthy. All of us have the same urge towards something of permanent worth, the same sense of awe and fascination before the mystery that lies beyond and within the cosmos, the same passion for love and joy, peace and fortitude. If we judge the saving power of truth from its empirical effects we see that every form of worship and belief has a strange power which enables us to escape from our littleness and become radiant with a happiness that is not of this world, which transforms unhappy dens into beautiful homes and converts men and women of easy virtue and little knowledge into suffering servants of God. All truth is God's truth and even a little of it can save us from great troubles.

Besides, the truth of religion is, as Troeltsch declared, 'polymorphic'. The light is scattered in many broken lights and there is not anywhere any full white ray of divine revelation. Truth is found in all religions, though in different measures. The different revelations do not contradict but on many points confirm one another. For the Hindu, religions differ not in their object but in their renderings of its nature.

The Hindu attitude to religious reform is based on an understanding of the place of religion in human life. A man's religion is something integral in his nature. It is like a limb, which grows from [illegible] from [illegible] we mutilate his human[illegible] and force it into an unnatural shape. We are all prejudiced in favour of what is our own. In spite of all logic we are inclined to believe that the home into which we are born is the best of all possible homes, that our parents are not as others are, and we ourselves are perhaps the most reasonable excuse for the existence of the human race on earth. If strangers are sceptical, it is because they do not know. These prejudices serve a useful purpose within limits. Mankind would never have progressed to this high estate if it had not been for this partiality for our homes and parents, our art and culture, our religion and civilisation. If each pushes this prejudice to the extreme point, competition and warfare will result, but the principle that each one should accept his own tradition as the best for him requires to be adopted with due care that it is not exaggerated into contempt and hatred for other traditions. Hinduism admits this principle of historical continuity, recognises its importance for man's advancement, and at the same time insists on equal treatment for others' views. Trying to impose one's opinions on others is neither so exciting nor so fruitful as joining hands in an endeavour to attain a result much larger than we know.

Besides, truth will prevail and does not require our propaganda. The function of a religious teacher is only to assist the soul's natural movement towards life. The longing for an ideal life may be hidden deep, overlaid, distorted, misunderstood, ill expressed, but it is there and is never wholly lacking. It is man's birthright which he cannot barter away or squander. We have to reckon with it and build on its basis. It does not matter what conception of God we adopt so long as we keep up a perpetual search after truth. The great Hindu prayers are addressed to God as eternal truth to enlighten us, to enable us to grasp the secret of the universe better and better. There is no finality in this process of understanding. Toleration in Hinduism is not equivalent to indifference to truth. Hinduism does not say that truth does not matter. It affirms that all truth are shadows except the last, though all shadows are cast by the light of truth. It is one's duty to press forward until the highest truth is reached. The Hindu method of religious reform or conversion has this for its aim.

Conversion is not always by means of argument. By the witness of personal example, vital changes are produced in thought and life. Religious conviction is the result, not the cause of religious life. Hinduism deepens the life of spirit among the adherents who belong to it, without affecting its form. All the gods included in the Hindu pantheon stand for some aspect of the Supreme. Brahma, Vishnu, and Śiva bring out the creative will, saving love and fearful judgement of the Supreme. Each of them to its worshippers becomes a name of the Supreme God. The *Harivamśa,* for example, tells us that Vishnu is the Supreme God, taught in the whole range of the Scriptures, the *Vedas,* the *Rāmāyaṇa,* the *Purānas,* and the epics. The same description is given of Śiva, who has Rudra for his Vedic counterpart.[20] He becomes the highest God. Śakti, the Mother Goddess, in her different forms represents the dynamic side of Godhead. Whatever form of worship is taken up by the Hindu faith it is exalted into the highest.

The multiplicity of divinities is traceable historically to the acceptance of pre-existing faiths in a great religious synthesis where the different forms are interpreted as modes, emanations, or aspects of the one Supreme. In the act of worship, however, every deity is given the same metaphysical and moral perfections. The labels on the bottles may vary, but the contents are exactly the same. That is why, from the *Ṛig-Veda* onwards, Hindu thought has been characterised by a distinctive hospitality. As the *Bhagavad Gitā* has it: 'Howsoever men approach me, so do I welcome them, for the path men take from every side is mine.' Hinduism did not shrink from the acceptance of every aspect of God conceived by a common search for truth. Every one is a Hindu who strives for truth by his heart. For what counts is the attitude of sincerity and devotion and not the conception, which is more or less intellectual. Kierkegaard says: 'If of two men one prays to the true God without sincerity of heart, and the other prays to an idol with all the passion of an infinite yearning, it is the first who really prays to an idol, while the second really prays of God,'[21] Dominated by such an ideal, Hinduism did not believe in either spiritual mass-production or a standardised religion for all.

The great wrong, that which we can call the sin of idolatry, is to acquiesce in anything less than the highest open to us. Religion is not so much faith in the highest as faith in the highest one can reach. At whatever level our understanding may be, we must strive to transcend it. We must perpetually strive to lift up our eyes to the highest conception of God possible for us and our generation. The greatest gift of life is the dream of a higher life. To continue to grow is the mark of a religious soul. Hinduism is bound not by a creed but by a quest, not by a common belief but by study and reflection, by purity of life and conduct, by devotion and consecration to high ideals, who believes that religion rests not on authority but on experience.

PERFECTION

Whatever view of God the Hindu may adopt, he believes that the Divine is in man. Every human being, irrespective of caste or colour, can attain to the knowledge of this truth and make his whole life an expression of it. The Divinity in us to be realised in mind and spirit and made a power in life. The intellectual apprehension must become embodied in a regenerated being. The Divine must subdue us to its purpose, subject the rebellious flesh to a new rhythm, and use the body to give voice to its own speech. Life eternal or liberation or the kingdom of heaven is nothing more than making the ego with all its thought and desires get back to its source in spirit. The self still exists, but it is no more the individual self but a radiant divine self, deeper than the individual being, a self which embraces all creation in a profound sympathy. The *Upanishad* says: 'The liberated soul enters into the All.'[22] The heart is released from its burden of care. The sorrows and errors of the past, the anxiety of unsatisfied desire, and the sullenness of resentment are no more. Its is the destiny of man where there is a perfect flowering of the human being. To embody this eternal greatness in temporal fact is the aim of the world. The peace of perfection, the joy of heaven, is realizable on earth. Perfection is open to all. We are all members of the heavenly household, of the family of God. However low we may fall, we are not lost. There is no such thing as spiritual death. As long as there is a spark of spiritual life, we have hope. Even when we are on the brink of the abyss, the everlasting arms will sustain us, for there is nothing, not even an atom of reality, where God does not abide. Men of spiritual insight take upon themselves the cross of mankind. They crown themselves with thorns in order that others may be crowned with life immortal. They go about the world as vagrants despising the riches of the world to induce us to believe in the riches of their world. When they gaze into men's eyes, whatever their condition of life, they see something more than man. They see our faces not merely by the ordinary light of the world but by the transfiguring light of our divine possibilities. They therefore share our joys and sorrows.

YOGA

To gain this enlightenment, this living first-hand experience of spiritual illumination, the aspirants submit themselves to long years of protracted search, to periods of painful self-denial. To be made luminous within we have to pay a heavy price. We must reduce the vast complex of actions and reactions we call human nature to some order and harmony. The appetites which call for satisfaction, the zest for life and the animal propensities, our unreasoned like and dislikes, pull us in different directions. This raw material requires to be subdued into the pattern of self. We must attain an integrated vision, a whole life, health and strength of body, alertness of mind, and spiritual serenity. A complete synthesis of spirit, soul, flesh, an affections requires a radical change-over, so that we think and live differently. We have to endure a violent inward convulsion. As a first step we are called upon to withdraw from all outward things, to retreat into the ground of our own soul and find in the inmost depth of the self the divine reality. The world of things in its multiplicity is revealed as a unity. The vision of the true self is at the same time vision of unity (*ekatvam anupaśyati*). He beholds all beings in himself and himself in all beings.[23] 'There one perceives no other, hears no other, recognises no other, there is fullness.'[24] A life that is divided becomes a life that is unified. Yoga is the pathway to this rebirth or realisation of the divine in us.

There are not only many mansions in God's house but many roads to the heavenly city. They are roughly distinguished into three—*Jnāna, bhakti,* and *karma*. God is wisdom, holiness, and love. He is the answer for the intellectual demands for unity and coherence, the source and sustainer of values, and the object of worship and prayer. Religion is morality, doctrine as well as a feeling of dependence. It includes the development of reason, conscience, and emotion. Knowledge, love, and action, clear thinking, ardent feeling, and conscientious life, all lead us to God and are necessary for spiritual growth. A relatively greater absorption in one or the other depends on the point we have reached in our inner development. When the goal is reached there is an advance in the whole being of man. Religion then ceases to be a rite or a refuge and becomes the attainment of reality.

JNĀNA

When *jnāna* is said to lead to *moksha* or liberation, it is not intellectual knowledge that is meant but spiritual wisdom. It is that which enables us to know that the spirit is the knower and not the known. By philosophical analysis (*tattva-vichāra*) we realise that there is in us a principle of awareness by which we perceive all things, though it is itself not perceived as an object in the ordinary way. Not to know that by which we know is to cast away a treasure that is ours. Yoga in the sense of the stilling of outward activities and emotions and concentration on pure consciousness is adopted to help the process of development. When we attain this *jnāna* there is a feeling of exaltation and ecstasy and a burning rage to suffer for mankind.

BHAKTI

While Hinduism is one of the most metaphysical of religions, it is also one that can be felt and lived by the poor and the ignorant. By the pursuit of *bhakti* or devotion we reach the same goal that is attained by *jnāna*. The devotees require a concrete support to their worship and so believe in a personal God. *Bhakti* is not the love which expects to be reciprocated. Such a love is a human affection and no more. Prayer becomes meditation, the worshipful loyalty of will which identifies itself with the good of the world. If you are a true devotee of God you become a knowing and a virtuous soul as well. The *bhakta* knows how to identify himself completely with the object of devotion, by a process of self-surrender.

My self I've rendered up to thee;
I've cast it from me utterly.
Now here before thee, Lord, I stand,
Attentive to thy least command.
The self within me now is dead,
And thou enthroned in its stead.
Yea, this, I Tuka, testify,
No longer now is 'me' or 'my'.[25]

The distinction between God and worshipper is only relative. Love and knowledge have one and the same end. They can only be conceived as perfected when there is an identity between lover and beloved, knower and known.

KARMA

Ethical obedience is also a pathway to salvation. Hinduism desires that one's life should be regulated by the conception of duties or debts which one has to discharge. The debts are fourfold: (i) To the Supreme Being. One's whole life is to be regarded as a sacrifice to God. (ii) To the seers. By their austerities and meditations the sages discovered truth. We become members of a cultured group only by absorbing the chief elements of the cultural tradition. (iii) To our ancestors. We repay these debts by having good progeny. The Hindu social code does not ask us to impose an unnatural order on the world. We discover the intentions of nature in the constitution of men and women and it is our duty to act agreeable to them. Marriage is not merely of bodies but of minds. It makes us richer, more human, more truly living, and becomes the cause of greater love, deeper tenderness, more perfect understanding. It is an achievement which requires discipline. If it is not the expression of spirit, it is mere lust. There are innumerable shades between love, the spiritual unity expressed in physical unity, and lust which is mere physical attraction without any spiritual basis, and which has created prostitution both within and without marriage. The great love stories of the world, even when they involve a breaking of human laws, are centred, lifted up, and glorified by their fidelity, by the fact that they do not pass. (iv) To humanity. We owe a duty to humanity which we discharge by means of hospitality and goodwill. Those who adopt this view are not content with merely earning their bread or seeking their comfort, but believe that they are born not for themselves but for others.

Hinduism does not believe that the use of force is immoral in all circumstances. The *Bhagavad Gitā,* for example, lays stress on the duties of the warrior and the claims of the nation. There is a place for politics and heroism, but wisdom and love are more than politics and war. In order to remain within the bonds of a class or a nation we need not free ourselves from the bonds of humanity. Real democracy is that which gives to each man the fullness of personal life. Animals are also included under objects to be treated with compassion. All life is sacred, whether of animals or of fellow men. We shudder at cannibalism and condemn the savage who wishes to indulge in this habit of our ancestors, though the slaughtering of animals and birds for human consumption continues to be regarded as right. The Hindu custom allows meat-eating but prefers vegetarianism. On days dedicated to religious functions meat-eating is disallowed. Our right to take animal life is strictly limited by our right to self-preservation. and defence. The true man is he in whom the mere pleasure of killing is killed. So long as it is there, man has no claim to call himself civilised. While Hinduism has within its fold barbarians inheriting the habits of wild ancestors who slew each other with stone axes for a piece of raw flesh, it aims at converting them into men whose hearts are charged with an eager and unconquerable love for all that lives.

In the priestly codes there is a tendency to confuse virtue with ceremonial purity. To kill a man is bad, but to touch his corpse is worse. The great scriptures, however, disregard technical morality and insist on the spirit of self-control and love of humanity. To be able to fulfill the obligations expected of man he must exercise self-control. Not only what we accept but what we renounce contributes to our making. Threefold is the gate of hell that destroys the self: lust, anger, and greed. We must make war upon them with the weapons of spirit, opposing chastity to lust, love to anger, and generosity to greed. The *Veda* says: 'Cross the bridges hard to cross. Overcome anger by love, untruth by truth.' The *Mahābhārata* says: 'The rules of *dharma* or virtuous conduct taught by the great seers, each of whom relied on his own illumination, are manifold. The highest among them all is self-control.'[26] Unfortunately, in our times, the man of self-control is regarded as a weak man.[27] It is for developing self-control that austerities and asceticism are practised, but when self-control is attained these rigorous practices are unnecessary. Insistence on discipline or self-control avoids the two extremes of self-indulgence and asceticism. Discipline does not mean either the starving of the senses or the indulgence of them.[28]

There is enough scope for repentance also. 'If he repents after he commits the sin, the is destroyed. If he resolves that he will never commit the sin again, he will be purified.'

The *sannyāsī* is not one who abstains from work. Meditation and action both express the same spirit. There is no conflict between wisdom and work. 'It is the children of this world and not the men of learning who think of wisdom and work as different. The peace that is won by the knower is likewise won by the worker. He sees in truth who sees that wisdom and work are one.'[29]

KARMA AND REBIRTH

The world is not only spiritual but also moral. Life is an education. In the moral sphere no less than the physical, whatsoever a man soweth that shall he also reap. Every act produces its natural result in future character. The result of the act is not something external to it imposed from without on the actor by an external judge but is in very truth a part of the act itself. We cannot confuse belief in *karma* with an easy-going fatalism. It is the very opposite of fatalism. It deletes chance, for it says that even the smallest happening has its cause in the past and its result in the future. It does not accept the theory of predetermination or the idea of an overruling providence. If we find ourselves helpless and unhappy we are not condemned to it by a deity outside of ourselves. The *Garuda Purāna* says: 'No one gives joy or sorrow. That others give us these is an erroneous conception. Our own deeds bring to us their fruits. Body of mine, repay by suffering.' God does not bestow his favours capriciously. The law of morality is fundamental to the whole cosmic drama. Salvation is not a gift of capricious gods but is to be won by earnest seeking and self-discipline. The law of *karma* holds that man can control his future by creating in the present what will produce the desired effect. Man is the sole and absolute master of his fate. But so long as he is a victim of his desires and allows his activities to be governed by automatic attractions and repulsions he is not exercising his freedom. If chains fetter us, they are of our own forging and we ourselves may rend them asunder. God works by persuasion rather than by force. Right and wrong are not the same thing and the choice we make is a real one.

About future life there are three alternatives possible: (i) The soul dies with the body, since it is nothing more than a function of physical life. Hindu religion does not accept this mechanical view. (ii) The soul goes either to heaven and eternal bliss, or to hell and eternal torment, and remains there. For the Hindu, the doctrine that the soul has only one life, a few brief years, in the course of which it determines for itself an eternal heaven or an eternal hell, seems unreasonably and unethical. (iii) The soul may not be fit for eternal life and yet may not deserve eternal torment, and so goes from life to life. This life is not the end of everything. We shall be provided with other chances. The soul does not begin with the body nor does it end with it. It pursues its long pilgrimage through dying bodies and decaying worlds. The great purpose of redemption is carried over without break from one life to another. All systems of Hindu thought accept the idea of the continuous existence of the individual human being as axiomatic. Our mental and emotional make-up is reborn with us in the next birth, forming what is called character. Our strivings and endeavours give us the start. We need not fear that the spiritual gains of a long and strenuous life go for nothing. This continuity will go on until all souls attain their destiny of freedom, which is the goal of human evolution. If there is not a shred of empirical evidence for it, the same is true of other theories of future life also.

CONCLUSION

From the beginnings of Hindu history the culture has been formed by new forces which its had to accept and overcome, in the light of its own sold and enduring ideas. In every stage there is an attempt to reach a harmony. Only the harmony is a dynamic one. When this dynamic harmony or organic rhythm of life is missing it means that the religion stands in need of reform. We are now in a period of social upheaval and religious unsettlement the world over, in one of those great incalculable moments in which history takes its major turns. The traditional forms are unable to express the growing sense of the divine, the more sensitive insight into the right way of life. It is wrong to confuse the technique of a religion with is central principles. We must reform the technique so as to make it embody the fertile seeds of truth. In my travels both in India and abroad I have learnt that there are thousands of men and women today who are hungry to hear the good news of the birth of a new order, eager to do and dare, ready to make sacrifices that a new society may be born, men and women who dimly understand that the principles of a true religion, of a just social order, of a great movement of generosity in human relations, domestic and industrial, economic and political, national and international, are to be found in the basic principles of the Hindu religion. Their presence in growing numbers is the pledge for the victory of the powers of light, life, and love over those of darkness, death, and discord.

POSTSCRIPT BY THE EDITOR

The most important religious heritage of India from her ancient past is no doubt the doctrine of transmigration (*samsāra*) which is characteristic of all Indian religions and sharply distinguishes them from those with a Semitic ancestry, such as Judaism, Christianity, and Islam. A few ambiguous and inconclusive references in Vedic literature suggest that vague ideas of metempsychosis were known even among the early Āryans, but thoughts of the afterlife seem then to have been mainly centred on a heaven whither the souls of the righteous went on death, to feast for ever with their ancestors. Among the first fruits of the pessimism of the later Vedic period was the gnawing doubt whether even the soul of the dead might not be liable to further death. Thus the idea emerged that Death would hound the soul from world to world (*loke-loka enam mrityur vindet, Śat. Brh, xiii.* 3.5). The quest for permanence, finality, and complete psychological security is very evident throughout the later Vedic literature, where the Vedic heaven begins to seem inadequate and limited, in the light of the contemporary dissatisfaction.

A definite doctrine of transmigration appears for the first time in the *Brihadāranyaka Upanishad* (vi. 2, repeated with some amplification in *Chhāndogya Up*. v. 3-10). The teaching here enunciated, which has certain primitive features such as do not occur in the developed doctrine of *Samsāra,* is ascribed to the kshatriya, Jaivali Pravāhana, a chief of the tribe of Panchālas, who taught it to the brāhman Āruni Gautama, also known as Uddālaka Āruni, apparently one of the most vigorous thinkers of the period (perhaps c. 700 B.C.). Another passage in the *Brihadāranyaka* (iii. 2) tells how the great sage Yājnavalkya secretly taught to a questioner as a new and secret theory the doctrine of *karma,* that the good and evil deeds of a man automatically influence his state in future lives.

The first of these passages suggests that the doctrine originally appeared in non-brāhmanic circles. The second indicates that it circulated secretly for some time before it became public knowledge. From the later *Katha Upanishad* (i. 20-9) it appears that there was widespread doubt at one time about whether the personality survived at all after death, and the doctrine of transmigration is again here put forward as a new one, revealed by the god of the death to the boy. Nachiketas only after much importuning. In the latest of the principal *Upanishads,* however, it seems to have become widely accepted, while in the Buddhist tradition transmigration is axiomatic. There is no discussion on whether or not the personality transmigrates, but only on the mechanics by which it does so.

The evidence for the origin of this doctrine is very faint. It may have been borrowed from non-brāhman and originally non-Āryan elements in the Gangā valley, and have gained currency only against considerable opposition from conservative elements among the priesthood. The names of historical sages—Yājnavalkya and Uddālaka Āruni Gautama—are connected with it in the traditions. How this new and secret doctrine spread in a comparatively short period of time to become universally accepted is also quite unknown. We can only suggest that it was disseminated by wandering ascetics, outside the fraternities of sacrificial priests.

Once it was universally adopted, the idea of *Samsāra*, the unending, or almost unending, passage from death to rebirth and redeath, conditioned the attitudes of nearly all Indian and encouraged certain tendencies in the social life of India. The prospect of endless rebirth in a vale of tears, even when punctuated by long periods of residence in the heavens, was extremely distasteful to many of the more sensitive people of the times, as it still is, and the quest for psychological security in one changeless entity where there would no longer be fear of death and rebirth was redoubled. The proliferating religious thought of the *Upanishads,* Buddhism, Jainism, and other less-known heterodox movements owes much of its existence to the growth of this doctrine, which appears to have become universal by the time of the Buddha.

Transmigration must also have encouraged the doctrine of *ahimsā* (non-injury), which was specially supported by Buddhism and Jainism in their campaign against animal sacrifice, for this doctrine linked all living things together in a single complex system—gods, demigods, human beings, demons, ghosts, souls in torment, warm-blooded animals, even humble insects and worms, all possessed souls essentially the same. The man who tried to infringe the rights of brāhmans to whom land had been granted by the king was threatened in the title-deed with rebirth for eighty thousand years as a worm in dung.[30] On such premises it is understandable that the wanton killing of animals should be looked on as little better than murder, and meat-eating as little better than cannibalism, for the ant which a man carelessly treads on as he walks down the road may contain the soul of his grandfather.

The great majority of Indians still believe in this doctrine, and the concomitant doctrine of *karma,* that man is reborn in happy or unhappy conditions according to his works, and these doctrines, in their Buddhist form, have affected more than half of Asia. They provide a potent sanction against evil-doing, or at least against a man's infringing the ethical norms of his society, for this leads to inevitable suffering, while righteous conduct brings happiness to the next life.

Moreover the afflicted can learn to accept suffering with the thought that it is not sent at the whim of fate or chance, and is not the visitation of a capricious god, but is the just recompense for one's own evil deeds in past lives. This doctrine is not fatalism, and does not imply that the sufferer should not try to better his lot—rigid determinism, of the type propagated by the heterodox sect of the Ājīvikas, is strongly attacked in many classical Indian texts—but it makes suffering of all kinds intelligible, and gives hope to the sufferer who bears affliction patiently. Thus, as a source of consolation, it has done much to mould the Indian character and to shape the Indian way of life.

A further potent factor in the moulding of the Indian mind, a relic from the same axial period that produced the doctrine of transmigration, is the concept of endless cyclic time in a cosmos so immense that the mind boggles at conceiving its size. The simple and comparatively small universe of Ptolemy, which provided the traditional world-view of later Judaism, Christianity, and Islam, is intelligible and homely by comparison; and the traditional Semitic and Christian doctrine of linear time—commencing at a period some 4,000 years B.C. and likely to come to an end and give way to eternity in the comparatively near future—was equally intelligible, giving an urgency to man's life which might not be felt in a society which believed that time was infinite, with an infinite number of opportunities for the individual to rise or fall in the scale of being. The Hindu universe is closer to that of modern science than the Ptolemaic one, and for this reason among others Hindus, even orthodox ones of the old school, have little difficulty in accepting scientific theories on the nature of the cosmos or of man.

The forbidding universe of science differs from that of the Hindus in one particular, however. The Hindu world, in all its immense length and breadth, is completely and fully underline by the Divine. There is no corner of the cosmos where God, or the impersonal *Brahman* for the monistic Vedāntin, is not. Facets of the personality of the one Lord behind the many appear in all aspects of life on earth, and the immense empty spaces of the universe are full of deities, all aspects or partial manifestations of the One.

If the intellectual Hindu prefers to think of the One spirit as impersonal and to equate that One with the *Ātman,* the innermost kernel of his own being, the ordinary Indian of all times has thought of the One as personal—a High God who created for himself all the lesser gods and the whole cosmos. Complicated theogonies evolved in the period following the composition of the Vedic literature, and continue to develop throughout the pre-Muslim period and even after. New gods appears and old gods faded away and almost vanished, in response to the needs of the times. They formed two broad groups, crystallising round the two High Gods, Vishnu and Śiva respectively; and the fantasy and inventiveness of the whole folk, not merely of the learned brahmans, expressed itself in the richest collection of mythology and legend in the world—ranging in quality from the sublime to the grotesque and occasionally even to the repulsive.

The universe for the simple Hindu, therefore, despite its vastness, is not cold and impersonal, and though it is subject to rigid laws, these laws find room for the soul of man. The world is the expression of ultimate divinity; it is eternally informed by God, who can be met face to face in all things, but especially in the image in the temple or family shrine, for divine images undergo consecration ceremonies at which they are converted into channels of god-head, means whereby the god they represent can reveal himself to his worshippers. God, infinite and omnipresent, nevertheless, in his condescension, projects himself in the form of an image so that his simpler worshippers may feel nearer to him.

For the Vaishnavites, the worshippers of Vishnu, the god has in the past taken material form, in order to save the world from impending disaster. His incarnations (*avatāras*), especially those as Rāma and Krishna, have given the Hindus their most exuberant and vital mythology, legend, and folklore. Rāma and his faithful wife Sītā combine the ideals of heroism, long-suffering, righteousness, loyalty, and justice in a story so full of exciting incident that it has become part of the tradition not only of India, but also of most of South-East Asia. And Rāma's henchman, the gigantic monkey Hanuman, the archetype of the loyal helper, striding out with his mighty club, is still among the most popular of the lesser gods of Hinduism. He figures as the divinity of countless minor shrines throughout the length and breadth of India, and is the personification of the strong arm of the Lord, ever ready to help the righteous in the hour of need.

Krishna, probably even more popular than Rāma, is a divinity of a rare completeness and catholicity, meeting almost every human need. As the divine child he satisfies the warm maternal drives of Indian womanhood. As the divine lover, he provides romantic wish-fulfilment in a society still tightly controlled by ancient norms of behaviour which give little scope for freedom of expression in sexual relations. As charioteer of the hero Arjuna on the battlefield of Kurukshetra, he is the helper of all those who turn to him, even saving the sinner from evil rebirths, if he has sufficient faith in the Lord.

Śiva, the divine dancer and the divine ascetic, has a less vivid body of mythology and legend associated with him. He dwells in the heights of Mt. Kailāśa with his beautiful wife Pārvatī, his bull Nandi, and his two sons, the elephant-headed Ganesa and the six-headed

Kārttikeya. Despite its superficial forbiddingness, and its bizarre elements, this group of divinities forms a sort of paradigm of family life. Often worshipped in the *lingam*, a much-formalised phallic symbol, Śiva represents the eternal power through which the universe evolves. As the divine dancer, subject of some of the most wonderful bronze sculpture in the world, Śiva dances new steps in never-ending variety until at length, in a very fierce and wild dance (*tāndava*), he will dance the universe out of existence, later to create a new one by yet another dance.

Stories and legends like these are perhaps almost as important as the austere monism of the intellectual *Advaita* of Professor Radhakrishnan. It is they that have provided the raw material for most of India's early art and literature, and they have given courage and consolation in face of adversity to countless millions through the centuries. Moreover they have provided India with her main source of entertainment.

Hinduism has its dark side. Psychopathic self-torture has long been part of it. Evil customs such as widow-burning, animal (and sometimes even human) sacrifice, female infanticide, ritual suicide, religious prostitution, and many others like them have in the past sometimes been practised in the name of the eternal Āryan dharma. But let it not be thought that Hinduism is morbid, gloomy, or forbidding. It is fundamentally a cheerful religion. In its temple courts children play unforbidden; at its temple gates the beggar finds his most profitable place of business. And all the larger temples are places of pilgrimage on holy days, centres of jolly religious fairs, to which peasants come from many miles around, not generally with feelings of guilt, fear, and sin, though awe is certainly present, but with the intention of combining religious business with pleasure, just as did the pilgrims of Chaucer's *Canterbury Tales*. Here they are refresh after hard weeks of labour in the fields, the burden of material care left behind in their villages. The dust and weariness of the road are washed away in the ritual bath in the sacred river or tank beside the temple. For a while they visit the shrine and pay their respects to the god who, like a mighty potentate, sits within it. As a symbol of his grace towards them they receive from an official the *prasāda,* in the form of holy water, sandal-wood ash, or red pigment, which they rub on their foreheads. Then, freed from earthly care, they enjoy their holiday among their fellows, secure in the knowledge of God's love, as they understand it.

We do not intend to disparage the Hinduism of the intellectual and the mystic, the Hinduism of the kind expounded by Professor Radhakrishnan. But let us remember the other Hinduism, the Hinduism of the artist and poet, with its rich mythology and legend, the Hinduism of the simple man, with its faith, its ritual, its temples, and its sacred images. Both are part of India's heritage, and it is impossible to pronounce objectively on their relative merits or importance; but there is little doubt which has the more strongly affected the majority of the inhabitants of the subcontinent for more than 2,000 years.

—*S. Radhakrishnan.*

References

1. Sir John Marshall, *Mohenjo-Dāro and the Indus Civilisation,* 1931, Vol. I, p. 106
2. Ibid. Vol. I, p. viii.
3. *Bhāgavata Purāna,* iv. 2. In the *Padma Purāna, pāshandins* are said to be 'those who wear skulls, ashes, and bones, the symbols contrary to the Vedas, put on matted locks and the barks of trees, even without entering into the third order of life and engage in rites which are not sanctioned by the Vedas'. *Uttara-khanda,* Ch. 235.
4. See Clement Webb, *Religion and Theism,* 1934, p. 36.
5. *Ṛig-Veda,* x. 90.9; *Brihadāranyaka Upanishad,* ii. 4.10.
6. Purushābhāvat...nishtha, *Mimāmsā-nyāya-prakāśa,* 6.
7. *Vivarana-prameya-samgraha,* p. I.
8 *Nirukta-pariśishta,* XIII. ii.
9. Cf. Augustine's statement that if one knows the object of one's belief, it cannot be God one knows.
10. i. 2-4.
11. *Bhāshya on Brahma Sūtra,* iii. 2.17.
12. See *Katha Up.* i. 2.7; also *Bhagavad Gitā,* ii. 29.
13. *Lankāvatara-sūtra,* 16.
14. *Mādhyamika-kārikā,* xv. 24.
15. *Brihad-aranyaka Up.* iii. 9, 26.
16. See Sankara's commentary on *Chhāndogya Upanishad,* viii.
17. 'In us too, all that we call person and personal, indeed all that we can know or name in ourselves at all is but one element in the whole. Beneath it lies even in us, that wholly other whose profundity impenetrable to

any concept can yet be grasped in the numinous self-feeling by one who has experience of the deeper life.' Rudolf Otto, *The Idea of the Holy*, E.T., p. 36.

18. *Brihad-ārunyaka Upanishad*, i. 4, 10.
19. The Supreme is 'all that which ever is, on all the world' (*Sarvam idam yatkiñca jagatyām jagat.* Isa Up. i).
20. *Atharva-śiras Up.* v. 3.
21. Quoted in *The Tragic Sense of Life* by Unamuno (3rd imp.), p. 178.
22. *Mundaka Up.* iii. 2.15. 23 *Iśa Up.* 6.
24. *Chhāndogya Up.* vii. 24. 25 Nicol Macnicol, *Psalms of Marāthā Saints*, p. 79. ·
26. *Śantiparva*, cliv. 6 25 Ibid. 34. 28 See *Bhagavad Gita*, vi. 16-18.
29. Ibid. v. 4-5.
30. This threat, occurring in many copper-plate grants, gives the lie to those neo-Hindu apologists who declare that it is impossible for the soul inhabiting human beings to fall to the state of an animal. Modern Hindu and their supporters may believe this, but it has no basis in any classical Hindu source.

12. Hindu Ideal of Life

What a people does in relation to its gods must always be one clue and perhaps the safest, to what it *thinks*.—Jane Harrison.

The Srautasūtras present in a rationalised form the great sacrificial cult dating at least from the Indo-Iranian age but further developed and elaborated by the Bharadvājas, Viśvāmitras, Vasisthas and other great priestly families in India. The Śrauta sacrifices are the exclusive preserve of these Brahmin priestly classes, and even when intended for the benefit of Kings and rich patrons had to be performed by them alone. The common people had little or nothing to do with the Śrauta-sacrifices directly. Yet, everyone in the state doubtless believed in the profound and beneficial efficacy of these elaborate ritual ceremonies, which therefore, were not without considerable influence on society.

The Grhya ritual, as we have seen, is predominantly magical in spirit,—the bizarre Grhya ceremonies being themselves regarded as the efficient and sufficient cause of the expected results even without the agency of the gods (the names of gods in the Grhya mantras are hardly more than magic words without any personal appeal). The Srauta ritual, however, at least of the Rgvedic age when the poetry of the mantras was still a vital and moving factor and had not degenerated into meaningless magic formulas, is much different. The Rgvedic Srauta sacrifices may be described as ritualised prayers,—their mantras are actually the prayers of a primitive and virile people addressed to benevolent gods, and it is these gods (and not the ritual) who are regarded as the real agents in conferring gifts and blessing on the sacrifices. But then, already in the Ṛigveda, there are passages which clearly suggest that the gods themselves were thought of as unable to resist the compelling persuasion of the Śrauta-sacrifices![1] So, if the Grhya ritual is on the whole penetrated by motives of direct magic, the

Śrauta ritual, it must be admitted, is the embodiment of indirect magic at the best. Whether the Śrauta-ritual in its oldest form-in the Indo-Iranian or still earlier times—was absolutely free from the magic element will never be fully ascertained.

Everything in the Śrauta sacrifices is performed by the Brahmin priests, the Yajamāna himself having to do nothing but bestow the Daksinā, observe the Sāmskāras such as sleeping on the ground, etc., and in special cases recite some mantras under the direction of the priests. The number of priests varies. Only the Adhvaryu is required for the Agnihotra. For the Agnyādheya as at new and full-moon sacrifice are required three more priests, viz. Āgnīdhra, Hotā and Brahman. A fifth priest Pratiprasthātā is necessary for the Cāturmāsya-sacrifice, and at the Paśubandha we have the sixth priest Maitrāvaruna apart from the Śamitā. But no less than sixteen priests are necessary for the highly complicated Soma-sacrifice. The Hotā there appears with three assistants, namely the Maitrāvaruna, the Acchāvāka and the Grāvastut; the Adhvaryu has as his assistants the Pratiprasthātā, the Nestā and the Unnetā; the Udgātā has under him the Prastotā, the Prathihartā and the Subrahmanya; the assistants of the Brahman are also three in number, viz. The Brāhmanācchamsin, the Potā and the Āgnidhra. According to the Kausītakins a seventeenth priest Sadasya is necessary for the Soma-sacrifices; his function is to supervise the whole ceremony. From the view-point of actual practice, however, the grouping of the priests is somewhat different, for the three assistants of the Brahman and one of the assistants of the Adhvaryu, namely the Nestā, are in practice helpers of the Hotā.

Nearly all the manual work connected with the Śrauta-sacrifices is performed by the Adhvaryu-priests, the others have only to recite, chant or mutter respectively the Rk-verses, the Sāmans and the Yajusmantras. The Hotā with his assistants is in charge of the recitation of the Rk-verses, the Yajus-mantras are muttered chiefly by the Adhvaryu-priests, and the Sāmans are chanted by the Udgāta and his assistants. Without special qualities, both inherited and acquired, no Brahmin can become a professional priest, nor can every member of the three upper castes become a Yajamāna at will. Both parties have to prove their *bona fides* before a sacrificial session is undertaken. This is necessary, for the Yajamāna may cheat the priest in respect of Daksinā, and the priests in their turn may do incalculable harm to the Yajamāna by allowing intentional lapses in the course of ceremonies.

A certain number of sacrifices are regarded as basic forms (*prakritis*) of which the rest are supposed to be mere variations (*vikrtis*). Thus the new-and full-moon sacrifices are the Prakrti of all other Istis: the Agniṣṭoma is the Prakṛti of the Dvādaśāha and the Ekāhas, and the Dvādaśāha in its turn is that of the Ahīnas and Sattras, etc. Each sacrifice is divided into its principal (*pradhāna*) and Auxiliary (*aṅga*). parts. The Pradhāna constitutes the distinguishing feature of a sacrifice and therefore has to vary from one sacrifice to another, but the Aṅgas, of minor importance, are repeated in practically the same form in many sacrifices. Thus the Pradhāna of the full-moon sacrifice consists of the Puroḍāśa aṣṭākapāla for Agni, the Puroḍāśa ekādaśakapāla for Agni-Soma, and the Upaṃiśuyāga for Viṣṇu or Agni-Soma, etc.; all else, such as the Prayājas and Anuyājas, are mere Aṅga's which are of no importance in themselves but serve as complement to the Pradhāna. The Aṅgas of a sacrifice are known collectively as the *tantra*: a single Tantra may serve several Pradhānas if their time and place of performance are the same. The Tantra reappears in practically the same form in Vikrtis, only the details varying sometimes.—The sacrificial offerings are of two kinds, Viz. *yajatis* and *juhotis* respectively. Like all Homas not specifically excepted, they too are offered into the Āhavanīya-fire. The *yajatis* are offered by the Adhvaryu in standing posture after the Puronuvākyā and the Yājyā; the latter ending with the Vasat-call the *juhotis* on the other hand are sacrificed by the Adhvaryu sitting with right knee bent, and the offering is accompanied only by Svāhā-call (no Anuvākyā or Yājyā); hence the *juhotis* are also known as *upavistahomas*. The Puronuvākyā of the Yajati-homa is an invocation to the deity, its Yāyā-verse (preceded by the formula *ye yajāmahe*) referring to the offering. The order to recite the Puronuvākyā is given by the Adhvaryu or the Maitrāvaruna. In the latter case the Adhvaryu at first addresses to the Maitrāvaruna the Sampraisa *"agnaye presaya" "somāya presaya"*, whereupon the Maitrāvaruna addresses to the Hotā the Praisa *"agnaye nubrūhi"*. Before the Yājyā the Adhvaryu says to the Āgnīdhra *"ozin śrāvaya"*, and the latter replies *"astu śrausat"*. Then the Adhvaryu commands the Hotā to begin recitation by saying to him *"Agnim (Somam* etc.) *yaja"*, and the latter thereupon begins the Yājyā with the Āgur-formula *ye yajāmahe* mentioned above. The seventeen mantra-syllables, namely *"asrāvaya" "astu-śrausat" "yaja" ye yajāmahe"* and *"vasat"*, are regarded as a constant feature of Śrauta sacrifices (see Nilakantha on MBh. XII. 47.48).

In the case of Soma-sacrifices the situation is infinitely more complex, for there we have over and above the usual paraphernalia the recitations and chants of the Hotā and the Udgātā and their assistants. The three characteristics of a Soma-sacrifice are the *graha* (cup), the *śastra* (hymn) and the *stotra* (song of praise) as already mentioned in the Śatapatha Brāhmana (VIII. 1 3.4). In the Agnistoma there are altogether twelve Śastras of Hotr-priests and twelve corresponding Stotras of the Sāma-singers. Of the five Śastras of the morning pressing, two (*ājya* and *prauga*) are recited by the Hotā himself and the rest by his assistants (*hotrakas*); corresponding to these there are from the side of the Udgātr-priests the *bahispavamāna-stotra* and four Ājyastotras known as *dhuryas*. At the midday pressing there are two Śastras of the Hotā (*marutvatīya* and *niskevalya*) and three if the Hotrakas; corresponding to these five Śastras we have the *mādhyandinapavamāna-stotra* and four others known as *prstha-stotras*. At the evening pressing there are only two Śastras (*vaiśvadeva* and *āgnimāruta*), both recited by the Hotā himself; corresponding to them the two Stotras *ārbhava-pavamāna* and agnistomasāman, the latter also known as *yajṇāyajṇīya*.

The Śastras are recitations, but the Stotras are songs chanted on the melodies (*sāmans*) collected in the Sāma-samhitā (the *text* of the SV. is altogether of secondary importance, giving, as it does, only the words on which these melodies have to be chanted). Now, the same verse can be chanted according to one melody only, or according to various melodies; in the former case the SV. verse concerned is called *ekasāmin,* and in the latter case, *bahusāmin*. ON the other hand, the same melody may be chanted on different verses. The verses of the SV.-text have therefore often to be modified and touched up in various ways in actual chanting. This is done very often by Vikāra, as when "*agne*" is chanted as "*ognāyi*"; when "*vitaye*" is changed into "*voyi toyāzyi*" in chanting it is Viśleṣana; the word "*ye*" may be distended into "*yāzzyi*" by the process of Vikarśaṇa; if a word of the original verse is uttered twice in chanting it is Abhyāsa; ungrammatical Virāma too may be forced in this way,—thus "*grnāno havyadātaye*" may have to be chanted as "*grnānoha vyadātaye*"; most frequently however the Rkverse is accommodated to the Sāma-melody through the addition of meaningless Stobhas such as *authovā, hāu* etc. Detailed rules about these modification of texts in chanting are to be found in the Puspasūtra.

Every Sāman is artificially divided into several parts. The first part is the Prastāva which is introduced with *hum* and chanted by the

Prastotā; the second part is the Udgitha introduced with *om* and chanted by the Udgātā; then comes the Pratihāra introduced with *hum* and chanted by the Pratihartā; and then the Nidhana or finale chanted by all together. The Partihāra moreover is divided into the Pratihāra proper and the Upadrava chanted by the Udgātā (for further details see Paṇcavidha Sūtra).—If a single Sāman-melody is chanted on several verses (usually a Trca or a Pragātha) the whole is called a Stotra, and a Stotra in its turn, through various combinations and repetitions of its verse-chants, results in long Stomas, of which, again, different varieties (*vistutis*) are possible. These Viṣtutis, consisting of several Paryāyas, clearly show that the Sāman-chants were regarded purely as magical charms. The Pañcadaś-stoma, for instance, is based only on three verses artificially constructed out of Pragātha, i.e. a pair of verses of which the first is either a Brhati or a Kakubh and the second a Satobrhati (Rkprātiśākhya, XVIII. 1); the component Pādas of this artificial verse-triad arranged in various weird ways and embellished with appropriate Stobhas etc., are then made to yield the number of verses required in the Stoma.[2]—The two Sāmans which are certainly the most important in Soma-sacrifices other than the Agnistoma are the Brhat and the Rathantara chanted on alternate days of the Abhiplava-sadaha, while at the Prsthya-sadaha a different Sāman is chanted on each of its six days.

The ritual of chanting the Stotras is no less elaborate than that of the recitation of the Vājyā by the Hotā. For every Stotra, the Udgātr-priests must formally ask the permission of the Brahman and the Maitrāvaruna wit the words *"brahman stosyamah praśāstah"* and the latter grant it with a formula ending with *om stuta*. The Brahman should preferably be a Vasiṣṭha. The chant of the Udgātṛ-priests, already described above, is followed by the Śastra of the Hotā or the Hotrakas as the case may be,—for which the command is given to them by the Stotrakārin with the word *"esa"* after the last Pratihāra. The Hotā addresses to the Adhvaryu the Āhāva *"somsāvoz"* to which the latter replies with the Pratigara *"othā modaiva"* or *"Somsā modaiva"*. Then follows a *tūsnīmjapa* and then the *puroruc*, both by the Hotā. And so on.[3]—In the following we shall discuss at first the simpler Haviryajñas and then the more elaborate Somasamsthāh and other sacrifices.[4]

In contradistinction from the Gṛhya-ṛitual for which the household fire (*gārhapatya*) alone is sufficient the Śrauta-ritual requires two more, namely the Āhavaniya and the Daksināgni, though the

Gārhapatya-fire, as the only one which (in theory at least) is never allowed to go down and also as the representative of the sacrificer, is easily the most important of the three also in Śrauta-sacrifices. The other two fires are kindled with splinters from this Gārhapatya-fire.. When setting out on a journey the householder at first takes leave of the Gārhapatya and then of the Āhavanīya, and when returning home he at first greets the Āhavanīya, and then the Gārhapatya: this touchingly expresses the intimate relation between the Gārhapatya fire and the householder's hearth and home. The sacrificial food is cooked on the Gārhapatya-fire, but not sacrificed into it,—it is sacrificed into the Āhavanīya. The Āhavanīya-fire, situated to the east, is the gate to heaven through which the offerings to the gods have to pass, just as the Dakṣiṇāgni (the significant designation indicates its location) into which the offerings to the Manes are sacrificed is the gate to the under world.[5]

The elaborate ritual[6] of setting up the sacrificial firs extending over two days is technically known as Agnyādheya. A Brāhmana should perform this ceremony in spring, a Ksatriya in summer, a Rathakāra in the rainy season, a Vaiśya in autumn; but in winter it may be performed by all. At first two huts are set up for the Gārhapatya and the Āhavanīya, the fire-alters in them being round and square respectively. The altar of the Daksināgni, situated to the south of the Gārahapatya, is shaped like a half moon. New fire for the altars is produced by attrition and is placed on the Gārhapatya. This laying of the Gārhapatya-fire is accompanied by mantras varying according to the ancestral Ṛṣi-name of the sacrificer. Thus if the sacrificer is a Bhārgava the Gārhapatya-fire is addressed with the mantra *"bhrgūnām tvā devānām vratapate vratenā 'dadhāmi"*; in the case of an Āngirasa the mantra would be *"angirasām tvā devānām;* etc. (Āp. 5. 11. 7).[7] The Āhavaniya-fire is then kindled with a faggot from the Gārhapatya. When the faggot is carried from the Gārhapatya to the Āhavanīya a horse is to trot in front of it: the horse here clearly represents the fire-god.[8]. According to Kātyāyana the southern fire too should be kindled in the same way, but Āpastamba differing from him significantly lays down that the fire for the Daksināgni should be fetched from somewhere else or produced separately by attrition. The Daksināgni is doubtless the Agni Kavyavāhana of the older literature, just as Āhavaniya is the name of the older Agni Havyavāhana.[9] A pious Śrotriya or a powerful prince was expected to maintain these three fires; but there were people, held in the highest esteem, who maintained two more fires, namely the

Sabhya and the Āvasathya.[10] The place of the Sabhya-fire is in the Sabhā, and it is meant exclusively for the Ksatriya; a ceremonial game of the dice is played on the occasion of the installation of this fire. The purpose of the Āvasathya-fire, mentioned along with the Sabhya (Āp. 5. 17. 1) , is not clear. Hillebrandt suggests that it is the fire of the Āvasatha "retreat" in which guests from outside were entertained.[11]— The fires thus ceremonially laid by the Āhitāgni have to be maintained by him through life, and it is expected that his life would henceforth be free from all blemish. But if the fires installed at so much expense fail to produce the expected results or prevent mishaps the Āhitāgni is free to given them up and install new fires within a year (Punarādheya). It is a peculiar feature of this Punarādheya-ceremony that various case-forms of the word *agni* (e.g. *agnim, agninā* etc.) are used in the mantras employed in it (Ap. 5. 28. 6). And it is suggestive of the whole purpose of the ceremony that some of the implements used have to be repaired ones, not new.

The daily duty of offering sacrifices into the domestic fire, morning and evening, is no less binding on the Śrotriya (= Āhitāgni = Vaitānika) with a least three fires than on the ordinary Snātaka-householder with only one, but of course the duties of the Āhitāgni Śrotriya are in this regard much more onerous as clearly suggested by the description of the elaborate ceremony of Agnihotra in the Śrauta-sūtras. It is quite apparent from the significant rules about the kindling of fires for the Agnihotra that not only the continuous maintaining of three fires at least was largely a matter of theory but also that even the Gārhapatya fire was not unoften allowed to languish (see Āp. 6. i ff.). The southern fire, at all events, was not maintained continually. The chief offering at the Agnihotra is milk which should be milched preferably by an Ārya and not a Śudra, and that from front or back-teats of the cow according to the special desires of the sacrificer. The difference between the morning and the evening—Agnihotra is slight.—The ceremony of Prātaravaneka is mentioned as a non-obligatory adjunct to morning-Agnihotra (Āp. 6.20) while Agnyupasthāna is the similar non-obligatory adjunct to the evening—Agnihotra. Very probably this custom of performing Agnihotra twice daily had been developed already in the age of the Rgveda.[12]

Of periodical Śrauta sacrifices we have firstly to mention the Śrotriya New-and Full-Moon (Darśapūrnamāsa) sacrifice which is much more elaborate than that of the Grhya ritual and serves as the Prakriti of all Istis. The central feature of the New-moon sacrifice is the offering of a Purodāśa to Indra-Agni, that of the Full-moon being a similar Purodāśa to Agni-Soma. "Two days were required at new moon, but one might suffice at the full-moon."[13] The preliminary part of the ceremony is concerned chiefly with the preparation of the Vaitānika fires, taking of the vow by the sacrificer and various other details,—one of them being that the wife of the sacrificer should look at the Ājyasthāli set before her, but not before the Āgnidhra has twisted round her a tree-fold cord. The actual sacrifice begins with the recitation by the Hotā of the fifteen "kindling" (*sāmidheni*) verses.[14] The most interesting of the immediately following ceremonies is the Pravara, or enumeration of the Rsi-ancestors of the sacrificer (see Āp. 2.16, 5 ff.), who, if a prince, has to invoke the names of those of his Purohita in this connection (Āp, 2. 16. 10). There is also an invitation of the gods through Agni in the order in which they figure in the sacrifice. These two important ceremonies of the cult have to be performed in the interval between the first two Āghāras (i.e., the sprinking of the Āhavaniya with butter to prevent its languishing). After the second Āghāra takes place the ceremonial election of the Hotā by the Adhvaryu, and the Ṛṣi-ancestors of the sacrificer are again mentioned in this connection. An important feature of the sacrifice is the eating of the sacrificial offering by the priests, the special shares of the Brahman and the Āgnīdhra being the Prāśitra and the Saḍavatta respectively. Of the various supplementary offerings let us mention the four Patnisamyājas, at the third which , addressed to the wives of the gods, the wife of the sacrifice has to touch the Adhvaryu.[15]—An Āhitāgni should continue performing New-and Full-moon sacrifices all his life. If both sacrifices are performed on each new-and full-moon day the full course may be completed in fifteen years. The same result may be attained even in one year by performing both in the Dāksāyana form every day.

The next important recurring Śrauta-sacrifice is the Cāturmāsya, which is a generic name for the three seasonal festivals, viz. Vaiśvadeva in spring. Varuṅapraghāsas in the rainy season, and Sākamedhas in autumn. Common to all the Cāturmāsyas are the five initial offerings to Agni, Soma, Savitr, Sarasvati and Pūsan. At the Vaiśvadeva, with which the course of Cāturmāsyas should begin, these initial offerings are followed by a Purodāśa for Heaven and Earth. The chief characteristic features of the Varunapraghāsas are the offering of a ram and an ewe of barley, the former for Varuna and the latter for the Maruts, sex-marks being prominently indicated on the two figures, and the confession by the wife of the sacrificer as to the number of her lovers, either by word of mouth or by raising as many Kuśa-blades as she has had paramours.[16] These peculiar ceremonies clearly indicate that Varunapraghāsas was a ritualised folk-festival. The most important features of the Sākamedhas are the Pitryajṇa[16a] performed at the Dakṣiṇāgni and the Traiyàmbakahoma offered to Rudra who is asked to partake of it along with his sister Ambikā. The Sākamedhas is followed immediately or after an interval by an offering to Śunāsirau which is clearly an agricultural rite.—Corresponding to the Grhya first-fruit festival we have annual Śrauta Agrayana ceremonies prescribed for Āhitāgnis to be performed on new-or full-moon day according to the rites of the new-moon sacrifice (Āp. 6. 29. 2 ff.) for each of the new crops like rice, barley etc. in appropriate seasons.

These are the daily or periodically recurring *nitya* ceremonies which an Āhitāgni, under normal circumstances,is expected to perform all his life. But there are, besides, a host of *naimittikās* and *kāmyas* which the Āhitāgni may perform for the fulfilment of special desires or in celebration thereof. These are technically known as Istis. The Āgrayana ceremonies mentioned above are typical Istis in celebration of the fulfilment of desires; but there are other Istis aiming at the restoration of amicable relation, reconciliation between relatives, birth of a son, acquisition of wealth, etc. The Kāriristi prescribed for those who wish for rain shows many features of pure magic (see Hillebrandt, 66).

Śrauta animal-sacrifices form a category apart. From the description of these sacrifices it is quite clear that the purpose of the naive and bizarre ceremonies connected with them was to introduce into the sacrificial animal active magical potency for transference to the participators at the sacrifice through the simple process of consuming its flesh or otherwise (Oldenberg, p. 33 1). Similarly motivated animal-sacrifices are known among many primitive peoples.[17] What is of particular interest with regard to Śrauta animal sacrifices is that the peculiar form in which they appear in the texts seems to have been developed already in the Indo-Iranian age, for the ancient Iranian animal sacrifice as described by Herodotus shows striking points of similarity.[18]—The Śrauta-sūtras distinguish between two kinds of animal-sacrifices, viz. The Nirūdhapaśubandh, which is an independent animal-sacrifice, and the Agnisomiya connected with Soma-sacrifice.

An Āhitāgni cannot eat flesh unless he has performed the Nirūdhapaśubandha, and he has to continue performing it all his life, once or twice a year.

On the whole the Nirūdha animal-sacrifice follows the model of the new-moon sacrifice. But no less than six priests are necessary for it, namely the Hotā, Adhvaryu, Āgnīdhra and Brahman as at every Isti, and also the Maitrāvaruna and the Pratiprasthātā (see Caland *id* Āp. 7. 14. 4). The Maitrāvaruna receives a staff on stepping into the place of sacrifice which he retains till the end: he must not touch himself or anybody else with it before uttering the Praisas of which the purpose is to urge the Hotā to recite the Yājyās. A goat without any physical blemish is sacrificed for Indra-Agni or Sūrya or Prajāpati. In animal-sacrifices other than the Nirūdhapaśubandha various other animals, sometimes in very large numbers, are immolated, particularly oxen and sheep, the colour and quality of the victims varying according to the god for whom they are sacrificed. The preparation of the post (*yūpa*) to which the sacrificial animal is bound is elaborately described, the accompanying mantras assuring the tree which is cut down for the purpose that nobody bears it any ill-will, the size and shape of the post, as well as the particular tree that should be cut down, varying according to the special desires of the sacrificer (Āp. 6. 2. II ff.). The Yūpa is placed in a hole which is half within and half without the Vedi, and a cord is wound round it at a height varying as usual according to object in view. The Pāśuki Vedi at which the animal is to be sacrificed is set up east of the fire, and in the eastern third of it is constructed the Uttaravedi, and upon the latter the Uttaranābhi: at animal sacrifices the fire of the Uttaravedi takes the place of the Āhavaniya, and the latter that of the Gārhapatya. As special utensils necessary for animal sacrifices we have the Vapāśrapaṇī on which the omentum of the victim is grilled and the Hṛdayaśūla or the spit on which the heart of the sacrificed animal is roasted. When everything is ready, the victim is bathed in perfumed water and, after Agnimanthana, is bound to the post with a cord. Then follow, as at new and full-moon sacrifice, the kindling verses, election of Hotā, invitation of the gods, Āghāras, and the election of priests.

The sacrifice proper begins after this with eleven Prayājas, the Yājyās corresponding to them being supplied by the Āpri-hymns varying in different priestly families.[19] After the tenth Prayāja the Svaru and one edge of the double-edged knife are anointed with butter and placed on the head of the sacrificial animal with the mantra *"ghrtenā 'ktau paśum trāyethām"* (Āp. 7. 14. 11)! Then the Adhvaryu hands the weapon to the Śamitā (who has to separate the limbs of the sacrificed animal with it) with the words "may this edge be sharp for you" (Āp. 7. 14. 14). What the Śamitā actually does to kill the victim is to strangle it with a cord (Āp. 7. 16. 5) while everybody else looks away, the Yajamāna reciting the significant mantras "you are not actually diving, nor are you being injured, you are going to the gods by convenient routes; where the virtuous and not the sinners go,—thee the god Savitā may install you" (Āp. 7. 16. 7). Just before the animal is strangled it is touched (with the roasting spit) by the Pratiprasthātā, the latter by the Adhvaryu, and the Adhvaryu by the Yajamāna,—all standing in a row (*pipilikavat*), the purpose of the ceremony being clearly to communicate to the participators the magic substance concentrated in the victim.[20] The omentum of the victim is then taken out and roasted on a spit over the Śāmitra (i.e., the slaughterer's fire) and finally placed on the Uttaravedi. Now comes the eleventh Prayāja, after which the whole omentum, with butter poured over it, is sacrificed along with pieces of gold, while the Śamitā holds the opening, through which the omentum has been taken out of the victim's stomach, closed with his fist (Āp. 7 19. 3). After a number of the minor ceremonies immediately following, the various limbs and parts of the carcass (see Āp. 7. 22. 6) considered fit to be offered to the gods (*daivatāni avadānāni,* which may be compared to the *exta* of the victim sacrificed in Roman ritual; see Wissowa, *Op. cit., p. 352*) are sacrificed in the proper order, the unclean parts being thrown into a pit west of the Śāmitra-fire outside the altar-ground as the share of the Raksases. Of the various ceremonies following this central feature of the sacrifice let us mention the eating of the Idā and the meat by the priests and the sacrificer, the eleven Anuyājas, the after-offering to the sacrificial grass (*prastara*), the offering of the tail of the victim to the wives of the gods, the prayer imploring Varuna to forgive sin, etc.—The ritual literature knows also Naimittika and Kāmya animal-sacrifices performed on special occasions or for the attainment of special desires.[21]

Now we come to the Soma-sacrifices, which, in contrast to other sacrifices, are offered, not to particular gods, but to the whole body of divinities, as also in the Avesta (Oldenberg, p. 45[2]). Historically considered, they should perhaps be regarded as the result of syncretism between the fire-cult, probably of Indo-European antiquity,[22] and the

Soma-cult at least of Indo-Iranian age.[23] That the intoxicating Soma-juice should be the central element of these amazingly elaborate ritual ceremonies is natural enough. To the primitive Indo-Iranians its wondrous effect on body and mind could but appear to be the result of direct divine influence, and so to come into communion with the gods, what cold appear to them more obvious than to partake of the beverage which visible produced that effect? The same motive explains also the drinking of wine at Dionysian orgies of ancient Greece.

The basic form of all Soma-sacrifices is the Agnistoma,[24] a sacrifice lasting one day only (*ekāha*) but requiring several days of preparation, and characterised by twelve Stotras and as many Śastras as mentioned above. The Ukthya is a modified form of the Agniṣṭoma, requiring at the evening-pressing not two Stotras and two Śastras as at the Agniṣṭoma, but five of each,—there being thus, fifteen Stotras and fifteen Śastras at the Ukthya; the three additional Śastras are called Ukthāni,—whence the designation of the whole ceremony. The Soḍaśin, in its turn, is a modified form of the Ukthya, its distinctive feature consisting of a sixteenth Stotra and a sixteenth Śastra. The other Ekāhas are the Atirātra (nocturnal vigil, twenty-nine Stotras and as many Śastras), the Aptoryāma (thirty-three Stotras and as many Śastras), the Atyagniṣṭoma (perhaps a special form of Sodaśin), and the Vājapeya which should have been in origin a popular festival in celebration of victory.[25]—"Ahīna" is the technical term signifying Soma-sacrifices lasting from two to twelve days, the longest Ahina being thus the Dvādaśāha. Between the Ekāha and the Ahina there is no difference excepting in duration, the latter being in fact a succession of Ekāhas variously modified and combined. The Aśvamedha is an Ahina of three-days.—The Dvādāha holds an intermediate position between Ahīnas and Sattras, i.e. sacrificial sessions of at least twelve days, but usually extending over one year: the Dvādaśāha may thus be performed both as an Ahina and a Sattra. A Mahāsattra is an extended Sattra of twelve years. The Ahīnas are performed by officiating priests in the interest of laic Yajamānas, but at the Sattras there is no room for Yajamānas as such, all the participating priests themselves being at the same time Yajamānas also, though one of them formally assumes the role played by the Yajamāna at the Ekāhas and Ahīnas. There is therefore no prospect of Daksinā at a Sattra.

The chief element of a Sattra is the Saḍaha, a period of six days, of which tho varieties are known in the cult: the Pṛṣṭhya-ṣaḍaha, on each of the six days of which a different Sāman is chanted, and the Abhiplava-ṣaḍaha, at which the Sāmans Bṛhat and Rathantara are chanted on alternate days. A chain of Pṛṣṭhyas and Abhiplavas variously arranged, along with other elements, would constitute a year-long Sattra like the Gavāmayana, of which the second half-year is the exact replica of the first, but in the opposite order, so that the beginning of the second half is identical with the end of the first and the beginning of the first half is identical with the end of the second. Dividing these two symmetrical halves stands the Visuvat performed on the solstitial day. The whole session of Gavāmayana is concluded with the Mahāvrata which shows many highly interesting features of folk-festivals such as the dance of women in a ring round the fire with water-pitchers.[26]

Even Agniṣṭoma, the simplest of Soma-sacrifices, is so complex that it requires no less than two hundred and sixty separate ritual acts according to the enumeration of Caland-Henry. And each of these two hundred and sixty is by no means a simple ritual act,—some of them are in fact elaborate rituals by themselves! The first of the ritual acts preparatory to Agnistoṃa is of course Diksā, of which the purpose is to chasten the mind and the body of the prospective sacrificer. The period of this chastening may vary from one day to one year. But the preparatory ceremonies with specific relation to the Agniṣṭoma are performed during the three Upasad-days immediately following the period of Dīksā, so that there would be altogether four preparatory days if the Dīksā is of one day only. The first Upasad-day is devoted chiefly to the purchase of King Soma. The mode of this purchase is very peculiar,—clearly suggesting a semi-ritualised form of an ancient Soma-myth. The vendor of Soma, a Kautsa or a Śūdra, should be actually beaten, and his goods taken away from him be force; later however he is given gold or a cow as price for his merchandise.[27] After the purchase, King Soma proceeds towards the sacrificial ground in his chariot while "the Subrahmanya utters the formula, whence he derives his name."[28] inviting Indra to pratake of the Soma. The metaphor of royalty is maintained throughout the ritual. After the royal procession comes the royal reception and then the formal installation of the King on the throne. He is also entertained with an elaborate guest-offering (*ātithyeśti*). The ceremonies of the first Upasad-day, including two Pravargvas (milk-offerings) in the morning and afternoon[29] and two corresponding Upasads,[30] are concluded with a light meal (*vratana*) in the evening. The special feature of the second Upasad-day is the preparation of the Mahāvedi, the Uttaravedi, the

Cātvāla and the Uttaranābhi. On the third Upasad-day, the second Pravargya and Upasad are performed at noon and not in the afternoon as on the previous two days, the evening being devoted chiefly to the offering of a goat to Agni and Soma (*agnīsomīya paśu*). [31] The principal animal-sacrifice connected with the Agnistoma (*savaniya paśu*) takes place on the great Sutya-day following immediately after the third Upasad-day, the Vapā being sacrificed at the morning-pressing, the Paśu-purodāśa at the midday-pressing, and the Angāni at the evening-pressing.[32] Of the bewildering number of complex ceremonies performed on the Sutya-day round the three pressings, no adequate idea can be given within the space at our disposal. The Daksinās, consisting sometimes of "all the sacrificer's goods save his eldest son."[33] have to be paid at the second pressing after the Nārāśamsa-cups have been deposited. The whole ritual is concluded, as usual, with an elaborate sacrificial ablution (*avabhrtha*) after the evening-pressing.

The Agniṣṭoma is the model of numerous Ekāhas,[34] such as the Viśvajit, after performing which one has to pass twelve nights in different places,—three of these twelve among Nisādas. The Sādyahkra, of which six varieties are mentioned, is essentially a simplified Agniṣṭoma, all the ceremonies connected with it, from Diksā to Avabhrtha, being performed in one day. Much more interesting are the four Vrātyastomas of which the object was formally to accept within the Aryan fold the non-Aryans or those Aryans who had forfeited their privileges through neglect of social duties (*patitasāvitrīkas*).[35] The most astounding of the Ekāhas is the Gosava for the attainment of cattle, after performing which one is expected to live like an animal for one year, completely disregarding all decencies of human life.[36] This is clearly a case of sympathetic magic.

The three greatest Śrauta-sacrifices, namely Rājasūya, Vājapeya and Aśvamedha, were all in origin popular festivals of political significance. The utterly non-religious and sometimes revolting character of some of the rites involved in them clearly suggest the culture of an age when Brahmanism, wisely pursuing a policy of compromise instead of trying to suppress outright the crude practices obtaining among the Aryan warriors and the aborigines of India, thought it better to throw over them the mantle of ritual sanctity. The Rājasūya[37] is a primitive coronation ceremony transformed into a Soma-sacrifice of one Sutya-day preceded by a year of preparation. The Purohita, the officers of state, the people and the King's son (whose name is once intentionally mispronounced for that of his father in the ritual!) take active part in the ceremony, of which the most interesting feature is the mimic expedition for booty in course of which the King defeats all his adversaries.—At the Vājayeya, which literally means the "drink of victory,"[38] the supremacy of the royal sacrificer is established in the same way by means of a chariot-race at which he beats his competitors.[39]—The Aśvamedha,[40] the famous horse-sacrifice of ancient Indian ritual, performed by princes desirous of extending their dominions, is of immemorial antiquity. It has been proved that the main features of the Aśvamedha appear in essentially the same form also in the horse-sacrifices not only of other Indo-European tribes,[41] but also in those of many non-Indo-European peoples.[42] The revolting practices mentioned in the ritual texts and also in literature in connection with the Aśvamedha were clearly a legacy of past barbarism which the Brahmins were cautious enough not to tamper with too hastily.

Human sacrifice (Purusamedha) too is mentioned in Indian ritual literature (see Hillebrandt, 77), but it is significant that the Śatapatha Brāhmana (vi. 2. 1. 39) gives the name of the man who was the last to actually immolate a human being at the Agnicayana instead of a surrogate victim, and the Purusamedha of the Śrauta-sūtras has been declared by Oldenberg (*op. cit.,* p. 362) to be the product of pure fantasy. Yet in view of the persistence of literary tradition about human sacrifices it would perhaps be going too far to altogether deny their existence in India in early times. If the highly cultured Athenian soldier-statesman Themistocles could have sacrificed three Persian princes at the battle of Salmis, it need not be surprising if it is discovered that some Indian princes too had on some occasions actually performed human sacrifice to placate the spirits of the people. According to Lecky, "the sacrifices of children to Saturn were very common" in the African province of the Roman Empire at the time of Constantine (*History of European Morals* [Issued for the Rationalist Press Association, Limited, 19 11], vol II. p. 14, col. I). "The gentle vegetarian Porphyry knows that in Chios, according to tradition, there had been a Dinysos called Omadius, the Raw One, and that the sacrifice he used to exact was the tearing of a man to pieces" (Harrison, *op. cit.,* p. 484). In Rome, even apart from the Gladiatorial combats which owed their origin to the Etruscan custom of immolating human victims at burial, human sacrifice become a part of the popular religion and is known to have been actually performed from before the second Punic War onward (Wissowa, *Religion und Kultus der Romer,* p. 54).

It will be clear from this rapid survey of the principal Śrauta-sacrifices that they are composed of very heterogeneous elements. The two chief strains in them were doubtless the Indo-European fire-cult elaborated in India separately in the Ātharvanic ritual, and the Indo-Iranian Soma-cult[43] which, though later than the fire-cult in origin, attained supremacy over the latter, both in Iran and India, through the assiduous efforts of energetic priestly guilds. But Zarathustra, through his reforms, revived the languishing fire-cult in Iran, and, reinforced by Zarathustrian ethics, it became the central feature of the Iranian religion. In India, however, the Soma-cult reigned supreme ever afterwards, the fire-cult being relegated to a subordinate position by the priestly families. Nevertheless, in Grhya-ritual, i.e. in the intimate life of the common people, the fire-cult maintained its own in spite of the priestly predilection for the cult of the exhilerating Soma.[44]

—B. Ghosh

References

1. See Oldenberg, *Die Religion des Veda*[2] p. 3 19. Formulas used in Roman religion too were regarded as possessing similar power of compelling the gods (see Wissowa, *Religion u. Kultus der Romer,* p. 333).

2. See Weber, *Indische Studien,* VIII, p. 25; Hillebrandt, *Ritualliteratur,* p. 101; Caland, Introd, to Translation of *Pancavimśa Brāhmana;* Keith, *Religion and Philosophy,* p. 314.

3. For further details see Hillebrandt, *Ritualliteratur,* pp. 102-3; Keith, *Religion and Philosophy, loc. cit.*

4. The following is based chiefly on Hillenbrandt's *Ritualliteratur* and the *Apustamba Śrautasūtra*

5. See Oldenberg, *Op. cit.,* p. 350.

6. Described in detail by Hillebrandt. 59.

7. This unusual variation of the mantras strongly suggests that the fire-cult was originally developed by each of the great priestly families separately from the habitual adoration of the hearth-fire. Expressions such as *agnir bharatasya* (RV. 7. 8. 4) should be interpreted in the light of this passage of the Āp. Śr. S. rather than otherwise (as for instance Oldenberg. *Op. cit.,* p. 132 who emphasises only the point that Agni was intimately connected with the household).

8. Sūrya's horse is conventionally called *bradhna* in the RV. Originally the word must have signified some colour (cf. RV. 10.20.9), and a reddish colour at that (cf. RV. 1.6.1). This conventionalisation of the designation of Sūrya's horse suggests that already in the Rgvedic age

Sūrya came to be specially associated with this animal. But not Sūrya alone, for Indra's horse too has a similar conventionalised designation in the RV., namely *hari.* It is possible at any rate that the ritual fire was contemplated as the sun.

9. Cf. Sat. Br. 2. 6. 1. 30: *havyavāhano vai devānām kavyavāhanah Pitinām.* Similarly Manu I. 95: *havyāni tridivaukasah kavyāni cai 'va pitaṛah.*

10. On these two fires are particularly Hillebrandt. *Vedische Mythologie*[2] vol. I. pp. 128-30.

11. *Vedische Mythologie*[2], Vol. I. p. 129 7.

12. So Oldenberg, *Op. cit.*, p. 438 f.n. 1.

13. Keith, *Religion and Philosophy,* p. 319.

14. Actually there are only eleven verses; the number fifteen is attained by repeating thrice the first verse and the last (see Caland *ad* Āp. 2. 12. 2).

15. The Śrāddha-ceremony of Piṇḍapitryajṇa has to be performed by the Āhitāgni in the afternoon of every new-moon day.

16. This is supposedly the only case in Vedic ritual where sin is regarded as a moral defilement and not a merely physical one removable by appropriate magical ceremonies (so Oldenberg. *Op. cit.*, p. 324). Yet the penitentiary character of many of the Prāyaścittas is so transparent that it would be certainly going too far to deny them any urge from moral compunction.

16a. In which Caland, *Uber Totenverehrung bei einigen der idg. Volker,* pp. 78 f., believed to have discovered traces of a very ancient sacrifice to the Manes dating from the Indo-European era.

17. Cf. the ancient Cretan custom of eating raw the flesh of the Dionysian bull in whom the god was supposed to have been incarnated (Harrison, *Prolegomena,*[2] pp. 482-5; Nilsson, *A History of Greek Religion,* p. 95). What may be called an eye-witness' account of this revolting Greek custom of omophagia will be found in Merejkowski's interesting novel *Naissance des Dieux.*

18. Oldenberg, *Op. cit.*, p. 342.

19. According to Bergaigne quoted by Hillebrandt, *Ritualliteratur,* p. 16, these Āpri-hymns used at animal-sacrifices are the best proof of the previous existence of different sacrificial cults in different priestly families in the earliest period, though a persistent effort to rationalise them into a homogeneous system set in already before the oldest Brāhmanas.

20. Cf. Oldenberg. *Op. cit.*, pp. 497 f.

21. See Hillebrandt, *Op. cit.*, 67 (end).

22. Keith, *Religion and Philosophy,* Appendix E.

23. Caland-Henry, *L'Agnistoma,* vol. II. p. 469.

24. Described in all its details by Caland-Henry, *Op. cit.* Oldenberg too, in his inimitable language, has given a brief but beautiful description of it (*Op. cit.*, pp. 457-9).

25. See Caland-Henry, *Op. cit.*, Preface, p. VIII.

26. See Caland-Henry, *Op. cit.*, Preface; Keith, *Op. cit.*, pp. 349-52.

27. For details of this ritual mimicry see Caland-Henry, § 34.

28. Keith, *Op. cit.*, p. 327.

29. See Keith, *Op. cit.*, pp. 332-3.

30. Caland-Henry, § 52 and 57.

31. On the occasion of this offering the Yajamāna and his relations, while ouching each other, are covered with a piece of cloth) Āp. 11, 16. 13-15). This interesting ceremony clearly symbolises family solidarity.

32. See Caland-Henry, § 41-15.

33. Keith. *Op. cit.*, p.330.

34. Hillebrandt, *Ritualliteratur,* 72.

35. Cf. the interesting description of Vrātyastoma in keith, *Op. cit.*, pp. 37-8; also Haraprasad Sastri, *Absorption of the Vrātyas.*

36. Āp. XXII. 13. 2-3: *upa mātaram iyād, upa svasāram, upa Sagotrām; atra yatrai 'nain visthā vindet tad vitiṣṭheta.*

37. For details see Hillebrandt, *Op. cit.*, § 74.

38. Oldenberg, *Op. cit.*, p.470.

39. Hillebrandt, *Op. cit.*, § 73.

40. Described in detail by Dumont, *L'Aevamedḥa.*

41. See particularly W. Koppers, *Pferdeopfer und Pferdekult der Indoger manen in Wiener Beiträge zur Kulturgeschichte und Linguistik, Jahrgang* IV (1936), pp. 279-411.

42. See Bleichsteiner, *Rossweihe und Pferderennen im Totenkult der kaukasischen Volker in Op. cit.*, pp. 414-495.

43. Which, according to Oldenberg. *Op. cit.*, p. 364, replaced an older honey-cult.

44. Can it be that the fire-cult was evolved by the Indo-European Daiva-worshippers and the Soma-cult by the Indo-Iranian Asura-worshippers?

13. The Fundamental Unity of India

The character of India is a single country is easily missed and lost in her continental extent and diversity. The whole is too large to be grasped as a unit and is realised only in parts. It is just like the blind men seeing the elephant in the old adage, each taking one of its limbs he could feel by his touch, for the whole animal. Or we are reminded by the story in one of the *Upanishads* of the quarrel for supremacy among the different members of man's bodily organism, not realising the common life by which each is sustained. It is difficult, indeed, to discover the One in the Many, the Individual in the Aggregate, the Simple in the Composite. Mere variety is, however, no proof against unity. It is, on the contrary, a sign of vitality, richness and strength.

The geographical unity of India is, however, patent on the map showing how the country is sharply separated from the rest of the world by almost inviolable boundaries, very unlike the disputed frontiers artificially settled between most of the countries of continental Europe.

And yet the question remains: How far is this fundamental unity of India realised by her people or exemplified in her history? Nature's gifts are of no consequence unless they are harnessed to the service of Man who must know how to explore, and take advantage of them.

The first condition of the progress of a people in political life and civilisation is its possession of a fixed and definite piece of territory which it can call and serve as its own mother country. A people that has not found a home for itself but lives in unstable and unsettled conditions, in unrest and uncertainty, lacks the conditions in which culture and civilisation can take their rise. The nomadic is one of the lowest stages of civilisation. The country is to a nation what the body is to the individual. It is necessary for its self-expression. The growth of the a nation, no doubt, depends upon several unities, such as those of language, religion, government common history and tradition, manners, and customs. But all these are secondary factors which have their roots in a common life in a common country.

The early progress of the Indians in culture and civilisation was owing to their first grasp of India as their common motherland. Accordingly, they applied to the whole of India the designation of Bharatavarsha. The Puranas expressly define the term Bharatavarsha as "the country that lies north of the ocean (i.e. the Indian Ocean) and south of the snowy mountains (Himalayas), marked by seven main chains of mountains, viz. Mahendra, Malaya, Sahya, Suktimat, Riksha (mountains of Gondwana), Vindhya, and Paripatra (western Vindhyas up to the Aravallis); where dwell the descendants of the Bharatas, with the Kiratas (barbarians) living to its east, the Yavanas (Ionians or Greeks) to its west, and its own population consisting of the Brahmanas, Kshatriyas, Vaishyas, and Shudras (i.e. the Hindus)". (See Wilson's *Vishnu-Prana,* ii, 127-9.) The modern name India for the country is not an indigenous appellation but a foreign import. India was known to foreigners in older times by its river *Sindhu,* which the Persians pronounced as *Hindu* and the Greeks as *Indos,* dropping the hard aspirate. But the name Bharatavarsha is not a mere geographical expression like the term India. It has a historical significance, indicating the country of the Bharatas, of Indo-Aryan culture of which the Bharatas were the chief bearers. Once their country was settled, the Indo-Aryans built it up with all their devotion. It engaged their deepest sentiments of love and service as expressed in their literature. One of the commonest prayers for a Hindu requires him to recall and worship the image of his mother country as the land of seven sacred rivers the Ganga, Yamuna, Godavari, Sarasvati, Narmada, Sindhu and Kaveri, which between them cover its entire area. Another prayer calls up its image as the land of seven sacred cities, Ayodhya, Mathura, Maya (modern Hardwar), Kashi, Kanchi (Conjeevaram), Avantika (Ujjain), Dvaravati (Dwarka), representing the important regions of India. The spirit of these prayers is further sustained by the peculiar Hindu institution of pilgrimage. It expects the Hindu to visit in his life the holy places associated with his faith. Each of the principal Hindu faiths or sects has its own list of holy places, Vaishnava, Shaiva, or Shakta, and these are distributed throughout the length and breadth of India and not confined to a single province. Thus the different sects are at one in enjoining upon their respective votaries a pilgrimage to the different and distant parts of India and thereby fostering in them a live sense of what constitutes their common mother country. In the same spirit, Shankara established his four *mathas* (religious schools) at the four extreme points of the country, *viz.* Jyotir-matha in the north (near Badri-Kedar on the Himalayas), Sharada-matha at Dwarka in the west, Govardhana-matha at Puri in the east, and Shringeri-matha in Mysore. Sectarianism is thus an aid to nationalism in Hindu culture. In some of the sacred texts like the *Bhagavata-Purana,* or *Manu-Smriti* are even found passages of patriotic fervour describing Bharatavarsha as the land fashioned by the gods themselves (*devanirmitam sthanam*) who even wish to be born in its as heaven on earth, for the spiritual stimulus of its environment, and above these is the culminating utterance—"Mother and Mother-country are Greater than Heaven!"

All these prayers and passages show that the Hindu has elevated patriotism into a religion. In the words of a distinguished British critic, "the Hindu regards India not only as a political unit naturally the subject of one sovereignty—whoever holds that sovereignty, whether British, Mohammedan, or Hindu—but as the outward embodiment, as the temple—nay, even as the goddess mother—of his spiritual culture...He made India the symbol of his culture; he filled it with his soul. In his consciousness it was his greater self."

But besides religion, the political experiences of ancient Hindus also aided them in their conception of the mother country. The unity of a country is easily grasped when it is controlled by a single political authority. The ancient Hindus were familiar with the ideal and institution of paramount sovereignty from very early times. It is indicated by such significant Vedic words as *Ekarat, Samrat, Rajadhiraja, or Sarvabhauma,* and such Vedic ceremonies as the *Rajasuya, Vajapeya,* or *Ashvamedha,* which were prescribed for performance by a king who by his *digvijaya* or conquests made himself the king of kings. Some of the Vedic works and later texts like the *Mahabharata* or the Puranas contain even lists of such great kings or emperors. And apart from these prehistoric emperors, there have been several such emperors in historical times, such as Chandragupta Maurya, Ashoka, Samundragupta, Harsha, Mihira Bhoja, and in later times, Akbar and Aurangzeb. Some even performed the horse-sacrifice in declaration of their paramount sovereignty, such as Pushyamitra, Samudragupta, Kumaragupta I, Adityasena and Pulakeshin I. Thus the institution of paramount sovereignty has had a long history in India. Its conception was quite consistent with the ideals set in their sacred works for kings who were encouraged to cherish as quite legitimate and laudable the ambition, which became them as Kshatriyas, of extending the area of their authority up to the limits of their mother country.

The unity of the country also manifests itself in the impress of a distinctive culture stamped upon it. That culture has been developed by its predominant people, the Hindus, numbering nearly 240 millions. The Persians had already defined India as the land of the Hindus, *Hindusthan.* Indeed, "India and Hinduism are organically related as body and soul". Hinduism has imparted to the whole of India a strong and stable cultural unity that has through the ages stood the shocks of political revolutions, being preserved in its own peculiar system of social self-government functioning apart from, and offering but few points of contact with, the State, indigenous or foreign. India is predominantly a land of villages, and these villages were recognised as self-governing republics, with a complete apparatus of local institutions for the conservation of indigenous culture, unaffected by political changes at the top or in the central government. What are the characteristic features of this indigenous Indian culture called Hinduism? These are indicated in the indigenous definition of Hinduism as *Varnashrama-dharma,* the religion based upon the two-fold division of *varnas* (castes) and *Ashramas* (stages of life), the most distinguishing and unifying feature of Hinduism. In its origin, as seen in Vedic literature, it rested on the division of society into four castes or self-contained social groups, the Brahmana, the Kshatriya, the Vaishya, and the Shudra. These in course of time became subdivided into any number of sub-castes. Now the Hindu all over India are divided into hundreds of castes and sub-castes. The principle of the caste-system, which is an outstanding peculiarity of India, is much misunderstood. It chiefly concerns one's private, domestic and religious life, and not public life. It only interdicts marriage between different castes (mainly on grounds of eugenics) and interdining especially eating from the same plate or eating the food that has been contaminated by unclean touch. Eating is recommended as the individual's private act, an act of prayer to God "the Giver of our daily bread". But the division into castes is only a part of the Hindu system. The other part is the division of the individual's life into well-defined stages or *ashramas* through which it should pass in its normal course. These *ashramas* are those of (1) the *Brahmachari* or the student,

(2) the *Grihastha* or the householder, (3) the *Vanaprastha* or the hermit, and (40 the *Sannyasi* or the ascetic absorbed in contemplation. The third stage of life should begin at fifty when a householder should retire from the world and family life and to the service of others. The last stage of life is meant as preparation for its end through the severing of all possible earthly ties. As has been already pointed out, Hinduism in its external social aspect is thus made up of two limbs, the caste-system and the *Ashrama-system*. Unfortunately more emphasis has come to be laid on the caste than on the *ashrama*. Caste divides and that on the basis of birth. But the *ashrama* system unites, binding all castes in its common rules to lead life-along a regulated course of development by natural stages.

The vehicle of this Hindu culture is Sankskrit. The unifying influence of Sanskrit can hardly be overstated. This has been well pointed out by Williams (*Hinduism,* p. 13): "India, though it has more than five hundred spoken dialects, has only one sacred language, and only one sacred literature, accepted and revered by all adherents of Hinduism alike, however diverse in race, dialect, rank, and creed. .That language is Sanskrit and that literature is Sanskrit literature—the only repository of the Veda or 'knowledge' in its widest sense; the only vehicle of Hindu theology, philosophy, law, and mythology; the only mirror in which all the creeds, opinions, customs, and usages of the Hindus are faithfully reflected; and (if we may be allowed a fourth metaphor) the only quarry whence the requisite materials may be obtained for improving the vernaculars or for expressing important religious and scientific ideas."

This distinctive Indian culture in course of time so far unified the country that the country and the culture came to be identified and became synonymous terms. The country was the culture and the culture the country, the kingdom of the spirit, transcending territorial limits. Since its introduction to India at the time of the *Rig-veda,* this Indo-Aryan culture had accordingly spread through the ages in ever-widening circles and regions known successively as Sapta-Sindhu, Brahmarshidesha, Brahmavarta, Madhvadesha; Aryavarta, Jambudvipa, or Bharatavarsha.

Efforts on History: In spite of this fundamental unity of India, the vastness of its size, and the variety of its physical features and social conditions, had their own natural consequences to its history and political development. It has been always difficult to organise the whole of India as a unit and have it governed from one centre under a common sovereign or political authority. The result has been that what may be strictly called Indian history as an organic whole or a unified development like English history or the history of France has been rarely achieved. More often the history of India has resolved itself into a number of subsidiary, subordinate, and unconnected histories, without continuing as a common history for the whole of India. Instead of developing from one centre under a common direction, it has developed very often from different, and even mutually independent centres, losing its unity in the variety of separate and local histories of different peoples, and regions, evolving along their own independent lines and offering but few points of contact or agreement and more of conflict between them. Thus the political history of India has to be often traced and studied in parts and fragments, in interruptions and isolated restorations, and in many missing links. It has been shaped through the ages by so many different peoples and governments such as Maurya, Kushana, Andhra, Gupta, or Gurjara, for the north, and Pallava, Chalukya, or Chola in the south, or Moslem, Maratha, Sikh and British in later times, functioning from different and changing centres like Pataliputra, Purushapura, Paithan, Nasik, Ujjain, Kanauj, Badami, Kanchi, Kalyani, and Tanjore; or Delhi, Poona, Lahore, and Calcutta, the headquarters of different political authorities in different epochs of Indian History. It was only once in Hindu India that the whole of India had a common history under the control of a common government, the Maurya empire under Ashoka who made his authority felt all over the country, and even Afghanistan and Baluchistan as parts of an extended India, of which he became the paramount sovereign.

It must, however, be noted that apart from its size, the conditions of ancient times, the difficulties of communication in the pre-mechanical ages, which have now yielded to the power derived from coal, electricity, or oil, did not permit the establishment of a large empire or a centralised administration. A government to be effective, to get its authority habitually obeyed in the different and distant parts of a large area, had to be very much decentralised, giving full scope to local self-government. Thus there was inevitably more of local life and history throwing into background the general life and history of India. Indian history thus becomes a mere collection of local and disconnected histories and but seldom the record of one common political development affecting India as a whole.

It is, however, to noted that behind this diversity of local history, there has always been in the background a kind of an all-Indian history which is from the nature of the case not political, but cultural in its character, the history of thought which transcends local limits and administrative boundaries. The whole of India bears the impress of certain common movements of thought and life, resulting in the development of certain common ideals and institutions which distinguish the civilisation of India from all other civilisations of the world, and marks it out "as a unit in the history of the social, religious, and intellectual development of mankind". (V. A. Smith: *Early History of India,* 4th ed., p. 5.)